Llanos Mestenas

MUSTANG PLAINS

Agnes G. Grimm

Library of Congress Catalog Card Number

68 - 19625

Printed by

Waco, Texas

Binding by
Library Binding Co
Waco, Texas

Dedication

To my husband, Joe, whose patience, encouragement, and faith were invaluable to the continuance and completion of this work.

Preface

Alonso de Piñeda explored and mapped the littoral of the Llanos Mesteñas in 1519, and liked the region so well that he spent forty days at the mouth of the Rio Grande. About 1534, Alvar Nuñez Cabeza de Vaca mapped his way across these plains after savouring the pitaya and nopal cacti as a captive of the Coastal Indians. South American scholar-historian German Arciniegas contends that Amerigo Vespucci mapped the Texas coast even sooner, in 1498.

An amazing stream of conquistadors, explorers, soldiers, missionaries, and settlers of most races and creeds have had a hand in the unique development of the Llanos Mesteñas region.

Early Spaniards, who were the first civilized people to arrive, used the descriptive term, "Los Llanos de las Mesteñas," when referring to the area between the Nueces River and the Rio Grande. To them, the term meant, "The plains filled with unclaimed livestock running wild." For here they found vast delta plains of rich native grasses, divided by their mother-streams edged with cypress and live oak and by caliche hills beginning to cover themselves with cacti, ocatilla, agarita, ceniza, and such. Herds of elk, deer, antelopes, javalinas, turkeys, and a large variety of game birds abounded—preyed upon by puma, coyotes, rattlesnakes, and roving bands of Indians.

Horses, cattle, and the lowly burros, whether escaping from their masters or being abandoned by them to the hostile savages and the vast loneliness, multiplied prodigiously—usurping much of the land from the smaller native animals.

By 1840, the horses had increased to herds rivaling those of the bison that roamed the plains farther to the north. Thus, the Spanish word "mesteñas" came to mean wild horses, and was anglicized to "mustangs."

Livestock, from the mesteñas of the early Spaniards to the blooded animals of today, have played a major role in economic and cultural development of this controversial region south of the Nueces. The Llanos Mesteñas and Mustang Plains eras vanished in 1930 with killing of the last drove of wild mustangs in Duval County and with emergence of "The Brush Country."

In *Llanos Mesteñas: Mustang Plains*, the author has endeavored to reflect some authentic gleams from each facet that has flashed through the centuries in the development of this decidedly different Texas region.

v

Acknowledgments

I wish to extend my thanks and appreciation to all who have offered me encouragement, information, and technical assistance of any kind; and especially to my brother, Bryan Glasscock, who shared his acquired documents, rare books, knowledge and encouragement; to pioneer residents and descendants of pioneer settlers who shared their knowledge, documents, pictures, and hospitality; to librarians, archivists, clerks, and other personnel at the General Land Office, at the University of Texas, at A & I University at Kingsville, at Del Mar College in Corpus Christi, at public libraries, and courthouses throughout South Texas, who were unfailingly patient and gracious; to members of the By-Liners of Corpus Christi and the Texas Press Women, especially Dee Woods and Sister Mary Xavier; to A. C. McCoy, who had faith in my plans for "Llanos Mesteñas" and consigned my first twenty-five stories for newspaper publication, and to other editors and staff members of the *Alice Daily Echo and News* who helped me "find my way around;" to Guadalupe Salazar who helped with some difficult Spanish translations; to William R. Gardner, Alice Public Schools Instructional Materials Center Director, and his wife, Betty; to Dr. W. W. Farrar, Alice Public Schools Curriculum Co-ordinator, and his wife, Evelyn; to Robert R. Mullen and John G. Gonzalez for their counseling and encouragement; to J. E. Conner, professor emeritus of history at A & I University; and to my children, especially Kathryn and Gilbert.

Table of Contents

Maps and Illustrations

Following Page 4

xi

These Pictures Follow Page 148

'Villa de Laredo' Marker
Republic of the Rio Grande Capital
Casa Blanca of San Diego—Four Pictures
Old Mexican Cart—Two Pictures
Restored Casa Blanca
Zachary Taylor's Headquarters
Fort San Ygnacio-Trevino—Six Pictures
Guidon Store
St. Francis de Paula Church
Father Bard
Marker from first bridge to span Nueces River
Ruins at Carrizo Springs
Old Tumlinson Blockhouse
Ruins of Camp Bullis
Monument Near Zapata
Fort Duncan Monument
Old Bridge Near Fort Duncan
Fort Merrill Monument
Fort Ewell Monument
Los Ojuelos Ruins
Stockade Fence
Old Amargosa
Old Cuevitas
Former Fort Brown Building
Fort Clark Building
Fort Duncan Building
Ringgold Barracks
Parapet Roof in Freer Area
Pablo Perez Grave
La Mota Fort
Schoolhouse built 1904
Burial Place of Don Pedrito Jaramillo
Catarino Garza
Ranchhouse East of Benavides
Early Newspaper Building
Philip Pope Price
Old Collins Town picture
W. T. "Uncle Willie" Wright, Sr.
T. Salazar Store pictures
Don Jesús Store pictures
Judge Robert Roland Mullen
"Uncle Jim" Dobie Ranchhouse
Old Collins School picture
Deed in Old Kleberg
Sketch of Longhorn
Sketch of S.A.A.P. Train
Perez Grandchildren and others
Phil Hobbs' Store

xii

LLANOS MESTEÑAS
"Discovery and Treachery"

The site of the first attempt by the Spaniards to fortify Texas was about thirty miles inland, on the left bank of the Rio de las Palmas that Alonso de Piñeda had found and named. Piñeda was an engineer whom Governor Francisco Garay of Jamaica had sent to survey the Gulf of Mexico littoral in 1519. Nearly two centuries passed before the discovery was made that the Rio Grande del Norte, the Rio Bravo, and the Rio de Las Palmas were all parts of the same river, not different rivers.

Piñeda remained at the mouth of the Rio de Las Palmas for forty days—exploring, making friends with the natives, getting the barnacles off his ship, and otherwise readying it for his return trip to Jamaica.

The next spring, Governor Garay sent General Camargo to the mouth of the river to build a presidio. This was begun in the vicinity of present Brownsville.

Three years later when Francisco Garay arrived with a detachment of 750 officers and men in 16 ships, instead of a presidio, he found nothing but large numbers of hostile natives. It seemed that news of Cortez' rape of the Aztec Empire in Mexico had traveled northward, or that the presidial builders had acted similarly. Maybe a combination of the two.

Since Garay found it better not to land, he decided to pay an official visit to Governor Cortez of Mexico, who had received his domain from the King of Spain at the same time. Apparently, Garay had known Cortez when he was in Cuba making preparations to enter Mexico. This decision proved most unwise, for Cortez seized Garay's ships and imprisoned him and his men. He then claimed Garay's lands for himself.

In 1535, Cortez sent Captain Pedro de Alvarado to establish a presidio in the same area, but a bit farther inland—beyond the palms and Coastal Indians. Perhaps the other Indians would be less hostile.

In the meantime, a previously planned expedition left Cuba destined for the Rio Grande, but it did not arrive and was never heard from. It was presumed to have been destroyed in a hurricane.

According to some sources, Alvarado did build the presidio on a high bluff overlooking the river, about 70 miles inland from Brownsville. A Tejones Indian village was soon settled nearby. Not until 1682, however, did the Spaniards settle here permanently and name the village "Penitas" (pebbles).

This village is still in existence and is about nine miles west of Mission in present Hidalgo County, about a mile off Highway 83.

CABEZA DE VACA IN LLANOS MESTEÑAS

Cabeza de Vaca walked southward along the coastal plains of Texas, a captive of the Karankawa Indians, to the caliche hills south of the Nueces River to help gather prickly pears (which the Indians called tunas) for the yearly festival.

The Karankawas were inordinately fond of these cactus pears which, in all probability, included the low-growing pitáya which is native to the Jim Wells-Duval Counties area only. The pitáya was also a favorite of the pioneer families settling here. The fruit is round and about the size of a plump strawberry, but has a smooth red skin when ripe. Its flavor is best described as a combination strawberry-pineapple. A very few are still found in this area.

In crude containers, the Indians carried prickly pears down to one of the streams of running water—perhaps the Agua Dulce or San Fernando in 1534, the year that Cabeza de Vaca and his companions managed their escape—where a motte of live oaks and other native trees provided shade along with drinkable water on the tree-scanty plains.

Abundant prairie grasses provided the piece de resistance of deer or antelope or javelina and wild turkey. Perhaps the Indians found an alligator and speared and partly roasted it. Peyote, with its nine different narcotic properties, was an important part of the yearly prickly-pear festival and aided in the escape of the captives.

Cabeza de Vaca, after his escape and return to Spain, told of this area abounding with wild stock. Later cartographers designated this region between the Nueces Valley and the Rio Grande as "Los Llanos de Las Mesteñas (The Plains of the Unbranded (or Wild) Livestock." In those days, all stock, tame or wild, belonged to the King until bought by certain favored individuals or families. Others could merely tend them.

2

Except for cyclic periods of drouth, the creeks were filled with clear running water fed by numerous springs, and populated with alligators as well as fish, eels, crawfish, snakes, and frogs.

Along the coast for about one hundred miles midway present Corpus Christi and Brownsville, beds of shifting, blowing sand obliterated the prairies in varying widths of fifteen to sixty-five miles. Encina (live oak), nueces (pecan), alamo (cottonwood), palo blanco (hackberry), and cypress trees grew along creeks and river bottoms, and in mottes around springs.

Also breaking the prairies into smaller units were the white-topped caliche hills along the Gulf-Rio Grande escarpment. These hills were sprinkled with cacti, ceniza (purple sage), mountain laurel, and such plants that would grow in the thin alkaline soil.

Deer, elk, antelopes, javelinas, and similar animals lived in these plains, and thrived because the immense herds of roving buffalos did not travel this far south.

During Texas Revolutionary and Republican days, the wild horses became the most numerous of the wild livestock, and the term "mesteñas" became anglicized as "mustangs."

TEXAS' FIRST CATTLE DRIVE

Texas' first recorded cattle drive started at the northern rim of the Llanos Mesteñas region across the Rio Grande from present Eagle Pass. Here, at San Juan Bautista Presidio, an entrada (expedition) gathered for the purpose of crossing Texas and forming a settlement and a protective presidio on the banks of the Red River where the Arroyo Hondo carried water close by, which it emptied into the river a few miles to the south.

Following a short distance back of the entrada was a drove of 300 head of cattle; and close behind them was a drove of 400 head of sheep. This first cattle drive followed El Camino Real (later called the Old San Antonio Road), which was blazed in 1690, through San Antonio and eastward to Los Adaes at a point seven leagues from the French post at Natchitoches, Louisiana.

Both droves of livestock arrived at Los Adaes on October 20, 1721, forming a part of the settlement plans of Texas' first capital.

Four thousand head of horses were also brought into Texas,

accompanying the entrada as far as San Antonio, where some were left for the soldiers, missionaries, and settlers. Others were distributed along the way at various posts and missions, so that only a small fraction of the original drove arrived at Los Adaes.

With the return of Louisiana Territory to Spain by France in 1763, trade across Texas became increasingly profitable. That is, until Spain got into difficulties in Europe and eventually returned Louisiana to France in 1800. Piracy in the Gulf of Mexico, mostly indulged in by the English and the French and a few Americans, was generally aimed at the rich Spanish loot. This further weakened legitimate trade. By 1800, most of the Spanish trade was centered from San Antonio southward.

During this time, San Antonio was said to have a population of about 7000. The North Mexican States paid for manuractured products with silver ore, livestock, and hides—whether the trade was legitimate or not.

George W. Bonnel, in his *Topographical Description of Texas*, published in 1840, gives several graphic reasons that explain why all major cattle drives initially began from the Mustang Plains. An example, . . . "The Agua Dulce, the Las Pintas, and Salt Creeks are three small streams which enter Corpus Christi Bay west of the mouth of the Nueces. They all run through a fertile body of musquit (sic) prairie land, which is almost entirely destitute of timber. In travelling over these extensive prairies, the eye is only relieved by the immense herds of wild horses, and cattle which are forever in view." (The mesquit refers to grass.)

About the area around the Los Olmos Creek and nearby salt lakes, he writes that it is ". . . the best stock raising country in the world, and the wild cattle, horses, deer, and elk resort to it in the thousands." He describes the Los Olmos as being "a stream sixty miles long."

Since mesquite beans rarely seem to sprout unless they have been in the stomach of a cow or other ruminant, one can see that man did not begin the change of the prairies into brushland; he merely accelerated the change.

By 1850, great numbers of sheep had been brought into deep South Texas. These animals, by their grazing habits of pulling up shallow-rooted plants and by very closely cropping others, helped denude the land so that mesquite trees and other shrubby plants could more easily take root.

4

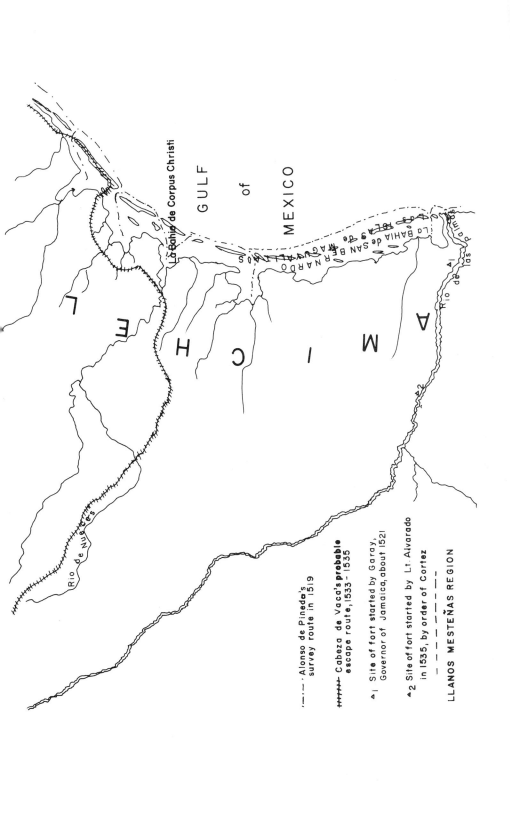

GULF of MEXICO

La Bahía de Corpus Christi

LA BAHÍA de SAN BERNARDO

ISLAS de MAGDALENAS

Río de las Palmas

Rio de Nueces

L E C H I C A M

·—·—· Alonso de Pineda's
survey route in 1519

++++++ Cabeza de Vaca's **probable**
escape route, 1533–1535

▲1 Site of fort started by Garay,
Governor of Jamaica, about 1521

▲2 Site of fort started by Lt. Alvarado
in 1535, by order of Cortez

LLANOS MESTEÑAS REGION

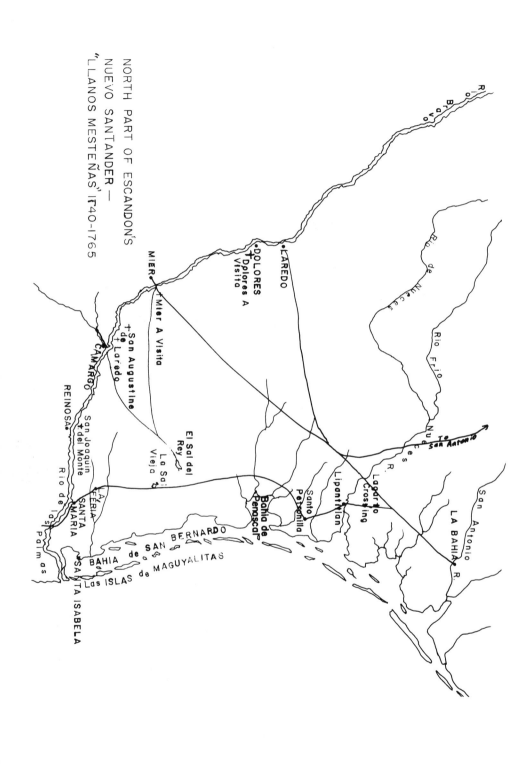

NORTH PART OF ESCANDON'S
NUEVO SANTANDER—
"LLANOS MESTEÑAS" 1740-1765

•LAREDO

•DOLORES
+Dolores A
Visita

MIER•
+Mier A Visita

+San Augustine
+de Laredo

CAMARGO

REINOSA•

San Joaquin
+del Monte

El Sal del
Rey

La Sal
Vieja

LA
FERIA

SANTA
MARIA

Bahia de
Peñascal

Santo
Petronilla

Lipantitlan

Lagarto
Crossing

To
San Antonio

BAHIA de SAN BERNARDO

SANTA ISABELA

Las ISLAS de MAGUYALITAS

LA BAHIA

San Antonio R.

Rio de las Palmas

Rio de Nueces

Rio Frio

Nueces R.

Rio Bravo

Rio Bravo

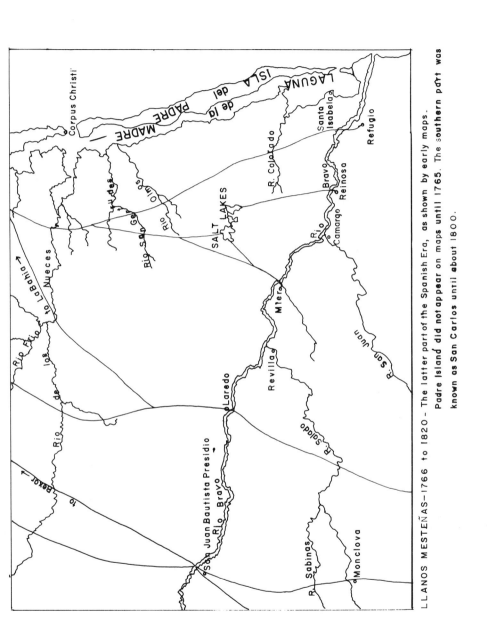

LLANOS MESTEÑAS—1766 to 1820 — The latter part of the Spanish Era, as shown by early maps. Padre Island did not appear on maps until 1765. The southern part was known as San Carlos until about 1800.

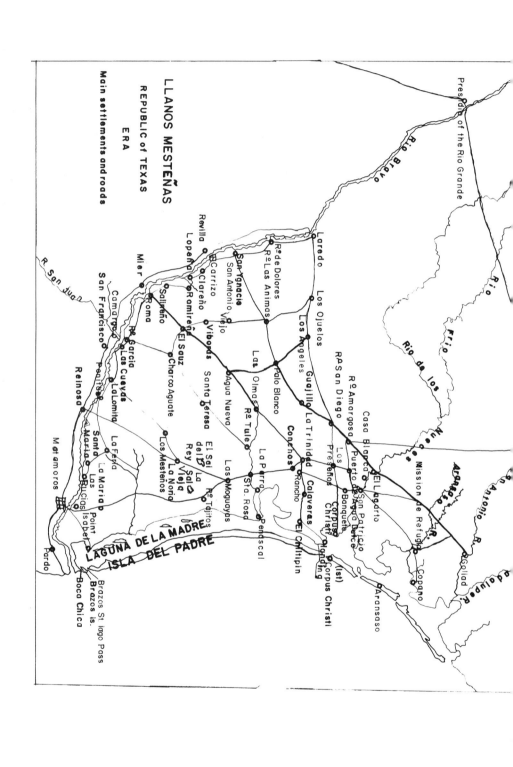

LLANOS MESTEÑAS
REPUBLIC of TEXAS
ERA
Main settlements and roads

Presidio of the Rio Grande

Rio Bravo

R. San Juan

Revilla
Lopeño
Mier
Roma
Camargo
San Francisco
Reinosa
Matamoros
Pardo

El Carrizo
Clareño
Ramireño
Salineño

San Ygnacio
San Antonio Viejo
Viboda
El Sauz
Charco Aguate

R.º de Dolores
R.º Las Animas
Las Olmas

R. García
Las Cuevas
La Lomita
Paalito
Santa María
Las Brucias

Laredo
Los Ojuelos

Los Angeles
Guajillo
Palo Blanco
Santa Teresa
Agua Nueva
R.º Tule
La Parra
El Sal
La Noria
Las Mesteños

La Trinidad
Conchos
Calaveras
Rancho
El Chiltipin
Las Moquayas
Sta. Rosa
R.º Tajitos
Pendscal

Casa Blanca
R.º Amargosa
R.ª San Diego
Los Presteños
Banqueta
Corpus Christi
(Ist) Kinding

Puerto Agua Dulce
San Patricio
El Lagarto

Mission de Refugio
Copano
Goliad
Aransaso

LAGUNA DE LA MADRE
ISLA DEL PADRE

Point Isabel
Brazos St Iago Pass
Brazos Is.
Boca Chica

Rio de los Nueces
Frio
R. de los
San Antonio R.
Guadalupe

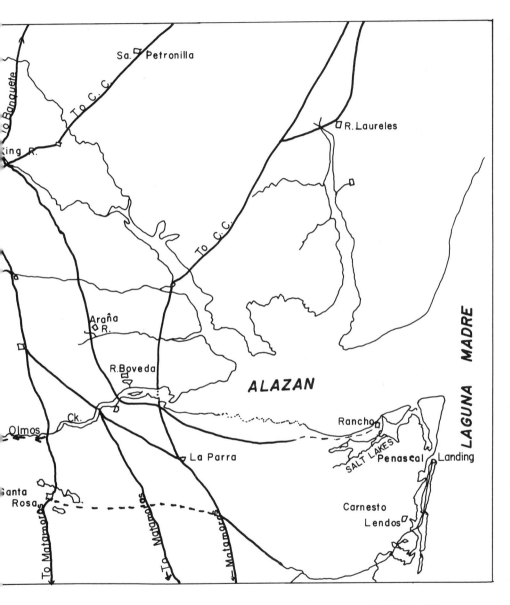

Sa. Petronilla

To C. C.

R. Laureles

To Banquete

ing R.

To C. C.

Araña R.

R. Boveda

ALAZAN

LAGUNA MADRE

Ck.

Olmos

Rancho

SALT LAKES

La Parra

Penascal Landing

Santa Rosa

To Matamoros

To Matamoros

To Matamoros

Carnesto Lendos

SMUGGLERS' PASS — AS MAPPED DURING THE REPUBLIC OF TEXAS ERA.

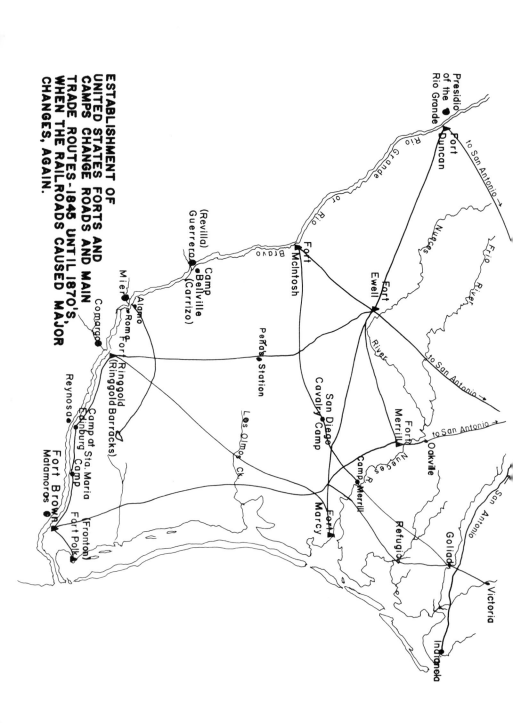

ESTABLISHMENT OF
UNITED STATES FORTS AND
CAMPS CHANGE ROADS AND MAIN
TRADE ROUTES-1845 UNTIL 1870'S,
WHEN THE RAILROADS CAUSED MAJOR
CHANGES, AGAIN.

Presidio
of the
Rio Grande

Fort
Duncan

to San Antonio

Rio Grande

Rio

Nueces

Frio River

Rio Bravo

(Revilla)
Guerrero

Camp
Bellville
(Carrizo)

Fort
McIntosh

Fort
Ewell

Mier

Comargo

Alamo

Roma

Fort
Ringgold
(Ringgold Barracks)

Peñas Station

River

San Diego
Cavalry Camp

Fort
Merrill

Oakville

to San Antonio

to San Antonio

Los Olmos Ck.

Camp Merrill

Nueces R.

Reynosa

Camp at Sta. Maria
Edinburg Camp

(Fronton)

Fort Brown
Matamoros

Fort Polk

Fort
Marcy

Refugio

Goliad

San Antonio

Victoria

Indianola

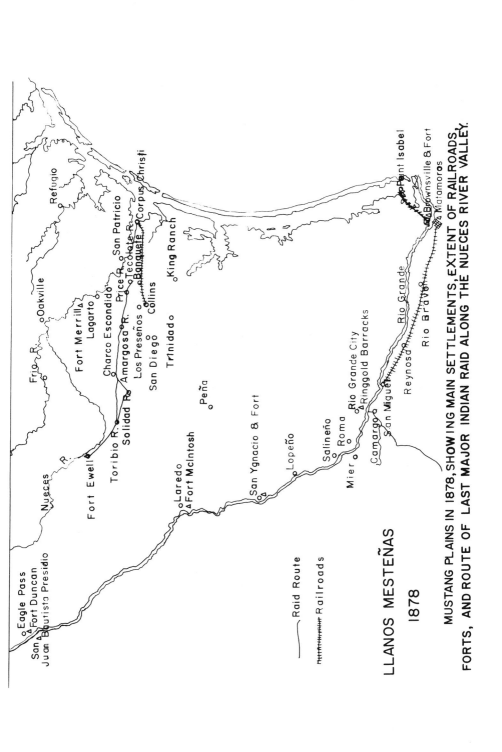

LLANOS MESTEÑAS
1878

MUSTANG PLAINS IN 1878, SHOWING MAIN SETTLEMENTS, EXTENT OF RAILROADS,
FORTS, AND ROUTE OF LAST MAJOR INDIAN RAID ALONG THE NUECES RIVER VALLEY.

Raid Route
Railroads

Eagle Pass
Fort Duncan
San
Juan Bautista Presidio

Nueces R.

Frio R.

Refugio

Oakville

Fort Merrill
Lagarto

Charco Escondido
Toribio R.
Solidad R.
Amargosa R.
Los Preseños
San Diego

Fort Ewell
Fort McIntosh
Laredo

San Ygnacio & Fort

Lopeño

Salineño
Roma
Mier

Camargo

San Miguel

Peña

Trinidad

San Patricio
Price
Tecolote R.
Banquete
Collins
King Ranch

Corpus Christi

Rio Grande City
Ringgold Barracks

Reynosa

Rio Grande
Rio Bravo

Point Isabel
Brownsville & Fort
Matamoros

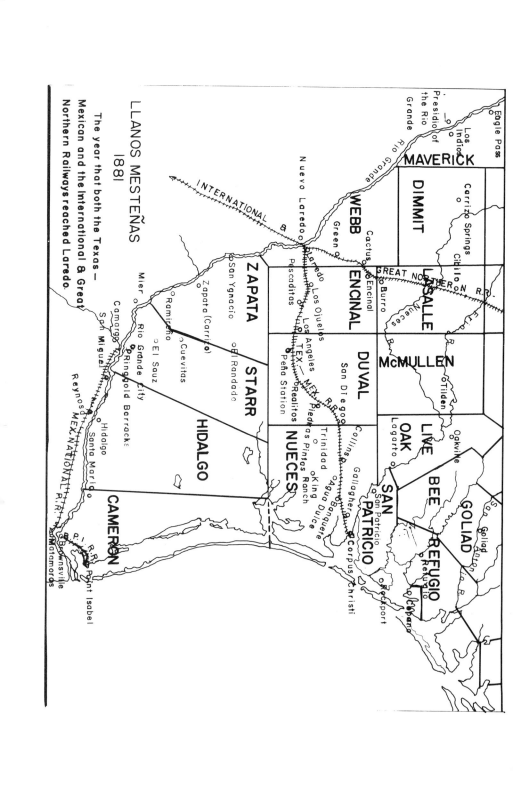

LLANOS MESTEÑAS
1881

The year that both the Texas –
Mexican and the International & Great
Northern Railways reached Laredo.

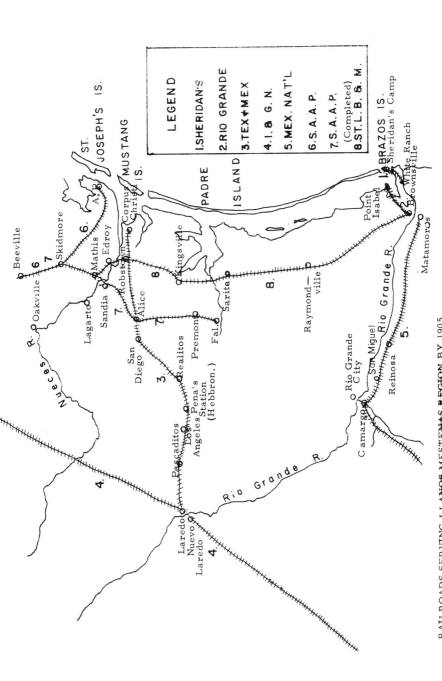

RAILROADS SERVING LLANOS MESTENAS REGION BY 1905

LEGEND

1. SHERIDAN'S
2. RIO GRANDE
3. TEX ✦ MEX
4. I. & G. N.
5. MEX. NAT'L
6. S. A. A. P.
7. S. A. A. P.
   (Completed)
8. ST. L. B. & M.

Poniente

Terrenos sigetos a los soberanos del: bene: Sobre terminos de Jamauli: pas y Nuevo Leon.

125 — B — 800 — 33 — 367 — H

Lindes Pentenbadss ʔ la Villa de los Aldamas

1

545

Río del Alamo

Juelas

Lindes pacificos con Revilla

Salinillas

Norte

Monte ... Nros. 125

2

L

75

250

430

140

4

Lindes con China ... Camargo Med.

258

G

700

100

100

Río Grande

Nocha buena

555

Lindes Pacifs con Revilla 400 s.

m.

500

6

K

112

Sur

242

b ... 230

Camargo

387

Lindes litrigiosos con

Y

400

83.44

184.11

L

N 320

7

Guardado

Chapote

Ceballo

92.20

Oriente

Lindes litrigiosos

Amplion terrenos a las Nueces 800 cond.

Lis ʔ cond.

Camargo

n

Nordeste

Resumen

1.ª figura vale 68.125
2. .... 15.550
3. 430
4. .... 19.460
5. liquida 1.315.097
6. .... 108.000
7. .... 317.520
         Suma 1.844.182

En condeladados cuadanadas
que son 18 A. sitios, y 4182 cond.ª cuadnados

Mier

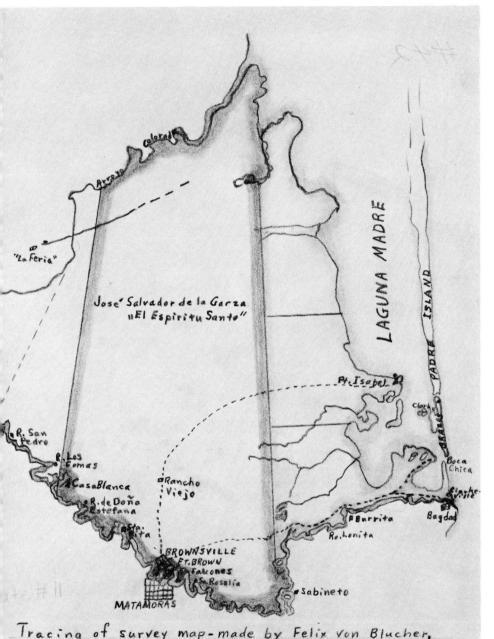

Colorado

Arroyo

"La Feria"

José Salvador de la Garza
"El Espíritu Santo"

LAGUNA MADRE

PADRE ISLAND

Pt. Isabel

Clark

R. San Pedro

Los Tomas

CasaBlanca

R. de Doña Estefana

Sta. Rita

Rancho Viejo

Boca Chica

Clarks...ville

Bagdad

Burrita

Ro.Bonita

BROWNSVILLE
FT. BROWN
Falcones
Sa. Rosalía

Sabineto

MATAMORAS

Tracing of survey map-made by Felix von Blucher,
First Official Nueces District Surveyor, about 1860.
Grant Made 1790 - El Espíritu Santo (in Genl. Land Of

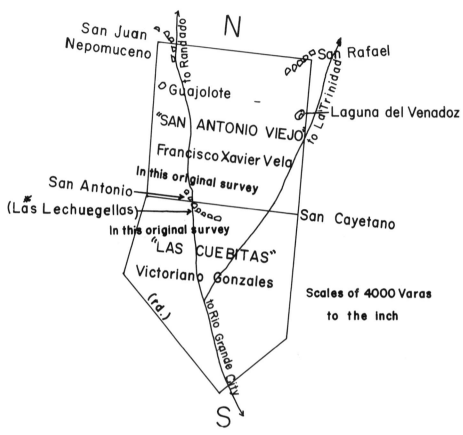

FROM FIELD NOTES OF A SURVEY... CALLED "SAN ANTONIO", MADE FOR HEIRS OF XAVIER VELA; GRANTED FROM THE STATE OF TAMAULIPAS, MEXICO TO FRANCISCO XAVIER VELA, DATED JULY 30, 1805. SAID SURVEY IS IN STARR COUNTY, SITUATED AT THE SAN ANTONIO WELLS, ON THE ROAD FROM RIO GRANDE CITY TO LAREDO, ABOUT 32 MILES NORTH OF RIO GRANDE CITY, BY WAY OF RANDADO. ✳(THIS SURVEY MADE SEPTEMBER 5, 1869.) MAPPED AS "CUEVITAS" BY 1879. PRESENT "GHOST-TOWN". INTERESTING RUINS EXTANT. DATE BURNED INTO RAFTER OF SETTLEMENT FORT, "SEPT-IEMBRE 13, 1871".

Agostadero de Los Ojuelos

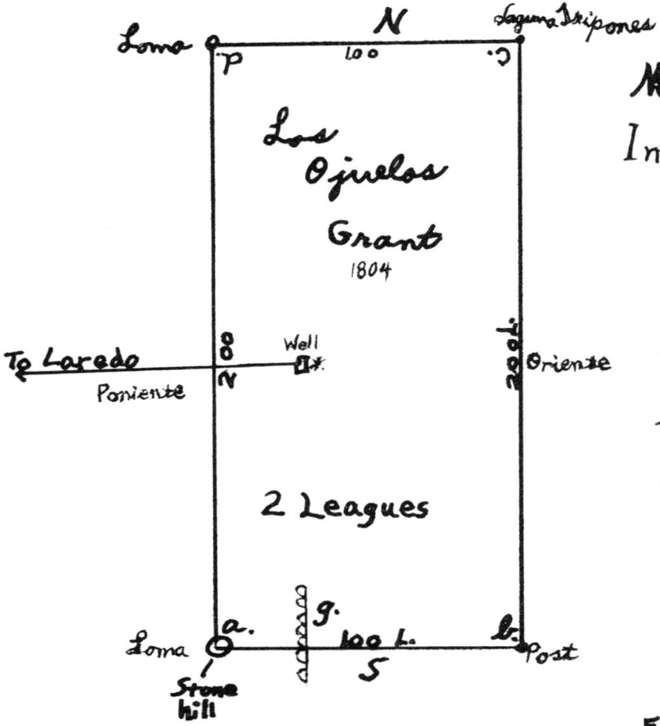

Medido para el C. Ysidro Gutierrez.

In Southeastern part of present

Webb County.

a. Lindero de la Leona

b. Sa. del alto atrabesado

c. Lg. de los Tripones

d. Jd. de la loma de piedras

g. Villa de Los Ojuelos

*. 88° Ne. from Santo Porcion

File 563-Dt. San Patricio-Ab.1393.

Laguna Tripones

C.

N

100

Los Ojuelos Grant 1804

Well

8 N

Poniente

To Loredo

Loma

2 Leagues

Oriente

g.

100 L.

S

a.

Stone hill

Loma

P

L. Post

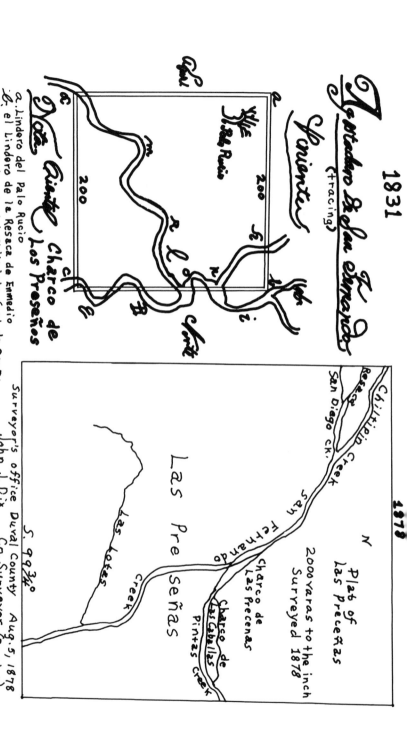

1831

Testadero de San Fernando
(tracing)

Poniente

200

200

Aqui

Villa
Viejo Ruia

Note: *Siente Charco de Los Preseños*

a. Lindero del Palo Rucio
b. el Lindero de la Reseca de Enmedio
c. A.B. es el Arroyo del Chiltipin: A. el de SanDiego
C. el el Pascidiso
d. el del Rincon: des la Reseca de Enmedia.
H. Charco de los Preseños: O. Charco de los Caballos
L. R.M.: el Arroyo de San Fernando al cual des prendiendose del chiltipin hase (?) curso
por depando de Norte a Sur nonsette haste la Laguna Meadne.... (Certified Nov. 16, 1831.)

u.s.e.

1878

N

Plat of
Las Preceñas

200 varas to the inch
Surveyed 1878

Chiltipin Creek

San Diego Ck.
Reseca

San Fernando

Charco de
Las Precenas

Charco de
Las Caballos

Pintas Creek

Las Preseñas

Las Lotes
Creek

Surveyor's office Duval County Aug. 5, 1878
John J. Dix Co. Surveyor (tracing)

S. 99¾°

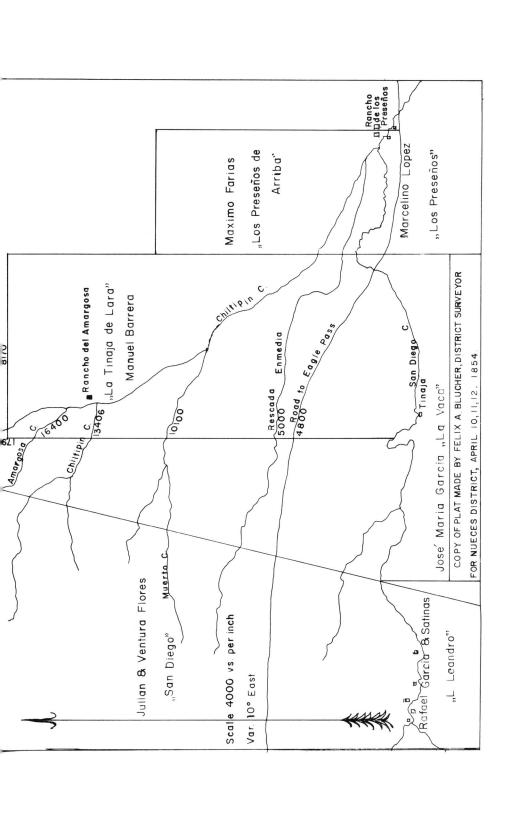

Julian & Ventura Flores

"San Diego"

Scale 4000 vs. per inch

Var. 10° East

Rafael García & Satinas

"L. Leandro"

José María García "La Vaca"

COPY OF PLAT MADE BY FELIX A. BLUCHER, DISTRICT SURVEYOR

FOR NUECES DISTRICT, APRIL 10, 11, 12. 1854

Rancho del Amargosa

"La Tinaja de Lara"

Manuel Barrera

Máximo Farias

"Los Preseños de Arriba"

Marcelino López

"Los Preseños"

Rancho de los Preseños

Amargosa C.

16400

Chiltipin C.

13406

Muerto C.

10100

Chiltipin C.

Rescada 5000

Enmedia

Road to Eagle Pass 4800

San Diego C.

Tinaja

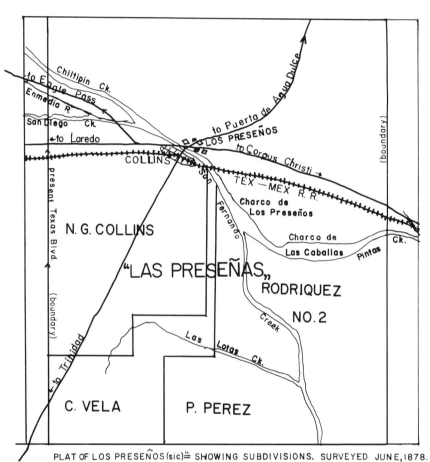

Chiltipin Ck.

to Eagle Pass

Enmedia R.

San Diego Ck.

←to Laredo

to Puerta de Agua Dulce

LOS PRESEÑOS

to Corpus Christi →

COLLINS

TEX — MEX R. R.

present Texas Blvd. (boundary)

(boundary)

N. G. COLLINS

San Fernando

Charco de Los Preseños

Charco de Las Caballas

Pintas

Ck.

"LAS PRESEÑAS,,

RODRIQUEZ

NO. 2

Creek

Las Lotas Ck.

←to Trinidad

C. VELA

P. PEREZ

PLAT OF LOS PRESEÑOS (sic)⁼ SHOWING SUBDIVISIONS. SURVEYED JUNE, 1878.
SURVEYOR'S OFFICE, DUVAL COUNTY, AUGUST 5, 1878. JOHN J. DIX, COUNTY
SURVEYOR. (⁼Note:Spelling as on plat and caption in public records.) Roads based on
Felix von Blucher's surveys. Compiled by Agnes G. Grimm.

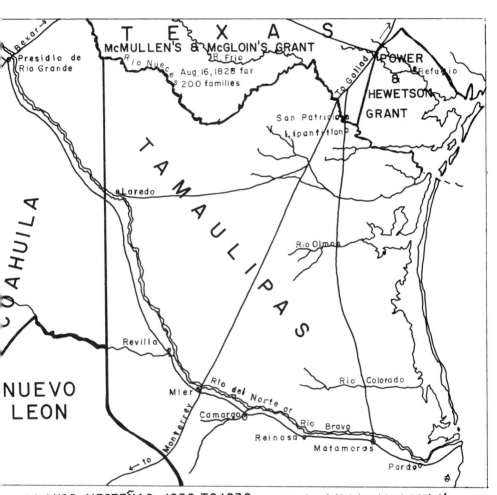

LLANOS MESTEÑAS—1828 TO 1836. Political subdivisions, as a part of Tamaulipas, Mexico during the Mexican Era of Texas.

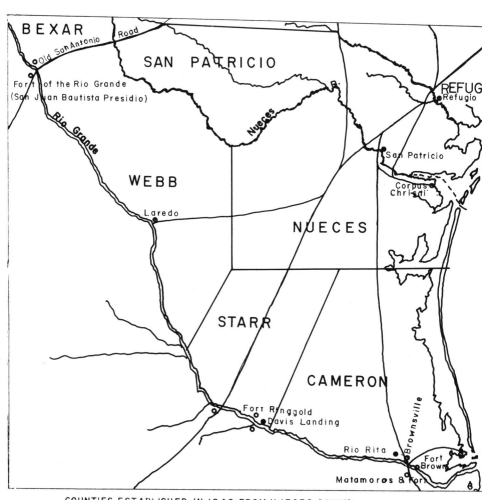

BEXAR

Old San Antonio Road

SAN PATRICIO

Fort of the Rio Grande
(San Juan Bautista Presidio)

REFUG
Refugio

Rio Grande

Nueces

San Patricio

WEBB

Corpus
Christi

Laredo

NUECES

STARR

CAMERON

Fort Ringgold
Davis Landing

Brownsville

Rio Rita

Fort
Brown

Matamoros & Fort

COUNTIES ESTABLISHED IN 1848 FROM NUECES COUNTY; also Refugio and
San Patricio Counties, which were original counties; also United States forts that
were established by 1848; and county seats.

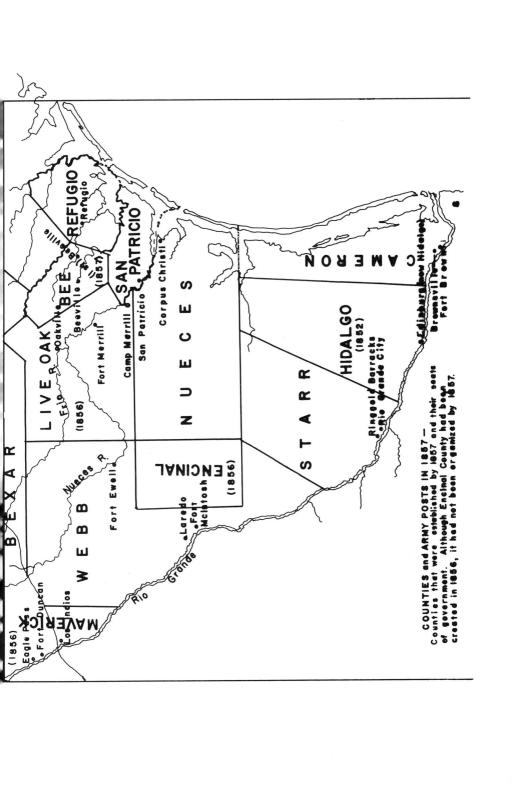

COUNTIES and ARMY POSTS IN 1857 —
Counties that were established by 1857 and their seats
of government. Although Encinal County had been
created in 1856, it had not been organized by 1857.

COUNTY BOUNDARIES
1858-1899

County boundaries of Llanos Mesteñas Region remained like this, with the exception of the creation of Aransas County in 1871, from 1858 until March 12, 1899.

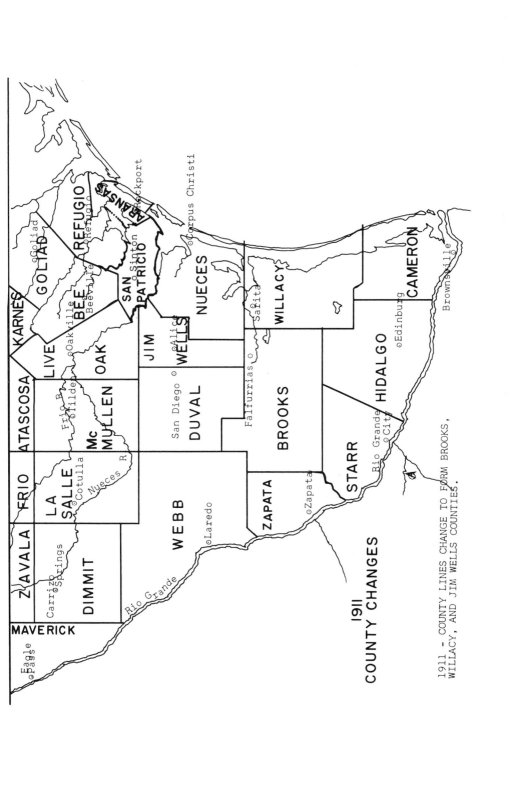

1911 - COUNTY LINES CHANGE TO FORM BROOKS, WILLACY, AND JIM WELLS COUNTIES.

1911 COUNTY CHANGES

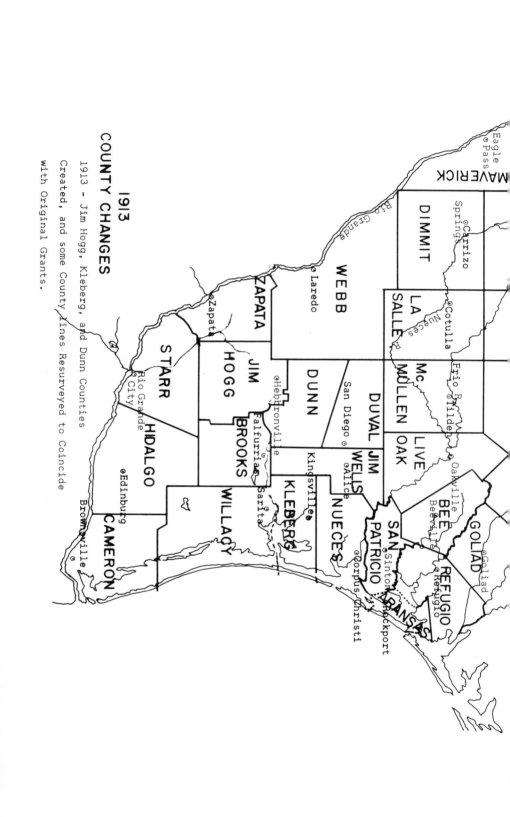

1913
COUNTY CHANGES

1913 - Jim Hogg, Kleberg, and Dunn Counties
Created, and some County Lines Resurveyed to Coincide
with Original Grants.

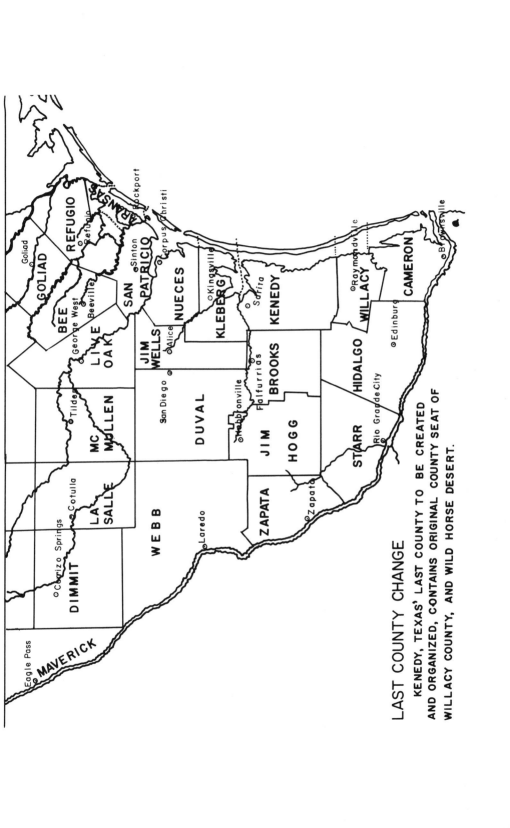

LAST COUNTY CHANGE

KENEDY, TEXAS' LAST COUNTY TO BE CREATED AND ORGANIZED, CONTAINS ORIGINAL COUNTY SEAT OF WILLACY COUNTY, AND WILD HORSE DESERT.

MAVERICK
Eagle Pass

DIMMIT
○Carrizo Springs

○Cotulla

LA SALLE

MC MULLEN
○Tilden

WEBB
○Laredo

DUVAL
San Diego ○

ZAPATA
○Zapata

JIM HOGG

STARR
Rio Grande City ○

HIDALGO
○Edinburg

CAMERON
○Brownsville

WILLACY
○Raymondville

KENEDY
○Sarita

BROOKS
Falfurrias ○

JIM WELLS
Alice ○
○Hebbronville

KLEBERG
○Kingsville

NUECES
Corpus Christi ○

SAN PATRICIO
○Sinton

LIVE OAK
George West ○

BEE
Beeville ○

GOLIAD
Goliad ○

REFUGIO
Refugio ○

ARANSAS
Rockport

Monument erected by the State of Texas commemorating Mission Dolores a Visita, located on Highway 83 in Zapata County near Falcon Dam and Reservoir.

Don Jesus de la Garza

IN THE VICINITY OF
THIS SITE WAS

MISSION MIER
A VISITA

ESTABLISHED IN 1750 AS A PART OF
JOSE DE ESCANDON'S PROJECT TO
SETTLE THE REGION AND CIVILIZE
AND CHRISTIANIZE THE INDIANS

Mission Mier a Visita Monument, erected by the State of Texas in 1936. On Highway 83, about 3.5 miles northwest of Roma.

Ruins of Old Dolores; rebuilt during 19th Century; in Zapata
County near banks of the Rio Grande.

Village Scene (deserted)

Reconstructed mission church at Ria Rita, first Anglo-American settlement in Lower Rio Grande Valley, and first county seat of Cameron County. Near Brownsville.

Abandoned convent, built in 1887, at Roma

Church at Santa Maria, built 1824

Old mission at Bentsen State Park near McAllen; erected about 1861.

ONE MILE NORTHEAST
IS THE SITE OF
FORT LIPANTITLAN
OCCUPIED IN 1831 BY
SOLDIERS OF THE MEXICAN ARMY

CAPTURED NOV. 4, 1835
BY VOLUNTEERS UNDER
CAPT. IRA WESTOVER

UNSUCCESSFULLY ATTACKED
JUNE 7, 1842 BY AN ARMY
UNDER GEN. ANTONIO CANALES

Fort Lipantitlan Monument, at site of old fort on south bank of the Nueces River across from San Patricio.

Old Camp Casa Blanca ruins near south bank of Nueces River in extreme southeast corner of present Live Oak County. Officially called "Camp Merrill." (See page 23) a & b (2 views)

Cattle drives routed through these pastures further accelerated the spread of brush.

During the Civil War years, a very severe drouth parched the Mustang Plains. Quite a bit of activity in the form of cotton smuggling and the obtaining of food, especially meat for soldiers, further helped to deplete the native grasses.

With the coming of the railroads, this South Texas frontier was opened wide for settlers. Their increased activities of stock raising and of plowing up numerous acres of sod, without proper knowledge of dryland farming, and more years of drouth and the depleting of underground water sources completed the change-over from prairieland to brushland by the early part of the 20th Century.

CHURCHES COME TO THE LLANOS MESTEÑAS

With the Franciscan monks as its vanguard in the New World, Christianity was extended to the Llanos Mesteñas in 1699 when San Juan Bautista (Saint John the Baptist) Mission was established for the purpose of Christianizing and civilizing the tribal Indians living in the vicinity. This mission was across the Rio Grande near present Eagle Pass.

However, the Indians inhospitably moved elsewhere, so the mission was abandoned. In 1701, the Presidio San Juan Bautista was established at a more favorable location a few miles to the south of the old mission site, complete with a chapel and priests. This presidio, later usually referred to by English-speaking Texans as the "Presidio of the Rio Grande," played an important part in Texas history for the next century and a half.

As part of the Escandón colonizing project of the middle 1700's, a number of sub-missions were established along the Rio Grande south of Laredo, which was established in 1755.

The first colony on the left (Texas) side of the Rio Grande was named "Hacienda de Nuestra Señora de Guadalupe de los Dolores." It was started in 1750, along with its mission of the same name, in the extreme northwest corner of present Zapata County.

Along the Nueces River, also as a part of the Escandón enterprise, Mission Nuestra Señora de la Sota was begun, along with a settlement, on the south bank of the river about a mile and a half west of the bay. But the Karankawa Indians who

5

inhabited the coastal prairies and islands were extremely hostile and cannibalistic. They proved so troublesome that the colonists and priests moved to the fort about thirty miles up the river that was built to protect the silver mining operations of the King of Spain.

During the Mexican Revolution, because of the withdrawal of Spanish troops from the frontier, the Indians moved back into the area with increased strength and hostility. Isolated missions and haciendas were destroyed, and trade routes were threatened.

Although the Mexican Government made a real effort, beginning in 1830, to settle the Llanos Mesteñas, no churches were established. Circumstances remained the same during Republic of Texas days.

At Corpus Christi, in the wake of Zachary Taylor's Army, with resultant increase in population, "English Catholic" services were reported to have been held in 1846, but no report of a church building has been found.

In Brownsville, Father Telmon of the Oblate Fathers built the first church in 1848. It was a wooden frame building that contained four rooms, each eight feet square, to house the clergy, in addition to the church. This was built and furnished at a total cost, including the land, of $1700. By 1893, a parish priest and five assistants were housed in a roomy clerical residence—in charge of a beautiful cathedral, plus ten chapels to be visited once or twice monthly, plus 285 ranches to be visited four times a year.

In Corpus Christi, the first resident pastor was Father Bernard O'Reilly, a native of Dublin, Ireland, who was sent here in 1853. The first recorded baptism signed by him was dated June 14, 1853. No church or chapel existed, but before the end of 1853, one was started in which services were being held by 1855, although the edifice was not completed until 1857. This first Saint Patrick's Church was rectangular, forty feet long and nearly as high. A small belfry rose from the middle of the facade.

Father Claude Jaillet arrived during the early throes of Reconstruction in 1866. He was the first Roman Catholic to be assigned a parish in the hinterlands of the Mustang Plains, away from the Lower Rio Grande Valley and away from the coast. He arrived in Corpus Christi in October of 1866, and was sent to San Diego, by way of horseback and alone, within a

6

week. Father Jaillet spoke only French, English, and German—the people of San Diego, for the most part, spoke only Spanish. Within six weeks, he was speaking and preaching in pure Castillian Spanish—as his Bishop had ordered. By the early summer of 1867, Father Jaillet had built a church 30 feet long by ten feet wide, of imported wood, at a cost of $700. The cost of the wood was $30.00 per thousand board feet; but it cost $40.00 per thousand to get it hauled from Corpus Christi.

At Collins, which thrived from 1878 until 1888, the only building erected for the purpose of being a church was built almost single-handedly by Father Peter Bard. He was the parish priest sent to assist Father Jaillet in 1877. By the early part of 1885, the church building was completed. It was of clapboard with a highrising roof, and even had a bell and bell tower. This church was strongly constructed. It was about 25 by 35 feet, so was not too difficult to move when the residents began abandoning Collins. It was moved to Alice (then Kleberg) in 1889 and was used as the only Catholic Church there until it burned in 1916.

The first Protestant Episcopal Church to be established in this region was in Brownsville. On April 17, 1851, the first organizational meeting was held. On April 20, in a building owned by Al Werbiski, the first church services were conducted by the Reverend William Passmore of North Carolina. He had been in Brownsville for two or three months. By 1854, the first church was completed and in use regularly.

The Presbyterian Church in Brownsville was a casualty of the Civil War. Some organization and a few services had been conducted under the leadership of the missionary, the Reverend Daniel Baker, who was from a Northern State. With the beginning of hostilities and with the division of the church national organization in 1861, no further interest was manifested until after the close of the war. The Presbyterian Church (South) appointed a missionary to reorganize the church at Brownsville, through the appeal and assistance of Edward Downey of Brownsville. By 1870, the first church building was completed, with the Reverend Mr. Greybill as its first pastor. This first church had a seating capacity of 300 persons.

Although the Methodist Episcopal Church, South (which was the Methodist Church in Texas for half a century following the Civil War) had no church building in Collins and no district organization, Methodists held services in the spacious lumber company building owned by Mrs. E. D. Sidbury, about eight years before the Alice Circuit was formed. In 1889, services were held in Kleberg (Alice) in the twenty-by-forty-foot log school building that was erected by George Hobbs and George Newberry and others. In 1895, the Alice Circuit was formed, with Brother W. A. Turner as Alice's first Circuit preacher.

In the present Jim Wells County area, the first Protestant Episcopal services to be held were in 1873, in the dining room of T. C. Wright's spacious home in Driscoll (name changed to Alfred in 1904). Bishops from San Antonio regularly visited and held services there, along with various San Antonio and Corpus Christi ministers, until 1903. At this time, the home burned and Mr. Wright died from burns received in the blaze.

The first building in Alice to be erected solely for the purpose of use as a church, was the Episcopal Church of the Advent, which was built in 1896. It was erected at the corner of Wright and Second Streets, where the present church stands. On January 7, 1896, the ground was broken to begin the mason work for the church. The cornerstone was laid January 9, by the Right Reverend J. S. Johnston, D. D., assisted by the pastor, the Reverend W. G. W. Smith. The following articles were put into the cornerstone: one copy of the King James version of the Holy Bible; one copy of the revised *Prayer Book of the American Church, 1892;* one each of *The San Antonio Express, The San Diego Sun, The Houston Post,* and *The Alice Echo;* and a few coins dated from 1880 to 1895.

The members shared their church with other Protestant Church groups who had not yet built church buildings.

ST. DENÍS TRIGGERS SPANISH ACTIVITY

Although early Spanish and Mexican governments did not consider the area between the Nueces and the Rio Grande as part of Texas, the French—since the time of St. Denís—considered the Province of Texas as continuing along the coastal prairies to the Rio Grande and following the Rio Grande as its border northwestward to the Pecos River (then mapped as the Rio Puerco), and due north to about 38 degrees latitude. The French mapped Texas as a part of Louisiana and belonging to France, because in 1714 the Frenchman Louis Júchereau de St. Denís crossed Texas from present Natchitoches, Louisiana to

8

Presidio San Juan Bautista on the Rio Grande without meeting a single Spaniard.

This feat so upset the Spaniards that they began, as fast as their unwieldy centrally-controlled government could allow, to travel through Texas and establish presidios, missions, and trading posts. They traveled through the coastal region and wrote about the extensive plains in the deep southern part filled with deer, elk, antelopes, javelinas, and turkeys.

Ranchers began to send their herds across the Rio Grande into the rich prairies. Forted haciendas were built. Horses and cows that escaped from military entradas, herdsmen, and missions were thriving and increasing unbelievably. Then the Indians began attacking in greater force, learning to master the horse, and attack more speedily and frequently; and again Spain withdrew into Mexico and lost interest in Texas. But when England and France again became interested in Texas, Spain decided to make another all-out effort to conquer the Indians and colonize the great region along either side of the Lower Rio Grande.

Finding an able man to settle and govern Nuevo Santander, as the province was called, was easy—José de Escandón filled the bill ably.

When Escandón made an extensive survey of the region in 1760, records show that the grant, "El Chiltipin," was inhabited by Blas María de la Falcón and his family, along with a company of royal soldiers and a score of retainers. He called his ranch, "Real de Santa Petronilla."

Herdsmen for Julian Flores occupied the ranch, "San Diego," as early as 1815. Juan Saenz, whose father was head herdsman for Señor Flores, was born at the ranch that year. This fact was recorded when he testified at the trial entitled "Hamilton P. Bee vs. The State of Texas" in 1860. Judge E. J. Davis, later to become the hated Reconstruction Governor of Texas, presided.

Mexican maps, including maps by Stephen F. Austin, show main roads through the Llanos de Las Mesteñas region as leading from Mier to the Lagarto Crossing of the Nueces River, and from Matamoros almost due north through Lipantitlán across the Nueces at San Patricio.

Had it not been for the Mexican Revolution, and had the Municipality of Mier continued to develop according to Escan-

9

dón's plans, Alice would have been included in the Mier Municipality. Present Texas Boulevard in Alice (extended north of San Diego Creek to the Nueces River) runs along the former Mier-Camargo boundary line. This is the line separating La Tinaja de Lara Grant, which was authorized by Mier Municipality, and Los Preseños de Arriba Grant, which was authorized by Camargo Municipality. South of San Diego Creek, the line extends, forming the boundary between the La Vaca Grant on the west side of Texas Boulevard issued by Mier Municipality, and the Los Preseños Grant in the Agostadero de San Fernando, issued by Camargo authorities.

JOSÉ DE ESCANDÓN'S PLAN

According to the Spanish way of thinking, it was necessary to learn something of a region before bringing in colonists. Before Nuevo Santander could be settled, the region must be surveyed. José de Escandón was given the project of conquering the Indians, learning the geography of the region, and taking a census of the plant and animal life between the Guadalupe River and the Rio Grande.

Escandón was appointed to the position July 9, 1746. By January 1, 1747, he was ready with the necessary men and equipment to carry out his plans to make a preliminary exploration of this virtually unknown region.

Within three months, he had carried out these plans. Previously, two large-scale and several lesser attempts had been made to establish settlements near the mouth of the Rio Grande; none had succeeded because of the extreme hostility of the natives.

The main points of Escandón's exploration plan were as follows:

1. With seven different surveying parties, each accompanied by a guard of soldiers, to enter the region from seven different points at one time. (The chief purpose for using so many groups was to awe the Indians. Heretofore, only one group had gone into the region at a time, and word of their coming had gone ahead of them.)

2. To survey and map the entire region in order to know the natives, resources, and best sites for missions and settlements.

Within three months, under Escandón's leadership, 12,000 square miles of virgin territory was explored, surveyed, and mapped. The native Indian tribes were located, named, and numbered; landform features were located and many were named; the plant life was identified; and the large herds of animals were located and their numbers were estimated. Before this survey, the Nueces was thought to be a tributary of the Rio Grande. Also, for the first time, Corpus Christi Bay was fully described.

A tribe of Negroid Indians was found near the mouth of the Rio Grande. The probable explanation of this surprising group is that they were survivors and descendants of survivors of three previous attempts at settlement along the mouth of the Rio Grande. The first was directly from Jamaica and the other two were from Cuba.

Already in existence were Presidio and Mission de La Bahía, Fort Lipantitlán across the Nueces from present San Patricio, and Santa Petronilla near present Chapman Ranch in Nueces County. These were described in Escandón's report.

In 1734, the Spaniards had erected a fort at the Indian village of Lipantitlán because it was at the best crossing of the Nueces River in this vicinity. The fort was occupied from time to time by Spanish soldiers.

Irish settlers brought into Texas by John McMullen and James McGloin settled across the Nueces from Lipantitlán and named the settlement for their patron saint, Patrick (San Patricio in Spanish). The Irish could not pronounce the word "Lipantitlán," so they called it "Le Panticlan."

The fort is better known for the part it played in the Texas Revolution. It fell into the Texans' hands with scarcely a fight because of the superior quality of their arms. By this time, the fort was almost in ruins, for the Mexicans had neither improved nor repaired it. It was described by the occupying Texans as a "poor second-class hog pen."

Following the Texas Revolution, while much of northern Mexico was still fighting for independence, Lipantitlán was occupied for several months by Mexican Federalists still trying to restore the Constitution of 1824. It was here at Lipantitlán that the Federalists in 1840, after they had been forced back across the Rio Grande for the third time, raised the flag of "The Republic of the Rio Grande" (also called "The Republic of the North") under the leadership of General Antonio Canales.

COLONIZATION BEGAN IN 1748

The Rio Grande was called "Rio Bravo del Norte" during Spanish colonial days while the relatively short-lived province of Nuevo Santander was created, surveyed, and colonized to a much greater extent than is generally recognized.

Within six months from the time of his appointment as governor of this new province between the Pánuco and the Nueces Rivers that was to be colonized, Don José de Escandón had surveyed and mapped the area, had submitted his recommendations, and was ready to start colonizing.

When Escandón and his surveyors mapped the region, they used many descriptive terms in naming areas. Some of these were: Ojo de Agua, Llano de Las Mesteñas, Charcos de Salada, Las Casteñas, Loma Blanca, Loma Verde, La Féria, Llano de La Flórida, Resaco del Gato, and Agua Poquita. Some of these places were already occupied by Indians, Mestizos, or Spaniards, and the names already in use were usually retained.

Escandón actually began colonizing in 1748 and led in the establishment of several municipalities and villages, most of which are still in existence. The municipalities of Revilla, Mier, Camargo, and Reynosa extended from the rim of the lower basin of the Rio Grande northward to the Nueces River.

Some missions and sub-missions were also established. In 1749 near the present town of Hidalgo in the Lower Rio Grande Valley, Mission San Joaquín del Monte a Visita, and two miles west of present Rio Grande City, Mission San Augustín de Laredo a Visita were established. In 1750, Mission Mier a Visita, 3.5 miles northwest of present Roma on Highway 83, and Mission Dolores a Visita, 25 miles south of Laredo near Highway 83, were established. These old sub-mission sites are marked by Texas State monuments.

José de Escandón established 23 settlements with about 6,000 settlers. By the end of the 18th Century, there were 15,000 inhabitants in the province of Nuevo Santander.

The municipalities of Mier, Camargo, and Reynosa were divided among the settlers in 1767. Beginning with the church plazas as the center, the municipalities were laid off in squares of 10,000 varas on each side for the towns; then the porciónes were surveyed.

Making them as nearly equal as the natural environment would allow, 111 porciónes—with an average width of 1500 varas and a depth of 12,500 to 20,000 varas—were allotted to the first settlers of Camargo. Eighty porciónes, with an average width of 1250 varas and of the same average depth as those of Camargo, were laid off and allotted to Reynosa's first settlers. Some of the porciónes from the Camargo survey extended into the Mier area. These were the only ones surveyed in the Mier Municipality. Similar porciónes surveys were also made south of the Rio Grande opposite those on the north side.

When the Mexican Government was organized following its revolution and freedom from Spain, the State of Tamaulipas was formed from the Nuevo Santander Province.

SOME EARLY SETTLEMENTS

José de Escandón, governor of the newly organized province of Nuevo Santander, reported to the Viceroy in Mexico City in October of 1775 that, since December of 1748, twenty-three settlements—totaling 6,334 inhabitants—had been made; and by August 18, 1757, thirty-four settlements had been established.

More of these settlements were south of the Rio Grande than to the north, with the majority along the river banks. However, nine had been made along El Sauz (also called Los Olmos) Creek in present Jim Hogg and Starr Counties.

Carnestolíndas, later called Rancho Davis and then Rio Grande City, was settled with a few families on March 10, 1753, at the mouth of El Sauz Creek. Others along the creek were El Sauz, Las Viboras, Las Cueb(v)itas, San Raphael, San Cayetáño, and Lechuguellas.

In the northwest corner of present Zapata County, La Villa de Dolores and the Mission Nuestra Senora de los Dolores were established August 22, 1750. A marker just off Highway 83 marks the mission and settlement.

Nearby, over a short primitive road through a ranch, are interesting ruins of the Old Dolores settlement that continued to exist into the 20th Century. A couple of the thick rock walls have been re-roofed and are being used for hunting lodges. Walls of about a dozen old stone houses are still standing, while many more foundations remain visible among the brush.

Of the greatest interest is an oblong ruins rounded at one end, and a row of casa hornos (outdoor baking ovens). Some of these old ovens are still intact, while others are in all stages of ruin. The construction of these old ovens, their caliche mortar baked into a lasting setting, is fascinating.

13

In 1755, Colonel José de Escandón had encouraged the settlement of La Villa de Vedoya with a group of fifty settlers at the mouth of the Nueces River. Mission Nuestra Señora de La Soto was begun nearby.

The Karankawa Indians, cannibalistic and foul smelling because of the fish oil they rubbed on themselves to repel mosquitoes, were loathed by many other Indian tribes as well as the Spaniards. They were so numerous and troublesome around the Nueces River near the coast, that the Spaniards soon abandoned both sites and joined the presidial soldiers about thirty miles upstream near the west bank of the river.

A fort was built here on a high bank near the mouth of Penitas Creek, about one and a quarter miles from where it flowed into the Nueces. Its twenty-foot walls built of caliche blocks protected the religious leaders, settlers, and miner-soldiers from the cannibal Indians roaming the vicinity.

Tomás Sanchez, founder of Laredo and a lieutenant under Colonel José de Escandón, reported mining operations on both the Penitas and nearby Barbon Creeks shortly after the establishment of the above-mentioned forted mission and settlement in 1755.

Captain Enrique Villarreal, commanding officer of a small garrison of soldiers near the mouth of the Nueces River in the vicinity of present Corpus Christi, reported to the King of Spain during the last decade of the 18th Century that a silver mine two days' journey from Corpus Christi Bay had been attacked and the entire mining crew killed. The captain was appealing for more soldiers.

He made this appeal directly to the King, because Spain's hold on the Mexican Government was deteriorating rapidly, and he complained that he had been largely ignored by the Viceroy. It will also be remembered that Laredo and other settlements and grants of land in Nuevo Santander were settled mostly by Castillians, so that this region remained generally loyal to Spain for a longer time than other parts of Mexico.

The old fort at Penitas Creek is on the Wallis Wade property, and the following description of its ruins was obtained from Mrs. Wallis Wade in 1964. She had moved onto the property as the 16-year-old bride of Wallis Wade, near the turn of the century.

The fort was built in the form of a hollow square, with a courtyard in the center and living quarters and other buildings along the outer wall, utilizing it to anchor roofs and strengthen inner walls. It was typically Spanish.

The outer walls were between eighteen and twenty feet high and three feet thick. The outer wall formed a parapet six feet above the roofs of the buildings lining it. Portholes were at intervals along the walls above the rooftops, and at two levels along the lower walls within the attached buildings.

Windows were small and near the ground, with heavy wooden shutters attached. The one massive door in the outer wall was of heavy hewn cypress logs. Inner doors and shutters were lighter and of cypress and mesquite, as were the roofs. Inner walls were finished with a smooth plaster of caliche composition.

The wood came from the Nueces River bottom nearby.

A well was in the center of the courtyard. Its five-foot square casing served a dual purpose—as an escape route and a container for water.

On the side toward Penitas Creek, about six feet below the top of the casing, was an oblong opening large enough for an average size adult to squeeze through. This opening led into a passage about a hundred yards long and four feet high, which widened gradually until it was six or eight feet wide at the far end which terminated at the steep bank of Penitas Creek. Near the middle of the passage was an offset, so constructed that light could not be seen from either end. The creek entrance looked like a cave.

During a severe flood during the early 1950's, about a hundred feet of the lower part of the tunnel caved off into Penitas Creek, changing its course. This left an opening that was visible as late as 1959 from a boat on Lake Corpus Christi, when the water level was fairly high. (This was pointed out to the author by Mrs. Wallis Wade, owner of the property, in 1959.)

J. Frank Dobie wrote of the removal of a treasure chest from these ruins near the turn of the 19th Century. Several persons in the Jim Wells County area were children of those involved in the episode and recall their parents speaking of it many times.

———

LAREDO

Tomás Sanchez, José de Escandón's aide and a lieutenant who had helped with the overall survey of the Nuevo Santander region, established the forted city of Laredo on May 15, 1755. This was the first independent city of European origin to be established in Texas. Heretofore, all settlements had been sponsored by the Church or the Military arm of the government. Sanchez refused aid from the Spanish government, and so organized his colony that it was able to support and defend itself.

In 1786, however, because of increased resistance of Indians along the frontiers of New Spain, Bernardo de Galvez, one of Spain's greatest military leaders, issued new orders for increased protection of these frontiers. The military strength of the northern part of New Spain was doubled, and divided into two departments. Nuevo Santander was put into Provincias Internas de Oriente, along with Coahuila, Texas, and Nuevo León, in December of 1786. General Juan de Ugalde was placed in charge.

Spanish troops were posted in Laredo in 1789, and the Presidio de San Augustíne de Laredo was formally established. The Comanches, because of their acquisition of horses and mastery over them, were roaming constantly farther southward and forcing the Apaches before them. Both Indian groups now used horses and were able to make destructive raids on outlying Spanish communities, missions, and even presidios.

Spanish politics, ever changeable, and becoming increasingly decadent, was rampant. In 1790, the military departments were again united, and Nuevo Santander, along with California and Nuevo León, was put under direct jurisdiction of the Viceroy.

During the years between 1810 and 1821, Laredo was a concentrating point for the Spanish Royal Troops in their fight with the Mexican Revolutionists. The citizens of Laredo took little active part in the Mexican Revolution and remained an independent settlement. In 1840, Laredo was named the capital of the short-lived "Republic of the Rio Grande."

TWO HUNDRED YEARS AGO

Two hundred years ago, the Spanish King allowed to be initiated what was the beginning of Spain's downfall in the New

World. It seems lamentable that, with the strong beginning made by the brilliant José Escandón in the Llanos Mesteñas region, such short-sighted persons should succeed him and his likeminded contemporaries in the governing of New Spain.

Escandón had been appointed Lieutenant-General of Sierro Gordo in 1740 and had achieved outstanding success in colonizing, establishing missions, and subduing the Indians. Because of this, he was chosen in 1746 to head the project of settling the territory between the Panuco River in Mexico and the Presidio de La Bahia del Espiritu Santo, then on the Guadalupe River at present Mission Valley.

It was absolutely imperative that this area be settled in order to protect the frontier provinces of Sonora, Chihuahua, Nueva Viscaya, Nuevo Leon, Coahuila, and Texas from foreign encroachment and from hostile Indians. Trade and safe communication between the coast and the landlocked frontier provinces had to be assured.

Nearly everybody who had any business with Texas and Mexico traveled the Old San Antonio Road (El Camino Real) during these years and until the pirates were ousted from the Gulf and the Caribbean. And all passed slowly through gay, fiesta-minded San Antonio, a delightful city of about 7000 at this time.

The following is an excerpt from M. E. M. Davis' well researched book, *The Story of Texas Under Six Flags,* which was published in 1897. This gives an authentic picture of trade through Spanish Texas and San Antonio.

. . . And all travelers halted at this lovely oasis in the wilderness. They were always loth to go away. For there were wonderful fiestas in the Churches of the Alamo and San Fernando, and solemn processions to the grand Missions of Concepcion and San Jose; there were stately gatherings in the houses of the Island Spaniards, and merry boating parties on the blue-green waters of the river San Antonio. There were gay dances on the plaza at night to the music of guitar and castanet, and Mexican jugglers throwing balls and knives by the light of smoking torches. Bands of Mexican muleteers jingled in from the presidio on the Rio Grande, driving before them trains of mules loaded with ingots of silver, on their way to Natchitoches, four hundred miles distant; caravans traveling westward with bales of smuggled goods crawled lazily through the narrow streets . . .

Escandón did a wonderful job in Nuevo Santander. By 1750, he had initiated the founding of several settlements, missions and sub-missions (a visitas). Among these were Santa Dorotea (present Goliad). Escandón recommended the transference of La Bahía Presidio and Mission to this settlement on the San Antonio River because of its more healthful climate and strategic position. The Mexican church colleges of San Fernando, the Holy Cross of Queretaro, and Guadalupe of Zacatecas cooperated fully with Escandón in furnishing priests and teachers.

Many settlements, missions, and sub-missions were necessary because of the vastness of the area and the hostility and extremely low cultural stage of many of the Indian tribes. Even so, the Jesuits had taxed themselves to the extreme, undergoing unbelievable hardships, as they had throughout New Spain.

But José de Escandón could not live forever, nor could the very able viceroy, Count de Revilla Gigedo, nor the other able contemporary leaders who had served their allotted times. They were replaced by too many crafty, selfish, ungodly, shortsighted men.

Like a "bolt out of the blue," Charles III, King of Spain, ordered the immediate expulsion of the Jesuits in New Spain in 1767; and in doing so, he knocked out a main prop of the Spanish Government. He kept the reason for doing so "buried in his royal heart." This was six years before Pope Clement XIV issued the official Brief of Suppression.

The Jesuits were given but a few days to end their business in New Spain and leave. This was a great blow to higher Catholic education and missions in the Llanos Mesteñas region as well as throughout New Spain. Since the new missions were not yet strong enough to sustain themselves, most of them in the newly settled region of Nuevo Santander were soon abandoned. No others replaced them for nearly a century.

LA ISLA DEL PADRE, LA FÉRIA, LLANO GRANDE, AND SAN CARLOS

La Isla del Padre, La Féria, Llano Grande, and San Carlos grants, under the jurisdiction of the municipality of Reynosa, were allotted by the King of Spain to Captain Juan José Hinajósa and José María de Ballí in 1776. Captain Hinajósa was alcalde of the municipality of Reinosa (Reynosa), and José María de Ballí was his son-in-law.

The above mentioned grants were surveyed under the direction of José Antonio de la Garza Falcón. However, before José María de Ballí could take possession of his land, he died, and others filed suit for the land in the La Féria grants.

Rosa María Hinojósa de Ballí, José María's widow, was unable to occupy the land left by her husband until 1790. The final decree was issued by the chief justice of the Province of San Luis Potosí on May 11, 1790, alloting the lands to the Ballís.

Rosa and her brother, Vicente Hinojósa, had each inherited twelve leagues of land north of the Rio Grande from their father about 1788. Vicente, who never married, gave his land to his sister, Rosa. Nicolás Ballí, priest-son of José María and Rosa, had been handling this land and ranching it in partnership with his mother since 1788. This was located around present Donna.

Nicolás Ballí inherited all of his father's land and half of his mother's property in 1790. Another son, Juan José de Ballí, decided to follow the career of his grandfather and became a Captain in the Spanish Army and Alcalde of Reinosa. José María, the youngest of the three brothers, became a sergeant in the army. He shared the other one-half of his mother's property with Juan José.

The long thin coastal island now known as Padre Island did not exist as such until 1766. Before this time, the land had been a group of islands separated by passes and known as Las Islas de Malaguitas, the most southern of which was named San Carlos de Las Malaguitas. This was the part of the coastal island that Padre Nicolás Ballí occupied in 1804. It had belonged to Captain Juan José Ballí, his brother, who died May 9, 1804. He left no children and willed the land to Nicolás. Very shortly after Padre Ballí occupied the land, area people began to refer to it as "Padre's Island." Soon the entire island was being mapped as Padre Island. Little was known of the center part of the island, much of which was inundated by high tides.

The lagoon between the islands and the mainland was mapped as the "Bay of San Bernardo" until after the islands became one and known as Padre Island. The water it sheltered then became known as "Laguna Madre." Small ships could navigate in this waterway as late as 1840. By 1846 it was so filled with sand that small ships could no longer negotiate the pass near Corpus Christi.

However, there must have been some navigable passes, for early maps show boat landings in the present Baffin Bay area, and quite a bit of smuggling continued to pass through here.

SOME CASAS BLANCAS OF THE LLANOS MESTEÑAS

Probably each present county area of the Mustang Plains has boasted of at least one Casa Blanca (important white house) during its history. As with trees, hidden treasures, and ghosts, the history of each goes back so far into time and so little has been recorded, other than by word of mouth, that each will have some conflicting and tangled history.

LA CASA BLANCA OF SANTA MARÍA — One of the first of these casas blancas was an hacienda built near the banks of the Lower Rio Grande and known as Santa María. It is about a mile east of present Santa María.

It has been called both "Casa Blanca" and "Rancho Blanco." The land on which it is built was a part of the La Feria Grant and was first allotted to the Ballí family by the King of Spain in 1790. However, they had first denounced and surveyed it in 1776, but José Marí Ballí (husband), had died before the grant had been lived on long enough to be perfected; and a Domingo Guerra immediately had filed suit for the land, claiming to have lived on it at La Flórida since 1770. The final decree returning it to Señora Ballí and to José María's other heirs was made by the Chief Justice of the Intendéncia of San Luis Potosí on May 11, 1790.

La Casa was enclosed by a thick wall of Spanish bricks. Brick was used throughout, even forming the floors to a depth of four feet. All walls were painted white.

The boat-landing for the hacienda was about half a mile to the south of La Casa Blanca. Here was the commissary-trading post. During the Mexican War, this almost windowless thick-walled building served as headquarters for General Zachary Taylor from time to time. After the war, the commissary-trading post resumed its interrupted career, but La Casa Blanca became an inn to serve those traveling along the Rio Grande— whether by boat, by hack, or on horseback. The Casa Blanca

20

Inn was a good day's journey from Brownsville and Matamoros to the southeast, and from present Hidalgo (called La Habitación as early as 1774) to the northwest.

Casa Blanca of Santa María has been restored almost to its former dignity, and is now a private residence.

JIM WELLS COUNTY "CASA BLANCA" — On Penitas Creek, fronting toward the Nueces in the present Sandia proximity, a fort of hand-cut white caliche blocks (called sillars) was erected by Spanish soldiers for protection of the King's nearby silver mine. Coastal Indians attacked the miners and mining operations so strongly and persistently, however, that the mine was abandoned.

The lode was probably not very rich, or the King would have sent more soldiers as was requested several times.

The land on which the structure stood became part of a sixteen sitio grant for the raising of livestock (ganado mayor).

Don Pancho Mentirose was the first civilian to occupy the old fort. Area Indians referred to him as "The Bad One," and his Spanish neighbors called him "The Liar," as his name implies. Mentirose soon returned to Mexico and either abandoned or sold his homestead rights to Don Joseph Agustín de la Garza Montemayor. Apparently, Mentirose had not proven his homestead, because this grant was first certified for Montemayor by the Captain of the King's Provincial Cavalry of the Frontier, by the Mayor of Camargo, by the Governor of the Colonial Province of Nuevo Santander, and by three Commissioners. Montemayor's first recorded payment to the government was stamped with the Provincio de Nuevo Santander seal and dated as payment for the years 1798-'99, at which time he paid forty-eight realis for sixteen sitios. Apparently he sold some of the land, because records show he paid but six pesos for the years 1802-'03 and the same for 1806-'07, which was for four sitios and three caballarías (105.75 acres equaled a caballaría).

When the Montemayors moved onto their land, they repaired and whitewashed the fort and lesser buildings, including the jacales for their domestic servants and other workers. Then the hacienda became known as La Casa Blanca.

Soon Montemayor's services were required by his country. When he returned with his family to La Casa Blanca, he found everything had been ruined by the Indians. Only the tall thick

21

walls of the old fort remained standing. His shepherds were missing and his livestock was scattered. Not only this, others were living on and claiming his property.

These claims were fought through the courts of Spain, of Mexico, and of the Republic of Texas, and carried into the courts of the United States before the case was settled in 1849.

Although there were other contenders for the land, two Ramirez brothers were the strongest. Because of this long court battle, La Casa Blanca began to be referred to as Fort Ramirez. The entire sixteen sitios of the Casa Blanca Grant were included in the battle. In 1849, the grant was partitioned as follows: the heirs of the Ramirez brothers received land along the Puenticítas Creek; the Herreras and the Garcias received the shares they had coming to their "Barranco Blanco" and "Agua Dulce" grants; and the Montemayor heirs received their four sitios and three caballarías, which included the old fort ruins.

Reasons for the Ramirez brothers claiming the land with the old fort ruins on it may have been because of the similarities in the descriptions of the Casa Blanca Grant and the Javoncillas Grant, which the Ramirez brothers had proved earlier.

Some of these similarities were: similar ruins were extant on each; the Falcon family owned land nearby each; El Macho Rancho was near La Casa Blanca Grant and Los Machos Rancho was near the Jav(b)oncillas Grant; a river bordering each grant flowed into a bay about the same distance away (the Spanish surveyors referred to both the Javoncillas and the Nueces as "Rios," with no distinction as to size). And to further confuse later settlers, the sons of Charles T. Lovenskiold bought parts of each grant following the Civil War.

A small lake through which the Nueces River flowed between present Calallen and San Patricio was named Santa Barbara by the Escandón surveyors. It has since been known successively as Lake Lovenskiold, Lake Mathis, and now as Lake Corpus Christi. Perhaps local Indians had first dammed the Nueces, causing Lake Santa Barbara, for it is known that a dam has been built or enlarged at this site, introducing each name change with an enlarged lake.

Lake Lampasisa and Lake Lampasazola near the Javoncíllas were probably referred to as "Lovenskiold's lakes." For O. C., F. S., and A. B. Lovenskiold bought about two thousand acres of land along the Javoncíllas and Los Olmos Creeks during the 1870's, and incorporated the Presidio Irrigation Company. This land included the above mentioned lakes and was situated between the Antonio Ramirez "Los Jab(v)oncillos" and the Antonio Gutierrez "Pasadixo" grants, and north and east of the R. de La Garza "El Paisano" grant. This land is located in parts of present Jim Wells, Kleberg, and Brooks Counties in the Premont-Falfurrias area.

CAMP CASA BLANCA — In 1852, on a creek near the Old Spanish Fort ruins on Penitas Creek called Casa Blanca, the United States Army built a supply camp of caliche blocks near the Nueces River to where flat boats could navigate—and another Casa Blanca came into being. It was first called Camp Casa Blanca because it was not only white, but was near the old high-standing ruins. However, because it was built to serve Fort Merrill, it was officially named Camp Merrill. As far as local residents were concerned, it remained Camp Casa Blanca. It was located in the southeast corner of present Like Oak County.

CASA BLANCA COMMUNITY — During the 1880's, the community of Casa Blanca was officially designated as a station-stop on the San Antonio-Aransas Pass Railroad. It had been founded as Wadeville, but because of duplication the postal authorities would not accept the name. Casa Blanca was then chosen as the name for the community, and was accepted by postal authorities. It was but eight miles south of the old fort ruins which were clearly visible across the prairies at that time.
The Casa Blanca community has vanished, but the cemetery remains, with the name "Wadeville" written in iron above the entrance. Fiery 90-year-old Mrs. Wallis Wade still sees that the cemetery is well taken care of (1968).

CASA BLANCA OF SAN DIEGO — The Casa Blanca of San Diego still stands on the high west bank above San Diego Creek where, until the 1930's, a spring always flowed. It has served as a trading post, a settlement fort, a general merchandise store, headquarters for a group of Confederates during the Civil War, a home, and a cantina. Ruins of a much more majestic white house not nearly so old (the Old Tobin House) stand beside it.
San Diego Casa Blanca was rather small, rectangular, and windowless when built. It had nine French doors instead. On the east side is a door, French like the others, but wide

23

enough to allow a yoke of oxen pulling a cart to enter. The west side originally had only one door and no windows, but a later owner closed in the patio with wooden walls having several windows.

This is the oldest building in San Diego. According to early settlers, it was built when the city obtained its first post office in 1852.

A company of Confederate soldiers under Captain Bedford Forrest used the building as a rendezvous while the Union forces had the Texas coast blockaded, and while they were in possession of Ringgold Barracks. Another source states that Captain Forrest erected the building at this time.

During the Prohibition Era, the building was known as "La Casa Blanca Club," but it did not remain a private club long. It remained vacant for several years before a family moved into it. After another interval, the family moved and it became a cantina again—which it is at the present time (1968). Marble columns still grace its bar.

San Diego's Casa Blanca is in very good condition, considering its age and lack of care. Its caliche sillar walls are two feet thick. Inside and outside doors are at each doorway. The inside doors are louvered, and the outside doors are heavy and carved in the traditional Spanish manner, thus providing La Casa Blanca with the traditional safety and coolness of the original blockhouses of the Mustang Plains.

These hand-cut caliche blockhouses with their parapet walls, such as those of the Casas Blancas of the Llanos Mesteñas, filled a distinct need during Indian and outlaw days of this region that lasted until the end of the 1870's, and they should be recognized as a distinctive form of Texas architecture.

LOS OJUELOS

Los Ojuelos—favorite Indian camping grounds for unknown centuries, site of Spanish and Mexican haciendas and Texas Ranger camps, settlement during the late 19th and early 20th Centuries—is now a ranch headquarters. The old caliche buildings are being restored, but the waters and the trees are no longer in such abundance. However, Hurricane Beulah returned a large amount of the water.

The big cats roamed in and along the arroyo that was fed by Los Ojuelos (Little Springs) in more affluent times, so the

24

Spaniards named it Arroyo Gato. When General W. L. Cazneau, in partnership with Colonel H. L. Kinney, established his trade route from Corpus Christi to Laredo in 1849, Los Ojuelos was an important stop.

In 1810, Eugenio Gutierrez received the Los Ojuelos grant from the Spanish Crown, and immediately began stocking it and making improvements. Unfortunately for Señor Gutierrez, two well-traveled Indian routes were nearby—one on either side. It seems that the roving Indians of the area were very fond of these springs in the prairie with a motte of trees nearby to protect them from the sun, and surrounded by low-rising hills to protect them from winter winds. They made themselves so troublesome that Don Eugenio was forced to leave.

Several years later, Isidro Gutierrez, Eugenio's son, cleared the title for two sitios of land and moved to Los Ojuelos with a group of workers. However, he was no more successful than his father had been in his dealings with the Indians, and was soon forced away.

Late in the summer of 1850, Rip Ford and his Texas Rangers occupied Los Ojuelos, moving here from their camp at San Antonio Viejo (Old San Antonio), about 34 miles by horseback to the southeast. Protection of the lucrative trade openly developing between Corpus Christi and Laredo, and of the increasing number of settlers moving into Webb County, warranted the move.

In 1857, José María Guerra, a descendant of the original grantee, moved to Los Ojuelos and built a blockhouse of native stone and extended the walls to enclose the springs. He encouraged immigrants from Mexico and built an irrigation system and a church.

About 400 people were living at the hacienda by 1861. Records show the village to be a stop on a regular pony express route by 1860. However, Los Ojuelos was on a mail route between Corpus Christi and Laredo in 1849, which was the route established by Kinney and Cazneau. Because of Indian trouble, the government, much to the disenchantment of local Texans, discontinued the mail route in early August of 1849. But Texans re-established it as a local route.

By 1910, the population had dwindled to fewer than 200, and the post office was discontinued. Mirando City was started nearby in 1920, after oil was discovered on the Mirando grant.

Oil was discovered on the Los Ojuelos grant in 1921, and

25

the population again began to climb. During the 1940's, children of the oil field workers were attending a common school at Los Ojuelos.

MEXICAN REVOLUTIONARY DAYS
IN LLANOS MESTEÑAS

Except for a few extremely well fortified ranches, the region between the Nueces River and the Rio Grande southeast of Laredo—our Llanos Mesteñas—became almost deserted after the withdrawal of Spanish soldiers during the first decade of the 19th Century. It became something of a no-man's land, peopled by roving bands of Indians and mustangers, mostly Mexican, one of which was about as ruthless as the other.

In 1830, the Mexican Government began encouraging Mexican citizens to move into this area, after they had completed a contract in 1828 with an Irish group to settle along the north side of the Nueces. Then Mexican soldiers were brought into the area—more to keep out American settlers than to protect their colonists.

Several companies of soldiers were at the old Spanish fort site near La Sal Vieja, in the northwest corner of present Willacy County. Lipantitlán, another Spanish fort site across the Nueces from San Patricio, was ordered rebuilt and occupied. Main cities along the south banks of the Rio Grande were all forted.

Since Indians were wary of armed soldiers, many Mexicans did claim land grants and many descendants of those receiving Spanish grants proved them. Among the grants were Las Cuevitas, San Antonio Viejo, and Randado in present Jim Hogg County. These still have ruins from this era of Mexican occupation.

In southwest Webb County, Los Ojuelos was reoccupied. Its large wells were a favorite watering and camping grounds for Indians and later immigrant travel.

Shortly after the Mexican War, "Rip" Ford headed a Texas Ranger camp at San Antonio Viejo and later at Los Ojuelos.

Survey notes of the above mentioned grants all record the surveyors setting posts at various points ". . . in the prairie." For then, this section of present Texas was still a prairie land and not a brush land.

Brazos Santiago Pass was forted on the island opposite

26

Santa Isabela (Fronton de Santa Isabela was the official Spanish name), which early American settlers called "Point Isabel," and which is now known as Port Isabel. This pass had one of the deepest natural harbors along the coast of Texas. It was frequently mentioned by early Spaniards.

Brazos Santiago Pass became heavily silted during early Texas statehood, thus ruining Port Isabel as a major Texas port. According to some authorities, competitors did this deliberately by the sinking of a ship at the edge of the pass.

THREE EARLY SETTLEMENTS

BANQUETE — Banquete, in western Nueces County, was the site of an early Indian village and camping ground. According to legend, it derived its name from a feast in 1830 held by the newly arrived Irish immigrants of San Patricio, local Indians, and Mexican soldiers and lesser Mexican officials. The purpose of the feast was to seal a lasting friendship.

AGUA DULCE — Agua Dulce (Sweet Water) in present Nueces County on Highway 44 is slightly south of the original "Puerta de Agua Dulce," which was an official port of entry into the Mexican State of Tamaulipas. The grant on which it was located was of the same name. It was at a crossing of Agua Dulce Creek that was on the road from Matamoros to the Lipantitlán Crossing of the Nueces River and on to Goliad, formerly known as La Bahía.

Trees grew along the creek, and the water was drinkable here, so that early travelers often camped at Agua Dulce. During the Republic of Texas days, a strong stockade was built and stood here for many years to hold captured mustangs that abounded throughout this area. Some early maps show a large lake in this area named "Charco Grande."

LOS PRESEÑOS — About ten miles southwest of Puerto de Agua Dulce was the ranch settlement of Los Preseños on San Fernando Creek, in the vicinity of the present San Fernando Creek bridge on Highway 44 east of Alice. The "Charco de Los Preseños" grant, issued to Marcelino Lopez, and "Los Preseños de Arriba" grant, issued to Maximo Farias, were directly north and south of each other, divided by San Diego Creek and a bit of San Fernando Creek, of which San Diego Creek is now a tributary. Originally, however, Chiltipín

27

Creek flowed to the east, separating the two grants, and a spring flowed into the creek bed just before San Diego Creek entered Chiltipín Creek. Then, the Chiltipín continued to the east, flowing through two lakes, the Charco de los Preseños and the Charco de Los Caballos. The Chiltipín Creek was later mapped as the Pintas. The flow from the spring turned south from Charco de los Caballos and formed San Fernando Creek, which, within a short distance, flowed toward the southeast.*

Los Preseños consisted of jacales only, but some were very nice, well-built and whitewashed. The community had the reputation as being a place where a traveler could get good food and supplies. It had a rather large trading post, which was built to serve traders traveling between Corpus Christi and Laredo and, later, Castroville, Eagle Pass, and area ranchers.

In August of 1849, a large body of Comanches surprised a group of eight mustangers at Los Preseños, killing two and badly injuring another. The Indians drove off the entire caballada belonging to the mustangers, after taking what they wanted of their supplies and destroying the rest. The Mexican residents hid themselves and were not attacked. Apparently, the Indians were just after horses.

When Collins was started across the creek to the southwest of Los Preseños in 1878, and the Texas-Mexican Railroad went through it, by-passing Los Preseños, most of the residents moved across to Collins and Los Preseños was no longer mapped.

FORT TREVIÑO Y SAN YGNACIO

Don Jesús Treviño received a land grant from the Mexican government in 1830, and promptly crossed the Rio Grande to establish the village of San Ygnacio.

This village still exists, with many of the old stone houses deserted and in various stages of ruin. Stone walls extend above the sagging roofs to form parapets, and iron bars are still over most of the windows and transoms. Highway 83 passes along the edge of San Ygnacio, which is in present Zapata County about 30 miles south of Laredo.

With the help of his settlers, Don Jesús built a fort on a high bluff overlooking the Rio Grande. This fort, still in good condition and occupied by Mrs. Aureliano Herrera, a descendant

*See map, Plate 14.

28

of Don Jesús, is thirty-six feet long, nine feet high, and twelve feet wide. The nine-foot walls were probably built first, because they form a courtyard with a wide, heavy gate on the north side. A large room was built along the wall on each side of the wooden gate.

A stockade was added to the south wall for the protection of the settlers' stock, especially horses, for both Indians and the Mexican mountain lions were extremely fond of horses. Then the rooms and north wall of the fort were covered with a caliche plaster. The fort faced north, and the plaster provided added protection against cold northers.

Although small, this fort furnished adequate protection for Don Jesús Treviño and the few settlers of the community for many years. Don Jesús died in 1842, leaving a daughter, Juliana, who had married Don Blas María Uribe.

In 1843 Don Blas began enlarging the old fort by adding an annex twelve feet wide by sixty feet long to each end, so that his completed fort formed a hollow square. He built these additional walls three feet higher than the old ones, and made the roof of the attached building three feet higher, also. Thus, all outer walls were but three feet higher than the entire roof of the finished structure.

Portholes for firing through were not built in the walls above the roof; just holes to allow for drainage. Four-by-sixes still extend about two feet directly below the holes, forming spouts. On two levels within the buildings, portholes were built at random places. They are difficult to see from outside the fort. Rooms were built onto the north, west, and south walls within the fort.

The gate was left in the old part of the fort as originally built. In 1851, José Villarreal made a sundial of native stone and fixed it upon a pedestal over the gate of the fort, now referred to as "Fort San Ygnacio." One starry night in autumn, he set it with the North Star.

The sundial (as of 1967) is still in good condition and can still be read. Only, it is thirty-six minutes slow by Central Standard Time, because Villarreal set it by Mexican time of 1851. Another unique feature of the sundial is that it is so set that it can be read from either side.

———

BURROS, JEHUS, AND STREETCARS

Seemingly, burros were wandering aimlessly along trails,

through streets and in the market plazas, but in reality they were looking for weeds, rags, paper, cigar butts—just anything chewable to eat. Wilder ones were browsing in the brush and tall grasses throughout much of the Llanos Mesteñas region, but not very far from villages for they preferred the protection and scraps generally afforded by man. Although found throughout the Llanos Mesteñas, burros were congregated in the largest numbers between the Rio Grande and the Arroyo Colorado. This immediate area was often referred to by Americans as "Jackass Prairie."

During the 1830's and until the mid-1870's, after United States trading vessels had discovered Corpus Christi and Brazos Santiago but before railroads had scattered the mustangs and longhorns and seared the rich native grasses and brought into the region trainloads of "snow-shovelers," the burro was the most commonly used beast of burden. Even the poorest ranchero could afford one.

Burros were easily caught and trained and were extremely strong for their size. The initial sight of a burro ambling along seemingly unconcerned, with a grown man on his back having to bend his knees at a ludicrous angle to keep his feet from dragging, never failed to elicit astonishment—and sympathy for the burro.

Burros did not have to be shod nor did food have to be taken along for them. They seemed to fare very well off the weeds and grasses they could nibble along the trails as they carried their loads. But they could not be hurried.

A native of this region, now (1967) nearly a century old and living in San Diego, says that she remembers when Old Amargosa was a wool and hide buying center, seeing burros carrying hides to be traded or sold. The hides were stacked on each burro to such an extent that they towered high above him. Nothing could be seen of the animal except his feet, and his tail when he switched it at an annoying insect—and occasionally a long ear drooped forward.

Down in Matamoros, burros were used to pull the streetcars that passed each other on the left at a snail's pace.

Burros pulled light, two-wheel carts in Mexico and along the lower Rio Grande in Texas. Water carts were the most frequently seen, carrying the water in one or two large barrels for sale to the poor. Burros generally pulled carts carrying bread from the bakeries to the market plaza. When the cargo was of light weight but bulky articles, the cart would be loaded as prodigiously as the above-mentioned burro.

Competing with the burro-drawn streetcars of Matamoros, and also of Brownsville, were horse-drawn two-seated hacks the natives called "jehus." Jehus were first introduced into Matamoros by Mr. William Neale while General Zachary Taylor's army continued to use his stagecoaches that the General had appropriated for army use when he took possession of the banks of the Rio Grande. General Taylor used the stagecoaches to provide himself and his officers with good transportation between his headquarters at Fronton (present Port Isabel) and his camps at Rancho Blanco, Fort Brown, and Edinburg (now Hidalgo).

MAPS OF AREA DATE AS FAR BACK AS EARLY 1800's

The earliest available map known to show the source of San Fernando Creek in present Jim Wells County is a plat drawn by an unknown surveyor for the State of Tamaulipas, Mexico. This plat bears the official stamp of the State, but not the name of the surveyor. It is titled, "Agostadero de San Fernando." Translated into English, it would be "Pasture lands of Saint Ferdinand."

This survey was filed in Camargo, August 2, 1831; in La Ciudad de Victoria, October 25, 1831; and certified by the State of Tamaulipas on November 16, 1831.

An interesting feature of the plat is that the west rather than the north is the direction shown above the map. "Charco de Los Preseños" is a sub-title shown below and to the right of the map. On some later plats, this survey is shown as "San Fernando," but on most it is simply "Los Preseños" or "Las Preseñas." Either the clerks or surveyors were not very good spellers, or they simply did not know Spanish well enough to be able to determine the sex of ponds and grants grammatically.

According to this 1831 plat, San Diego Creek joined Chiltipín Creek and San Fernando Creek simultaneously. The explanation for this lies in the source of the San Fernando, which was a spring. This spring rose to the surface of the ground in the channel of the Chiltipín shortly after its juncture with La Resaca de Enmedia. It flowed along with the Chiltipín past the mouth of San Diego Creek, on through El Charco de Los

31

Presceños (sic) and on into El Charco de Los Caballos. Here, near the southwest end of "The Lake (or Pond) of the Horses," the San Fernando broke through the banks and pursued its course to the southeast alone. The Chiltipín continued its meanderings through El Charco de Los Caballos and on toward the east, where it became a tributary of Petronilla Creek.

A slightly different version of the same area is shown in a survey made August 5, 1878. This plat was made to show the subdivisions of the original grant, for N. G. Collins had just bought about a third of the grant. His land included, roughly, the present area from the east boundary of the Alice Country Club west to Texas Boulevard. The north and south boundaries can be ascertained easily from the plat.*

This 1878 survey shows San Fernando Creek taking off from El Charco de "Las Preceñas" (spelling as on plat) rather than from El Charco de "Las Caballas." Note that even the name of the grant is changed from masculine to feminine. The creek that continues to the east through the lakes is now named Pintas Creek. Resaca de Enmedia is now shown as a tributary of San Diego rather than Chiltipín Creek. San Fernando Creek has deepened its channel and is shown to be clearly divided from El Charco de Las Preceñas. And the north is now shown to be toward the top of the map.

Other maps studied, both earlier and later, show Resaca de Enmedia to join Chiltipín Creek. However, the General Highway Map of Jim Wells County, Texas, prepared by the Texas Highway Department in cooperation with the United States Department of Commerce Bureau of Public Roads and Planning Survey Division, instituted a version all its own, as shown by the 1952 map.

On this map, La Resaca de Enmedia disappeared as far as its name was concerned and Muerto Creek took its place. As of spring 1967, however, Resaca Enmedia and Muerto Creek were again on official maps in the correct places.

While cogitating thusly in this area,—Chiltipín Creek had another tributary that suffered similarly. Amargosa (Bitter Weed) Creek, so named because of the extremely bitter weeds growing along its banks that at times the very waters were bitter, suddenly became Armagosa Creek. The word "armagosa" is meaningless. As of 1967, Amargosa Creek again has its correct spelling, also.

*See Plate 14.

What caused these changes? Simple evolution? mutation? ignorance? or was it prestidigitation?

LOS PRESEÑOS AND COLLINS

Settlement in the immediate Alice area seems to have started in 1831 with the filing of the "Charco de Los Preseños" grant in the "Agostadero de San Fernando," by Marcelino Lopez. In order for the grant to be certified, the land had to be improved, stocked, and have someone living on it. It was certified in Victoria, the capital of the State of Tamaulipas, Mexico, on November 16, 1831.

Adjoining grants to the north and east were issued in 1831 and in 1832. Where these grants met, ranch headquarters were built for mutual protection and companionship. Jacales were built on the northeast (left) side of San Fernando Creek on high ground to the north and south of the present Highway 44 bridge.

In 1846, Colonel Kinney of Corpus Christi marked a trade route to Castroville and to Laredo that led through this Mexican ranch village of Los Preseños. A fight between mustangers and Indians, and a smallpox epidemic have been recorded as happenings in Los Preseños. It was shown on maps until Collins replaced it.

The Los Preseños Grant was subdivided in June of 1878, and N. G. Collins bought the northwest portion.

He laid out the townsite of Collins along the southwest side of San Fernando Creek, across from Los Preseños. To get the Texas-Mexican Railroad to extend westward from Banquete (to where it had operated from Corpus Christi since January 1, 1876), N. G. Collins had to give the railroad owners one-half of his townsite.

With the arrival of the railroad in the fall of 1878, Collins began to grow. Several former residents of Lagarto, which had been by-passed by the San Antonio-Aransas Pass Railway, were among its new citizens, as were several families from Los Preseños and elsewhere. The postal service was now by rail, so Collins replaced Los Preseños on maps.

This picture is of the main street of Collins about 1889. The railroad station is in the foreground back of the horse and buggy. The two-story hotel is at the far right, and the Catholic Church that Father Bard built is barely discernible in the background between the horse and driver. The shuttered school-house is back of and to the right of the row of stores, behind the wagons.

This school picture is of the teachers and pupils at Collins in 1889. The man teacher is Hugo McIntyre, who committed suicide a few months after this picture was taken. The lady teacher was Miss Rachel Littig, who later married John Wright of Alice and taught music there for years.

With the extension of the Texas-Mexican Railroad to San Diego in 1879 and on into Laredo by 1881, Collins became increasingly important as a shipping and a mail center for ranchers between San Diego and Agua Dulce. Its population had increased to 500. But in 1888, the SAP* Railway by-passed Collins because the owners and Mr. Collins could not agree within a thousand dollars of each others offer. The southern terminal of the SAP Railway intersected the Tex-Mex Railroad about three miles west of Collins, on land belonging to the King Ranch.

People soon began moving to this railroad intersection and Collins started losing population. Late in 1890, the post office was moved and Collins was well on its way to becoming a ghost town.

LA TINAJA DE LARA GRANT ON TRADE ROUTE

About twelve miles almost directly west of La Puerta de Agua Dulce on a hill overlooking the broad valley of Chiltipín Creek at its juncture with Amargosa Creek, Manuel Barrera established the headquarters for his ranch. He named the ranch "Amargosa" for the bitterweeds that infested the banks of the creek and pastures in the area.

Amargosa Ranch was crossed by the main road from Mier, Tamaulipas, Mexico to the Lagarto (lizard or alligator) Crossing of the Nueces River, and on to Goliad. This had been a main route between Mier and Laredo and Presidio La Bahía since the middle of the 18th Century when José de Escandón began settlement of the area and caused the Presidio to be removed from its unhealthy site on the Guadalupe River.

A road led off this route at Amargosa Ranch directly northward to intercept the Cópano-San Antonio Road. And still another led from Los Encinos Ranch through Amargosa

*San Antonio-Aransas Pass.

34

and La Puerta de Agua Dulce Ranches eastward to Banquete, and on into Corpus Christi. These routes were first traveled by smugglers, for Cópano and Corpus Christi were notorious pirate rendezvous long before settlements were established. The famed Jean Lafitte was known to have frequented these natural ports.

By 1836, Manuel Barrera had improved his ranch and stocked it to the extent that he had received the deed to the grant, "La Tinaja de Lara," on which his Amargosa Ranch was located. It was a well-known ranch by 1849.

General William L. Cazneau's trade route from Corpus Christi to Eagle Pass, which he established in 1849, passed through the southern part of La Tinaja de Lara grant.

Large amounts of wool and hides were shipped from Corpus Christi to northern markets during the 1840's and '50's. *The Corpus Christi Star*, which replaced *The Gazette* the first of September, 1848, read like a modern Chamber of Commerce brochure. Trade with Chihuahua, Mexico through the Port of Corpus Christi had been established and a ship-building firm had begun operation.

But all was not well, for the Asiatic cholera was raging along the Texas coast, in New Orleans, and in Paris, France. Would it come to Corpus Christi and the ranches of Llanos Mesteñas? Indians were again invading the area. They had raided along the Nueces and around Laredo. Would this raiding increase?

―――――

POLITICAL EVOLUTION: LLANOS MESTEÑAS LIMITS DEFINED

During the Spanish Era in Texas, trade flourished through the old ports of Cópano, Corpus Christi, Penascal, and Santa Isabela. This trade was termed illegal by those desiring to profit through the exploitation of those living in the land-locked provinces of New Spain. Goods from these ports were carried along routes through the grassy plains, over the chaparral-covered caliche hills, by mottes of trees announcing springs, and along creek beds to crossings along the Rio Grande as far to the northwest as present Eagle Pass. These devious routes continued to be used in a lessening degree even into the Twentieth Century.

Because of this trade kinship, the limits of Llanos Mesteñas are defined as extending from the south bank of the mouth of the Rio Grande to the present Eagle Pass-Piedras Negras vicinity, and eastward to include most of the McMullen-McGloin Grant and the Powers and Hewetson Grant, then southward along the coast to the mouth of the Rio Grande. The Irish settlers in these grants were more closely aligned with the European settlers south of the Nueces than they were with the American settlers of Gonzales.

Since the first real efforts toward settlement of this area began in 1746, with the appointment of Lt. General José de Escandón to make a study of these coastal prairies from the San Antonio River (then called Seno Mejicáno) southward to Tampico, Mexico, we will begin with this era.

In 1748, the Province of Nuevo Santander was created, and Escandón was appointed governor. Nuevo Santander included the Llanos Mesteñas region, which was generally limited at the Nueces River Valley to the north, continuing to El Camino Real along the northeast from Laredo, and eastward to the coast. It also contained the Lower Rio Grande Valley south of the river. Laredo and Dolores were the only two settlements planned at this time to become local government seats of municipalities that were north of the Rio Grande.

Along the Rio Grande, the following municipalities were planned to extend to the Nueces River, with each established settlement to serve as the seat of local government. These settlements, all along the south bank of the Rio Grande, were Revilla (present Ciudad Guerrero, near the Falcon Dam), Mier, Camargo, and Reynosa (also spelled Reinosa and Rhinosa during the 18th and 19th Centuries). Present Alice would have been in the extreme east side of the Mier Municipality.

During Mexican Revolutionary years, Nuevo Santander as an organized province practically ceased to exist. The withdrawal of presidial soldiers from the region allowed hostile Indians, mostly Apaches who were being driven out of their homes by the Comanches, to raid at will.

In 1821, following Mexican independence, Nuevo Santander officially became a part of the Mexican State of Tamaulipas, whose northwest boundaries were extended in 1828 to include Laredo. The planned municipalities, with their existing seats of government along the south bank of the Rio Grande, were left unchanged. No extra strong forts or settlements were established along the Nueces River, which had been officially designated as the boundary line between Texas and Nuevo Santander in 1805. But settlers were encouraged to move into the vicinity, especially if from Mexico or Europe.

During the Spanish and Mexican eras, the region including Laredo westward to present Eagle Pass and along the Rio Grande to its juncture with the Pecos River, then east to the Nueces, was a part of Coahuila. This section had likewise received little protection from the Mexican Government.

The municipalities of San Patricio and Refugio, within the same lines as the grants to these Irish settlers, were established in 1828.

The first Congress of the Republic of Texas in 1836 changed the existing municipalities into counties, keeping the same seats of local governments. Since Mexico had established no lasting municipality seats north of the Rio Grande in the area south of the Nueces River and east of Laredo, this entire region became a part of the nearest county, which was San Patricio.

By 1837, San Patricio County was well organized and contained all of the area south of Bexar County and southwest of Refugio County.

With the annexation of Texas to the United States and the impending war with Mexico, the sudden influx of soldiers and camp followers to the Rio Grande made a change in local county organization imperative. Nueces County was created from San Patricio County in 1846, and it was organized immediately. Now, Nueces County consisted of the entire area between the Rio Grande and the Nueces south of Bexar County. Corpus Christi was named the county seat. This Nueces County area also included Laredo. Ex-President M. B. Lamar assumed command of the town in 1846, as an officer of the United States Army, and thus extended Texas government to Laredo officially for the first time.

TWO ENTREPRENEURS

After the Texans had won their Revolution, Europeans in increasing numbers, along with more adventurous and far-seeing Americans, came to the fringes of Llanos Mesteñas and settled near the Nueces Bay and along the Lower Rio Grande. Two of the more interesting of these entrepreneurs were Colonel Henry Lawrence Kinney, one of the founders of Corpus Christi, and Mr. William Neale of Matamoros and Brownsville.

37

It has been said of Colonel Kinney that whatever he found that he wanted, he considered his and endeavored to keep it. At his trading post stronghold which he had built on the south bank of Corpus Christi Bay by 1840, he employed a body guard of several "strong-arm" men. However, Mr. Peoples, editor of the *Corpus Christi Star* during the late 1840's and early 1850's, spoke very highly of Colonel Kinney.

About 1843, Colonel Kinney came out second best in an encounter with Mexican officials of Matamoros. He was reputedly attempting to take over an immense tract of land embracing Brazos Santiago and Point Isabel when he was arrested. General Pedro Ampudio had already ordered Colonel Kinney shot when Mrs. Neale learned of the situation. Mr. Neale was not in Matamoros at the time, so Mrs. Neale met with the General and was able to persuade him into releasing his prisoner.

Mr. William Neale was an Englishman whose career had begun on board the first frigate in the Mexican Navy of 1821. This vessel had been bought in England, and volunteer English sailors had been encouraged to man the ship. Firing from this ship had forced the surrender of Castle Uloa, the presidio guarding the harbor of Vera Cruz, Mexico.

After traveling extensively through Mexico, Mr. Neale went to New Orleans. After a few years there, he moved to Matamoros in 1834. Soon he owned property on both sides of the Rio Grande, and lived at Santa Maria and Brownsville as well as at Matamoros.

Trade was brisk, and smuggling across the Rio Grande was a profitable and honorable trade at this time. Mexican carts pulled by oxen were used to bring goods from Brazos Santiago, as the port at Point Isabel was called.

Mr. Neale established a stage line between Matamoros and Point Isabel about 1840. His stages had spoked wheels and were pulled by four high-spirited horses each. They were a sensation to the native Mexicans. The spoked wheels were as much a sensation to them as were the teams of horses. This was the beginning of the end of solid wheels on Mexican carts in this area.

During the Battle of Palo Alto, General Zachary Taylor's army captured Mr. Neale's stage coaches. They had been pressed into duty by the Mexican Army for use as ambulances. More than a year passed before Neale was able to get them back. After the close of the Mexican War until the raids of

Cortina, a period of about fifteen years, Mr. Neale continued to operate his stage line.

TWO REPUBLIC OF TEXAS PATRIOTS

Two of Texas' outstanding patriots, Lieutenant Archelaus Bynum Dodson and Sarah, his wife, contributed greatly to the development of this region along the Nueces River and south of it—largely through their fine descendants who grew up here.

Archelaus Bynum Dodson was born December 31, 1807, in North Carolina. He left for Texas in 1826 and settled in Harrisburg, where he met and married Miss Sarah Bradley in 1835.

Dodson and his bride were among the very first to answer in defense of Texas when the Committee of Vigilance and Safety sent out its call to arms on September 19, 1835. This call was issued because of information received in regard to General Cos' planned invasion of Texas.

The Harrisburg Company, of which Dodson was First Lieutenant, was one of the first to organize. Captain Andrew Robinson was its commanding officer, and James Ferguson was Second Lieutenant. It was known as the "Andrew Robinson Company."

Sarah Bradley Dodson designed, and made with the help of some other ladies of the community, the first tri-color Lone Star flag of Texas. When the Andrew Robinson Company was mustered into the Texas Volunteer Army, Sarah Dodson presented the members with her flag and it went into immediate use. Lt. Ferguson carried the flag from Harrisburg to Cíbolo, a few miles east of San Antonio.

From Cíbolo, the Dodson flag led the Volunteer Army into San Antonio—carried by an unnamed color bearer. It took part in the siege of San Antonio from December 6th to the 10th, 1835.

Archelaus Dodson returned to East Texas with Captain Robinson's Company early in 1836, with the Dodson Lone Star flag still leading. It was one of the two flags that flew above the cabin that housed the Convention of 1836 at Washington-on-the-Brazos, where the Texas Declaration of Independence was adopted.

The Dodson flag waved proudly above the Texans at the Battle of San Jacinto—but Archelaus Dodson was in sick bay with the measles, along with slightly more than 200 other Texans unable to participate in the battle, much to their disgust. This epidemic among the soldiers was due to their close contact with sick children they aided in the "Runaway Scrape."

Lt. Dodson had been among those detailed to insure the safety of women and children beyond the Brazos River. Because of illness and rain, camp was made just east of the Trinity River. The sounds of battle at San Jacinto could be heard in this camp. And here, Maria Louisa, the Dodson's first child, was born.

According to Miss Ruth Dodson, formerly of Mathis but now deceased, as told to her by her father, Milton Milam Dodson, and further substantiated in a letter written by him, is the following description of the Dodson flag as published in a 1932 issue of *Frontier Times*, and as verified by a granddaughter of Milton Milam Dodson now living in Alice, Texas, where the remains of Archelaus Bynum Dodson are interred in the Old Collins Cemetery at the edge of town.

"The flag was tricolored blue, white and red, and, because of not being able to get any bunting, was of calico. It was made in squares, with the blue next to the staff, white in the middle, and the outer square of red. A white star that measured about six inches from point to point was sewed in the middle of the blue square."

Of all the Texas Revolutionary flags, the flag by Sarah Bradley Dodson most nearly resembled the permanent Lone Star flag of Texas, adopted January 25, 1839. It is not known what became of the original Dodson flag.

Archelaus and Sarah Dodson continued to live in Fort Bend County until 1844, when they claimed their headright in Grimes County. Besides Maria Louisa, the children were Elizabeth Bradley, Milton Milam, Harriet Houston, Sarah Belvedier, and Thaddus.

Sarah Dodson died October 9, 1848, and was buried in the Bethel Cemetery, which was on land she and her husband had given to the Bethel community on which to build a church and a school, and to locate a cemetery.

In 1850, Archelaus Dodson married Katherine Maria (pronounced "Mariah" to rhyme with Josiah) McKnight McWhorter, a widow with several children. In 1860, Dodson brought his family to Live Oak County. Katherine Maria Dodson died in 1888 and is buried in the Perdido Ranch Cemetery in southern Live Oak County, which Dodson owned.

Archelaus Dodson spent the last six or eight years of his life on his other ranch about five miles south of Alice. Here he was cared for by two of his children, Mrs. William (Sarah Belvedier) Adams and Miss Elizabeth Bradley Dodson (Aunt Betsy to her nieces and nephews and all of their friends)). Archelaus Bynum Dodson died March 10, 1898.

Direct descendants of Mr. Dodson living in the Mustang Plains are all well known, substantial citizens who have done their full share in developing this part of Texas into a splendid place to live. Mrs. Susie Dodson (Henry) Roddy, daughter of Milton Milam, is the only one of his three daughters still living (in 1968). Her home is in Corpus Christi.

Lillie, George, and Archie (who died in his early 20's) were the only children of Sarah and William Adams who grew to adulthood.

George Adams married Mayme Wright, who is still living in Alice (as of 1968). Their children were Miss Lois Adams, who teaches in the Alice Public Schools; Mrs. Georgie (O. B.) Wilke, who also taught in Alice for about thirty years; and Mrs. Aleen (Hubert) Sain, also an Alice resident.

Lillie married Harry Garrett. Their two remaining children are Mrs. Edith (McGehee) Word Sr. of Alice, and Mrs. Mary (Byron) Johnson of Laredo.

Among descendants of Archelaus and Maria McWhorter Dodson are Mrs. Lucille Hobbs (Goode) Wier and Philip Hobbs, who are their grandchildren. Both still live in Alice. Mrs. Wier has a Bible that belonged to her grandmother. It is inscribed, '"To Katherine Maria McKnight from Father."

MUSTANGS

The Spanish horse, the Texas cow pony, and the mustang were all one and the same. Early Spaniards in Texas referred to all large livestock that ran wild—such as horses, cattle, deer, elk (probably their name for the mule deer that grazed in large numbers in South Texas), javelinas, and antelopes—as "mesteñas." However, they used the same term when referring just to the horses, so the pioneer Americans anglicized the term to mean just horses, and called the wild Texas ponies "mustangs."

These were the escaped descendants of the Arabian and other horses that had been brought to America by the early Spaniards. They were usually rather small, and were able to

41

travel long distances with no food other than grass. Occasionally, however, magnificent ones were seen, especially stallions.

Mustangs had "cow-sense" as well as "horse-sense." They were extremely agile and responded to the rider's touch instantly. As range horses, they were ideal for the work of cutting, roping, and branding, as well as for the roundup and the trail drive.

The area between the Nueces and the Rio Grande was the home of the mustangs. By the time the Americans came into Texas, mustangs were virtually natives of this plains region and were beginning to migrate into other areas.

The Llanos Mesteñas provided both the Texans and the Mexicans with mounts during the Texas Revolution.

Dr. James Grant came to Agua Dulce with thirty men to capture horses for use by the Texans stationed at Goliad under James Fannin. They probably chose La Puerta de Agua Dulce vicinity for their camp because of the good water and the oak trees along the creek that provided shade and posts for a corral. It was on the main road between Matamoros and Goliad, and mustangers had already built a corral there.

No Mexican soldiers were expected north of the Rio Grande for about three months. With characteristic enthusiasm, the Texans were intently corralling a herd of mustangs when a scouting party of Mexicans under General José Urrea surprised them.

Dr. Grant ordered Placido Benavides to escape to Goliad and inform Colonel Fannin of General Urrea's presence. Five others managed to escape also, but were later killed with Fannin in the Goliad Massacre. Six were captured and taken to Matamoros as prisoners. One of these, Reuben R. Brown, managed to escape and returned to Texas several months later. The others, including Dr. Grant, were all killed in the fight. The date of the so-called "Battle of Agua Dulce Creek" was March 2, 1836—the date that the Texas Declaration of Independence was adopted at Washington-on-the-Brazos.

A decade later, mustangs from this same area provided mounts for the United States Cavalry entering Mexico at the start of the Mexican War.

During the last quarter of the 19th Century and well into the 20th, the term "mustanger" had the same connotation as "buffalo hunter," for mustangs were being killed for their hides.

And, many local cowboys went without work rather than kill and skin mustangs.

The last surviving caballada in South Texas was said to have been in Duval County. The leader was a magnificent black stallion. The stallion was kept by the owner of the ranch on which the mustangs were grazing, but all of the mares and colts were shot and skinned in 1930. Their hides made a high stack at the hide buyer's store.

———

TRADE CENTER DURING
MEXICAN AND REPUBLICAN ERAS

Trade, largely in the form of open smuggling, flourished in the Llanos Mesteñas from 1834, when steamers from American and European countries started calling regularly at Brazos Santiago, through the 1840's. Actually, smuggling continued across the Rio Grande only slightly less open until after the Pancho Villa raids of 1916.

Indeed, smuggling had gained quite a foothold in this region, because it had been indulged since Spanish Colonial days of the 18th Century. Spanish colonists cared no more for unreasonably high taxes than did their neighbors, the English colonists.

By 1834, the Matamoros townsite had already been laid out and several substantial buildings had been erected. Trade with the Northern States of Mexico was brisk. Raw wool and hides, along with handcrafted pottery, baskets, leather goods, silver, and semi-precious stones were brought overland by oxcarts and burros to be traded or sold for cloth, pans, machinery, and other manufactured goods.

The present Main Plaza of Matamoros was then called the Market Plaza. It was filled with carts and drivers, many of whom brought their families along with their oxen and burros.

Until the mid-1850's, Mexican carts had solid wheels, cut from a single tree and kept from splitting by strips of iron or wood bolted across them. Some of the cart beds were also of one piece, but by mid-century, these were no longer made and seldom seen. Most of these carts had triple decks, with produce on one deck, goats and poultry on another, and the family on the other. It was their home.

In the center of Market Plaza was a pond—ostensibly for

ducks, but enjoyed equally by goats, bull frogs, and naked children.

Matamoros had been a cosmopolitan city almost from its inception. England and France did not cease trying to get a foothold in America throughout the 19th Century. Germany, with a very large number of immigrants in Mexico as well as in Texas, became increasingly interested as it became more powerful. And the unstable Mexican Government seemed to offer an easy back-door access—especially during the Civil War which was egged on by their maneuverings, and during the unhappy Reconstruction Days.

In the market place and on the streets of 19th Century Matamoros were Frenchmen, Englishmen, Irishmen, Americans, Germans, Texans, Africans, richly dressed and peon Mexicans, Indians, cowboys, and ranchers (caballeros)—interspersed with reboza-draped señoritas and richly dressed "Spanish" ladies. On the streets were magnificent horses ridden by their gold and silver bedecked masters—and burros ambling along with perhaps a barefooted peon ludicrously perched on his back. Carts pulled by eight to ten yoke of oxen, and small ones pulled by but a single ox, rattled along continuously.

Matamoros was a busy place in the 1830's and early 1840's. And also beautiful. Truckfarming flourished; hanging baskets filled with exotic flowers adorned courtyards, and lovely homes were well kept—until the Mexican War.

SMUGGLERS' PASS

The route through Santa Rosa to Corpus Christi and through Santa Rosa to Chihuahua, Mexico was known as "Smugglers' Pass," and had been so called since Spanish Colonial days. This particular Santa Rosa was a short distance due west of La Parra Rancho, in the northeastern part of present Brooks County. Apparently Santa Rosa was a headquarters or maintained a warehouse for smugglers. The Penascal Grant was between La Parra Grant and Laguna Madre, but both grants were bounded on the north by the south bank of present Baffin Bay. Two early settlements were on the coast in the Penascal Grant. These were Penascal, which maintained a landing and was due east of La Parra, and Carnesto Lendos, about five miles south of Penascal.

Early Spanish maps show Padre Island not to be a long continuous island, but broken by definite passes and called "Islas de Maguyalitas." In 1766, the islands were first shown joined. Not until after Padre Ballí had occupied the island formerly known as San Carlos but now joined to the other islands, did it become known as "Padre's Island." He managed it in partnership with his mother, Rosa María Hinojosa de Ballí, after 1804 when she inherited it. Some passes were open through the island at full high tide, even into the 1920's.

Before its native grasses had been ruined and before so much water had been taken from the ground by deep wells to the north, the streams in the Llanos Mesteñas were longer flowing, clear, and fed by occasional springs. Even during times of drouth, these springs provided waterholes for men and beasts.

The Spanish plan for colonization of this area fostered smuggling. Lands between Los Olmos Creek and the Lower Rio Grande were not considered for town settlement. Instead, this land was granted to wealthy cattle raisers of "good reputation." Most of these grants were large, embracing five to ten leagues. Among these were Espiritu Santo, La Mesteña Pitilas y La Abra, San Juan de Carixitas, La Barreta, Penascal, and La Parra.

The route by way of Smugglers' Pass to Chihuahua must have led through level land between Los Olmos Creek and San Antonio Creek, continuing in a northwesterly direction along Palo Blanco Creek and through Los Ángeles and Los Ojuelos on into Laredo, where trading would take place and repairs would be made. From Laredo, the regular route into Chihuahua would probably be followed.

Until after the treaty of Guadalúpe Hidalgo, the boundary claimed by Chihuahua extended to the source of the West Nueces in present Edwards County. The route to Chihuahua led through present Bracketville. It was probably here that the Smugglers' Pass route and Cazneau's Road intersected. Cazneau's route followed the Nueces from Corpus Christi northwestward through present La Salle County, then west through present Bracketville.

To Corpus Christi by way of Smugglers' Pass, the route lay directly northward from Santa Rosa, turning sharply northeastward near the site of the first King Ranch house on Santa Gertrudis Creek. From there, the road led through Santa Petronilla on into Corpus Christi. An alternate route probably followed a more easterly direction through the Oso Ranch, which belonged to Colonel Kinney during the 1840's.

According to Texas Ranger "Rip" Ford, Point Isabel was doing a $10,000,000 yearly import and export trade in 1859. The California Gold Rush had been responsible for much of this trade, which had to pass through Chihuahua. How much must have been smuggled during the 1840's and earlier!

Could this have had anything to do with the annexation of Texas and the Mexican War? Could this have been why England and France were so interested?

MUSTANG PLAINS BECOME BRUSH COUNTRY
Cowboys, Mustangers, and Traders

According to Texas Ranger "Rip" Ford, the term "cowboy" originated during Republic of Texas days as a descriptive term for those Texians engaged in capturing horses and cattle in the prairies between Laredo and Corpus Christi. The term was not one of reproach, but rather of admiration for their riding ability and skill in the handling of these grown-wild animals.

In writing of his initial trip to the Mustang Plains (Llanos Mesteñas) in 1849 to assume his duties as commanding officer of the Texas Rangers responsible for protecting the area, Rip Ford wrote ". . . between Laredo and Corpus Christi, we encountered countless droves of mustangs and deer, and in many places numerous wild cattle. . . . These (horses and cattle) were the increase of the animals abandoned by the Mexicans when ordered to vacate the country between the Nueces and the Rio Grande by General Valentín Canalizo, Commandante of the line of the Bravo and representative of the Mexican Supreme Government. . . . This line [was] given up by President Santa Anna in 1836 to the Republic of Texas."

Following the Mexican War during 1848 and 1849, while no United States troops were stationed here for protection of the frontier and before the Texas Rangers were reactivated, hundreds of mustang pens were scattered throughout the Mustang Plains, largely manned by lawless Mexican "mustangers" as savage as the Comanches who were invading the area.

Perceiving that the United States Government was not going to immediately send cavalry detachments for protection of the South Texas frontier, Governor George T. Wood ordered the immediate organization of a company of Rangers at Corpus Christi. By June 23, 1849, a company was organized. The Governor assigned Colonel "Rip" Ford to assume command of the entire Mustang Plains region. This area was bounded on the northwest by the Old San Antonio Road, on the north by the Nueces River, on the east by the Gulf of Mexico, and on the southwest by the Rio Grande. Quite an area for a handfful of men to guard. They had to reconnoiter the region drained by the Agua Dulce, the San Fernando, and the Santa Gertrudis, as well as give protection to caravans of traders.

Before 1850, Colonel H. L. Kinney, a Mr. Mann, General William L. Cazneau, and E. Fitzgerald of Corpus Christi, H. Clay Davis of Rio Grande City, B. F. Neal of San Antonio and Brownsville, and J. H. Blood of New Orleans had established trade routes to and through Laredo, Rio Grande City, Castroville, and Eagle Pass destined for the rich trade areas of the landlocked North Mexican states of Chihuahua, Coahuíla, and Nuevo León.

Heretofore, these states had been served largely by a trade route from St. Louis through the northern panhandle of the Republic of Texas. A very rich trade also traveled by way of the "Smugglers' Pass" from the ports of Corpus Christi and Penalasco (Baffin Bay). The newly established trade routes rather closely followed the old roads traveled by the contrabandistos in times past. Caravan leaders had little difficulty hiring knowledgable guides.

Trade caravans were made up of carts and wagons drawn by oxen or mules. For their return trip to the ports, these carts and wagons were loaded at the trading posts with hides, horns, bones for fertilizer, and handmade articles. Much of the trading post's barter was delivered to them on the backs of burros, piled high by inland natives.

This barter continued in like manner throughout South Texas until railroads were built during the 1870's. However, not until 1881, when both the International & Great Northern and the Texas-Mexican Railroads reached Laredo, did much change in trade routes occur. But not until after 1917 was Rio Grande City to receive freight other than by wagons drawn by yokes of oxen.

Because of the numerous grass fires started by the old wood-burning steam engines, early settlers generally blamed the railroads for destroying grass and thereby encouraging the

47

growth of brush. In reality, however, the railroads were just one of the steps in the transforming of the Llanos Mesteñas—Mustang Plains into Brush Country.

SOME CARRIZOS OF THE MUSTANG PLAINS

Carrizos apparently rimmed the Llanos Mesteñas when the first European explorers and early settlers first traversed the region, judging by the number of creeks and springs that were named "Carrizo." Carrizo is the Indian word for the wild reeds or cane that grew so abundantly in this region.

In the southeast part of present Live Oak County is a creek that was shown on early maps and as late as 1861 as "Carrizo." (Some early maps show the creek to be Correase.) In 1829, descendants of Don José Antonio and Don José Victoriano Ramirez claimed eight leagues of land in this area. They claimed improvements on the land had been made as early as 1813, including houses and tanneries of lime and stone.

By the end of 1845, Colonel Henry L. Kinney of Corpus Christi had established a trade route from Corpus Christi to Castroville. The Ramirez land was on this route, which crossed the Nueces west of Oakville.

The Ramirez family built their ranch house of hand-cut caliche blocks, with walls two feet thick that continued above the roof to form a parapet—as were most Spanish and Mexican-built blockhouses in this area, and as were blockhouses of most early South Texas settlers until after the cessation of Indian raids about 1880. The frontier ranch settlements of this section consisted of a stone or caliche (sometimes erroneously referred to as "adobe") blockhouse and several jacales. The blockhouse usually served as a combination trading post and home for the owners. The Ramirez Ranch was no exception, for it was on a well-traveled trade and immigrant route.

The Ramirez settlement was known by the Spanish term so frequently used, "Ramireña," which means "Ramirez lands." It is shown on early state maps, including Felix von Blucher's map, as "Ramireña." Felix von Blucher was the first official surveyor for Nueces County and also for San Patricio District.

With the increase in the importance of Corpus Christi as a port and the advent of the California gold rush in 1849, Ramireña became an overnight camping and supply point.

Carrizo Creek soon became known as Ramireña Creek. By 1870, the name Carrizo was no longer mapped as a name for this creek.

The oldest and most important of the Carrizos began as an Indian village on the north bank of the Rio Grande in present Zapata County. Whether with or without the permission of the Indian villagers is a moot question; nevertheless, the Spaniards established a fort here in 1770. A Spanish village grew around it, nurtured by the waters of the Rio Grande and protected by the occupying troops—until the Mexican Revolution.

General Alexander Somervell and his men occupied Carrizo in 1842, while foraging for supplies. Although the villagers professed friendship, the Texans were unable to get any supplies in either Carrizo or Revilla (present Guerrero), which was across the river. While at Carrizo, Somervell made the wise decision to return to Austin immediately.

In 1849, Colonel "Rip" Ford was placed in command of a detachment of Texas Rangers in this vicinity. He referred to the old fort as "Redmonds Rancho, formerly Carrizo."

When the United States Army established Camp Harney at Carrizo in 1851, it was usually referred to as "Bellville;" sometimes as "Carrizo or Bellville."

W. G. Freeman reported his inspection of the "Camp at Redmond's Ranch" on July 18, 1853. He described it as being 400 yards from the Rio Grande opposite Guerrero (formerly Revilla), Mexico, and as being the second largest town along the Rio Grande. Only Matamoros was larger. He further described Carrizo as having 3000 inhabitants living in 250 stone houses and several whitewashed jacales. He was enthusiastic in his description of the old fort as "a massive stone structure with parapet walls and loopholes for musketry . . . and suitable for mounting field artillery."

On April 11, 1863, some outlaws drove a herd of cattle past Carrizo and across the Rio Grande and into and through Guerrero. Owners of the cattle quickly alerted Captain Santos Benavides of the Confederate Army, who was formerly a Texas Ranger. Captain Benavides and thirty hand-picked men soon passed Carrizo in pursuit of the outlaws, but were unable to overtake them. However, they crossed the Rio Grande and entered Guerrero, where Benavides demanded an audience with the alcalde.

Mexican local authorities and a Mexican Army officer ordered him to leave. Benavides refused to do so until his interview with the alcalde. Presently, the alcalde appeared.

Although Captain Benavides' men did not catch the outlaws, they stopped raiding through Guerrero and Carrizo, for the Captain extracted a promise from the alcalde that he would no longer permit it—and he kept his word.

On December 23, 1863, the Commissioner of Texas for the Confederacy, George J. Durham, issued a directive naming the Confederate Tax Districts and local collectors. H. Redmond was named the local collector at "Zapata, formerly Carrizo." Zapata County was organized in 1858 and Zapata was named its county seat, but located at Carrizo. Several years passed before Carrizo lost its identity. Books published as late as the 1890's still mentioned that "Zapata had formerly been Carrizo."

CARRIZO SPRINGS

Carrizo Springs was the source of one of the few Texas creeks to flow due north. As with many other springs below the Nueces, its present flow is intermittent but generally nonexistent. The creek fed by the springs was named Carrizo Creek and it emptied its waters into scary Lake Espantosa, in the northern part of present Dimmit County. The springs and creek used the Indian name for the reed or "cane" that grew thickly around the springs and along the creek.

Fort McLaughlin, whose rocky walls formerly dominated the vicinity—some old-timers say since before the Civil War—until 1950 when it was torn down to make way for the new highway and become the foundation of Tri-Motor Sales. The old fort was built by a German contractor whose name, Kuechler, was carved on the cornerstone, according to early Carrizo Springs residents.

Settlement forts were necessary because settlers in this area were raided by Comanches, Kiowas, Tonkawas and other hostile Indian tribes until the late 1870's.

Besides Old Fort McLaughlin, the Old Tumlinson House was used for a settlement fort. Both were built of rocks and had walls two feet thick. The Old Tumlinson House is still standing (1968).

The city of Carrizo Springs was established in 1865 to supply the needs of the only industry in the area, cattle raising.

But artesian wells were discovered in the vicinity in 1890, making agriculture possible through irrigation. The farmers specialized, and Carrizo Springs became a main shipping point for Bermuda onions. Artesian wells no longer flow in the area to the extent they did formerly, so the area has largely reverted to stock raising. However, there is still some truck farming.

In 1888, the first bridge to span the Nueces River was built in Precinct One by Grey White, who was County Commissioner of Precinct One at that time. The picture of the bridge marker was taken in Ive White's front yard in August of 1958.

"Uncle" Charlie Vivian built a blockhouse near the east prong of Carrizo Creek soon after the Civil War, about five miles south of present Carrizo Springs city limits. In 1870, about 200 Indians attacked the ranch, but did not succeed in killing any of the occupants, nor did they burn the buildings. However, they did drive off a few horses that were in the pasture and shot some arrows into a cow and calf.

The men of the ranch had gone to a trading post about 25 miles away, leaving early in the morning, for supplies. The wife and mother, a daughter about twelve years old, a son about eight years old, and the family dog remained home.

The boy spotted the Indians in time for his mother to get the house closed tightly and for the three of them to run to the creek and hide among the reeds. The girl scooped up the dog and took him down to the creek with them, for if they left him he might reveal their hiding place to the Indians.

As the Indians approached, the dog refused to be quiet, and the girl had to hold the dog's head under the water until he was drowned in order to save themselves. Knowing that the Indians would see the wagon tracks and would assume the entire family was away from home, they had to be absolutely still and quiet.

Soon afterwards, Lieutenant John L. Bullis established a camp of Negro infantry on the east prong of Carrizo Creek about two miles above the Vivian Ranch. Only a chimney remains standing.

The Vivian Ranch was bought by a family named Lemon, who owned it for about twenty years, so it became known as the Old Lemon Ranch. In 1963, the Old Lemon Ranch was owned by the Bill Johnson family. At that time, they were restoring the old rock ranch house into the beautiful home it had formerly been.

UNITED STATES FORTS
COME TO THE MUSTANG PLAINS

Although the first United States military establishment to be erected on Texas soil with permission of the Texas Government had been Fort Marcy in Corpus Christi, it had not been for protection of the frontier from Indian depredations. It was an encampment for Zachary Taylor's Army in preparation for the Mexican War.

It has been ascertained also, that an underground magazine was built in 1849, when a depot for military supplies was established in Corpus Christi. These were used, probably, to combat Indians. This old magazine was about fifty feet square, and had only one entrance, which was located near the center of present block 14 on Chaparral Street.

In 1852, Camp Casa Blanca was established to serve as a supply station for Fort Merrill. The name "Casa Blanca" was chosen because of its proximity to, and perhaps partial use of, the old Spanish fort ruins that area settlers referred to as "Casa Blanca." The Spanish fort ruins are located in the extreme northeastern corner of present Jim Wells County near Sandia. Camp Casa Blanca ruins are in the extreme southeastern corner of Live Oak County.

Its name was soon changed to Camp Merrill, in honor of Captain H. W. Merrill—the same as Fort Merrill. Since it was closer to Corpus Christi and on a well-traveled route, it may have been garrisoned more constantly. It was more strongly fortified than Fort Merrill, but covered less area.

In regard to nearby Casa Blanca, *The Corpus Christi Star* of July 21, 1849, reported the following: "Great Cazneau train Departed for Chihuahua'—For more than a week previous the carts had been leaving, a few every day, for Casa Blanca, where they were to rendezvous, and our streets were filled with oxen and teamsters . . . a motley crowd—fair-skinned Germans, ruddy Irishmen, swarthy Mexicans contrasted with bronzed faces of keen Yankees and rough but ready Texans. 'Donner and blitzens' and 'Carrajos' and Anglo-Saxon oaths blended—not very euphoniously."

A Texas Ranger Company accompanied the wagon train filled with goods to trade in Chihuahua. Extra ammunition was obtained from whatever source was at hand, some probably from the Army magazine in Corpus Christi.

This Cazneau train arrived safely in Chihuahua by way of present Eagle Pass, and opened a trade route that competed with Indianola and San Antonio and ushered in a tempestuous era, which culminated in the brutal "Cart War."

THE UNITED STATES ARMY MOVES
TO THE RIO GRANDE

The Corpus Christi Gazette printed an "extra" March 8, 1846, with headlines stating that the United States Army was about to take occupation of the left bank of the Rio Grande. It stated further that the Army would not interfere with residents of either bank nor should anybody interfere with the Army in any way, either en route or on the Rio Grande. The order was signed by W. W. S. Bliss, Ass't. Adjutant General.

A depot was established in the vicinity of Sarita, where the main army was to rendezvous. The 2nd Dragoons, under command of Col. D. F. Twiggs, left the morning of the 8th, along with the Corps of Light Artillery headed by Captain John Erving. On the morning of the 9th, the First Brigade, commanded by Brevet General W. J. Worth, composed of a Battalion of Artillery and the 8th Infantry, were to leave. The 2nd Brigade was to leave the 10th, and the 3rd Brigade the 11th, all headed for the same destination. The route followed the old Matamoros Road, used since Spanish days.

En route to the Rio Grande, an incident occurred that really demoralized an entire regiment for awhile. . . . This incident happened in the middle of the afternoon, their second day out from Corpus Christi, while they were sleepy and tired and irritated by the gnats. They were entering a sandy area that was beginning to be overgrown with mottes of mesquite and scrub oak. The soldiers were marching monotonously along in the hot sun, when the corporal who was marching on the right flank of the column suddenly came face to face with a Texas Longhorn bull.

Startled, and being a greenhorn in Texas, he jerked out his revolver and fired at the bull, hoping to frighten him into running away.

Apparently the shot grazed the bull some place, for he considered this act on the part of the soldier downright irritating. He let out a bellow, lowered his huge head and charged the corporal—who didn't stay around to argue, but dashed straight into the column of unsuspecting infantrymen.

Undaunted by numbers, the longhorn charged headlong, scattering almost the entire regiment as if they were so many chickens. No one dared to fire for fear of hitting another soldier. After about half an hour of this fun, the old bull raced off into the brush unharmed.

POINTS ALONG THE RIO GRANDE

When Captain Rodriquez, in charge of the Mexican port-of-entry at Brazos Santiago across the channel from Point Isabel, heard of the approaching thousands of United States troops, he burned the customs house and the few other jacales, for General Garcia had been sent with but 250 soldiers to defend the port. He and Captain Rodriquez and the soldiers made double time down the beach to Boca Chica and crossed the Rio Grande, headed for the fort at Matamoros.

At Point Isabel, General Taylor selected the site for his supply base on a twenty-foot bluff commanding the bay. He named this base-to-be "Fort Fronton,"* left a detail to begin building it, and continued his journey to the Rio Grande. The date was March 26, 1846.

On the morning of March 29, the American troops began building a defensive earthen fortification directly across the Rio Grande from General Mejia's headquarters. The building of this fort and of Fort Fronton progressed simultaneously.

The Rio Grande fort was called Fort Taylor until Major Jacob Brown, commander of the 7th Infantry, was killed by a cannon ball on April 9th—the first fatality.

The fort at Point Isabel was selected as the main supply base because Santiago Pass had a channel eight feet deep at full tide, so that supply ships were able to land there. Fort Fronton was finished in early June and the name of the base was changed to Fort Polk, in honor of the President.

Fort Polk, rather than Fort Brown, was General Taylor's main base while operating along the Rio Grande. The hospital base was likewise maintained at Fort Polk.

---

*"Santa Isabela de Fronton" was the Spanish name for this land grant.

General Taylor maintained sub-bases at Rancho Blanco, about a mile southeast of present Santa María, at the riverboat landing; and at Edinburg, now called Hidalgo and which also maintained a boat landing at that time. The Rio Grande was navigable as far up the river as present Rio Grande City, called Rancho Garcia at this time.

WEBB, STARR, AND CAMERON COUNTIES

In 1848, Nueces County was relieved of 9,022 square miles by the creation of Webb County on January 28, Starr County on February 10, and Cameron County on February 12. Refugio and San Patricio Counties remained the same at this time. So did the part of Bexar County that extended into the Mustang Plains.

Although no Texas government had been extended over Laredo earlier, its residents had generally been friendly. Ex-Republic of Texas President Mirabeau B. Lamar very probably was chosen to occupy Laredo because of his friendship with planners of the "Republic of the Rio Grande," most of whom lived in or near Laredo.

Lamar, along with many other Texans, had dreams of a great Republic of Texas. It was Lamar who had gotten Colonel Henry L. Kinney to settle in Corpus Christi and encourage trade and promote friendship with Northern Mexico. He encouraged settlement in the region also.

According to friends and admirers of Lamar, he had made quite a bit of headway before Sam Houston again became president and sent several of his uncouth friends into this area to cause trouble with Mexico, thus frightening the majority of Texans into desiring annexation. At any rate, Lamar—the Southern Gentleman from Georgia—got along famously in Laredo. It was not long before the county was organized and named for one of Lamar's friends. James Webb had been a favorite advisor of Lamar during his term as president of the Republic.

Starr County, originally containing 1207 square miles, was named for James Harper Starr, another of Lamar's friends. He had been appointed by President Sam Houston, during his first term as President, to be Chairman of the Board of Land Commissioners of Nacogdoches County, and had done a splendid job. Starr became a friend of Lamar and served under him as Secretary of the Treasury. Upon examination of records in the City of Houston, to where the capital was moved by Houston, Starr found many errors in the way the department had been operated. He participated in the removal of the archives to Austin.

Davis Landing, also called "Clay Davis," was named the county seat when Starr County was organized. This was at the Carnestolindas Ranch that had been established by the Garcia family in 1767. Clay Davis settled here in 1845 and married into the family. He became interested in river commerce and built a landing here, directly across from Camargo. In 1848, Fort Ringgold was established, and "Clay Davis" was named the county seat. However, when the town was incorporated in 1850, its name was changed to Rio Grande City.

With an area of 3,308 square miles, Cameron County was established to include two-thirds of the coastal region, including most of Padre Island, between the Rio Grande and the Nueces. Ria Rita was the first county seat selected, but in December of 1848 Brownsville was named the county seat.

This new county was named for Ewen Cameron, a participant in the Battle of San Jacinto. Afterwards and until 1842, Cameron was the leader of a group of horsemen who came into this Llanos Mesteñas region between the Nueces and the Rio Grande to capture mustangs and longhorns, which they drove to market in San Antonio. Because of their expert horsemanship and boldness, these "hunters below the Nueces" became known as "cowboys,"—and Cameron's Cowboys were the most famous. Cameron and some of his cowboys participated in the Mier Expedition; and, although Cameron drew a white bean, he was executed at the express orders of General Santa Anna.

CIVIL WAR BUILD-UP

John H. Peoples, publisher and editor of *The Corpus Christi Star*, which began publication September 12, 1848, and which appeared each Tuesday, foresaw trouble with Indians and outlaws in the Mustang Plains following the Mexican War.

In one of his editorials, Peoples stated:

> It is time some cavalry companies intended for protection of the frontier had arrived. All our rangers either are mustered out or are being mustered out—leaving the frontier exposed. Thieving parties of Indians may now

make descent on the Rio Grande and country this side, ravage and return with plunder, without let or hindrance. To protect our citizens and traders on this frontier should be the first duty of the Government, whilst they are obligated by treaty of peace with Mexico to afford ample protection to Mexican citizens of the line. Infantry and artillery are ineffective. If dragoons cannot be sent here at once and in sufficient numbers—the best method is to re-engage some light companies of West Texas Rangers, who could be brought into service at once. The Secretary of War should lose no time.

. . . —consequences of termination of War with Mexico. Unprincipled Mexicans from the other side with worthless Americans, who have lived without labor as 'followers of the army', and who find a marauding life more congenial will—unless severely dealt with—commit many outrages . . .

Thus the basis of Texas participation in the Civil War was being laid immediately after the Mexican War. To show that Texans' disenchantment with their new federal government was not confined to this area, the following discussion and excerpt of an act passed in the last session of Congress from *The Galveston News* of September 17, 1848 was quoted in Volume I, Number 7 of *The Corpus Christi Star*. A portion of the quotation follows:

"Provided that nothing in this act contained shall be so construed as to express any opinion as to the true boundary of any state or territory contained therein."

"Our readers will recollect the speech made by Mr. Calhoun in South Carolina sometime since, on the subject of the Wilmot Proviso, in which he says: 'At the next session of Congress the contest will be renewed for California, New Mexico and the territory between the Nueces and the Rio Grande—for the North claims all that'. This taken in connection with the extract from the law quoted above, would seem to indicate that Congress by no means considers the question of jurisdiction over the territory between the Nueces and the Rio Grande as settled; but the people of Texas have made up their minds on the subject and the wiseacres in Congress may as well spare their breath and the people's time and money . . ."

With the recall of Texas Rangers to the frontier and the establishment of forts along the Rio Grande and the Nueces, along with payment for Republic of Texas lands desired by the United States, Texas remained happy, peaceable and reasonably prosperous. The slavery question was gaining momentum during this time, but was of little concern to the majority of the citizens, for few slaves were here.

A COUPLE OF DECADES AND A CENTURY AGO

About one hundred and twenty years ago, residents of the Mustang Plains had many views rather different from those of present-day citizens, and some surprisingly similar.

Although no Chamber of Commerce organization then existed, a similar spirit did exist. This is illustrated in an item in an 1848 *Corpus Christi Star* (the local weekly newspaper) titled, "Angora Wool." It states that this area has both the soil and the climate for breeding the Angora goat and that such should prove to be very profitable, "for not a fine shawl is made in the United States." Seemingly as an afterthought, the writer added that "this climate is also ideal for the breeding of silk worms." And included this clincher: "We have here fields more prolific than cotton and tobacco. Who will break the fallow ground?"

The enterprising editor spotlighted one of his advertisements a couple of weeks later, under the disconcerting title, "Out of Soap." It seems that Corpus Christi merchants were out of soap temporarily, because the bi-monthly steamer that commuted from New Orleans to Galveston had brought only twelve instead of the 120 cases that had been ordered. Secure in the knowledge that the ship was well on its way, all available soap had been sold to the traders who left by ox-train the day before, bound for Laredo. However, the editor pointed out that the situation was not nearly so bad as it seemed at first glance, and suggested that readers note Warren Kinney's advertisement of the arrival of 300 dozen shirts. . . . "Those who need and can't buy soap can buy extra shirts, for there will be soap within a few days."

In regard to governmental status, "By *La Europa* we learn that the difference between General Saunders, our minister at Madrid, and the Spanish Government, arising out of the arrest of his servant, has been settled. An immediate apology was made by their Minister, and the required exemptions granted, in addition to which the offending officers were dismissed. The

London correspondent of the *National Intelligence* says: "The opposition English papers compare the full, prompt, and satisfactory apology made to the American ambassador, with the yet unacknowledged degredation and insult passed upon the English one, and attributes the former to the firm and decided attitude which the American minister assumed. The comparison is by no means flattering to the British Government."

And as to homicide,—"The death of Joseph P. Wells at the hands of Captain Bodman, in self-defense, was announced October 24, 1848. It seems that Wells had a cocked five-shooter in his hand when he expired. . . ."

There is an item about the experimental steam car built by General Semple. *The Star* quotes the *Illinois State Register:* ". . . *The Register* expresses the conviction that a car can be made to run 10 MPH with perfect safety. Some of these days we shall have a steam car, as we already had a sail car on the beach of Galveston. Here it requires no experience to establish the practicability of such a car."

Republished in *The Corpus Christi Star* in January of 1846 is a "mod" resolution in regard to Anti-Capital Punishment by the National Society of Opponents of Punishment by Death, adopted in Philadelphia November 25, 1845. The Honorable George M. Dallas, Vice-President of the United States, was presiding.

Mutual concessions with England and Mexico were also reported to be the order of the day. This was intended as a criticism, for in January of 1846, Texas was still a Republic and certain United States citizens and foreign countries, as well as quite a few Texas citizens, were still fighting annexation.

ESTABLISHMENT OF SAN ANTONIO VIEJO

Outlaw and Indian depredations in the Llanos Mesteñas area began with renewed vigor following the Mexican War after the Federal government mustered out all Texas Rangers along with the regular army, leaving only a few infantrymen at Fort Brown.

The Corpus Christi Star, which succeeded *The Corpus Christi Gazette* in 1848, had much criticism to offer about the influx of bad men to this frontier in the wake of the United States Army. Many were mustered-out soldiers who chose to remain here. Their first prey were the Mexican-descent citizens of both sides

59

of the Rio Grande. All citizens were in constant danger, however.

In October of 1848, Ringgold Barracks was established and quartered with infantrymen. More infantry units, despite pleas for cavalrymen, were sent to occupy forts established at Laredo and Eagle Pass in 1849, and at Fort Merrill in March of 1850.

With Indian attacks increasing alarmingly all along the Texas frontier as well as throughout the Mustang Plains, Governor Wood was forced to reactivate the Texas Rangers for protection of the entire Texas frontier.

Late in 1849, John Salmon (Rip) Ford was made a captain in the Texas Rangers, and stationed in this region south of the Nueces. From Corpus Christi, he and his company of Rangers traveled by horseback to Santa Gertrudis Creek. They camped here while reconnoitering the entire area drained by the Agua Dulce, San Fernando, and Santa Gertrudis Creeks. This camp was due east of La Trinidad, a Mexican settlement. However, Captain John J. Grumble's men were posted in the northern part of the Mustang Plains, near the Nueces River and along the upper Agua Dulce. So Captain Ford continued to the southwest, and chose to locate his first post on San Antonio Creek, 32 miles north of Ringgold Barracks and nearly 140 miles from Fort Merrill on the Nueces. He made his camp at "San Antonio Wells," known to the Spaniards for at least a century, and probably much longer.

These wells were located on the "San Antonio Viejo" (Old San Antonio) Spanish Land Grant that Don Francisco Xavier Vela had received and surveyed in 1805. He had brought in a large number of livestock and had built a large rock hacienda. He had improved the wells and had built large stone watering troughs. When the revolutions broke out in Mexico, causing Spanish soldiers to be removed from the extreme northern frontier in order to help the Royal government, Indians reclaimed the region. They made a shambles out of the hacienda, but saved the wells and the watering troughs for their own use. These they understood.

These stone troughs were still in good condition in 1849;— and the Indians, joined by some driven by the Americans from the North and the East coast, were again returning.

The wells were in the midst of a motte of oak trees. Here the Rangers pitched their tents, forming three sides of a square. The fourth side of the square was formed by the crudely repaired main building of the old hacienda. The Rangers kept their supplies in this old building.

Ringgold Barracks had been the first fort established by the United States to protect trade and the frontier settlers. Because it was at the end of the steamboat line of the Rio Grande, a large amount of goods came through here destined for the northern Mexican States. Wanting to cash in on this trade, Colonel H. L. Kinney of Corpus Christi had opened roads at his own expense to Laredo and Mier during Republic of Texas days, and later to Eagle Pass, Presidio, and El Paso.

When Rip Ford established his camp at San Antonio Viejo, it was on the main trade route which was through Rio Grande City into Mexico, and through Camargo and Mier. But in 1849, Asiatic cholera struck Brownsville, San Antonio, Victoria, Port La Vaca, and other cities where soldiers returning from the Mexican War were posted while being mustered out. This was a great help toward establishing Corpus Christi as a port, for the Army by-passed Corpus Christi on its return and the cholera did not strike it at this time. This changed the main stream of trade in this region through Laredo, rather than Brownsville.

Since the flow of trade was reduced to a bare trickle through San Antonio Viejo, the Rangers moved their camp about 35 miles north to Los Ojuelos, which was on the main trade route into Laredo from both Corpus Christi and San Antonio de Bexar.

Called "San Antonio" in 1805 and "San Antonio Viejo" when occupied by the Rangers in 1849, the settlement was appearing on maps as "Cuevitas" by 1879. The "Cuevitas" Grant adjoined the San Antonio Viejo Grant to the north, and ranch headquarters were built near each other for safety and companionship. The community grew into one, occupying parts of both grants. As "Cuevitas," the ghost town is still shown on most road maps (sometimes spelled "Cuebitas").

Six or eight shells of houses, some of hand-cut caliche blocks (sillars) and others of smaller rocks, are still standing near the paved State Highway north of Rio Grande City. Foundations of several others are in evidence.

The San Antonio Viejo Ranch is now owned by the well-known East family. Their present headquarters and ranch house are several miles from the original "San Antonio" settlement, however.

———

Many interesting items are noted in several issues of the late 1848 *Corpus Christi Star*. Residents of Corpus Christi were really beginning to worry about the cholera, smallpox, and fever epidemics that were raging north of the Nueces and in the Lower Rio Grande Valley on both sides of the river. They were also worrying about the increase in raids and other Indian depredations. However, Corpus Christi as a port was showing a remarkable increase, as was overland trade.

The November 7 edition told of an accident happening to Colonel H. L. Kinney and a party of gentlemen guests returning to Barranco Blanco, Colonel Kinney's Ranch on the Nueces River. The horses became frightened at something, dashed off the road, and upset the wagon. No one was seriously injured.

The November 14 edition reported correspondence from Rio Grande City. Judge Norton of that city, in a letter to Editor Peoples of the *Star*, wrote that much excitement was growing out of the arrest of a band of robbers who had committed various acts of wholesale plunder and theft, principally directed against their Mexican citizens. "It is almost incredible," he wrote, "the number of mules and horses stolen this side of the river within the last two or three months. In one instance, five Mexicans were killed who were quietly herding their stock, and their entire caballada of 60 horses was taken. Most of those arrested are area men recently from the United States."

An item with this title, "San Antonio Transportation Line," in the same paper, told of the return of the train of wagons which left Corpus Christi the 21st of last month for San Antonio. A most successful journey was reported. Plenty of water and grass and level land made the journey profitable.

Another item in the same paper told of the arrival of a large party of fifty wagons and mules, and of another en route, for the purpose of trade. These traders were from Mier and Camargo, Mexico.

The November 21st edition stated that the traders from Mier meant $40,000 to Corpus Christi, and that they left this morning for Mexico.

The December 16th edition reported the finding of fossil foot marks on the Brushy (Creek), imbedded in soft argillaceous limestone. And that they were very distinct, with the stride so large that an ordinary size man could, only with difficulty, jump from one print to another.

MORE CIVIL WAR BUILD-UP

Since the majority of very early settlers to the Llanos Mesteñas, other than those from Mexico, were from Europe, it is highly possible that the main reason so many of these Texans were inclined to favor secession was because of the lack of protection by the Federal government of its frontier citizens from Indian raids. Following the Mexican War, the Rangers and U. S. soldiers were mustered out of the army or transferred out of this area very quickly, leaving the Mexican border region without protection.

Several issues of *The Corpus Christi Star* were highly critical of the Federal Government's policy in carrying out the Treaty of Guadalupe Hidalgo. Publication Volume I, Number 16, dated December 30, 1848, stated, ". . . if the government cares naught for American citizens, they can at least protect the Mexican citizens on *both* sides of the Rio Grande." (One section of the treaty promised the settlers of northern Mexico protection from Indians raiding from the United States.)

Volume I, Number 23, dated February 24, 1849, reported, "Indians Again—In regard to Indians again committing outrages since the Rangers have been withdrawn . . . The people have been told the government has soldiers and agents to keep them out . . . They have not done their duty." (This is an excerpt from a letter to the editor from Navarro County, Texas, dated January 10, 1849.)

Volume I, Number 19 of January 27, 1849, stated: ". . . Much discontent with the federal government spending money in protection of and road building in North Mexico and disregarding safety of and road building in Texas and other inland places along the southern border—but aiding a northern route which is impassable much of the year . . ."

Volume I, Number 45, dated July 28, 1849, reported: "Indian Depredations.—Mr. Dwyer besieged on the San Fernando by 50 or 60 Indians. Fifteen men under Lt. Rankin have started for his relief. Others have been reported near the Oso and the Alamo . . ." (area creeks).

Conclusion, "If the government does not adopt effective means, and that promptly, to relieve the frontiers of Texas, the

63

citizens will be forced to take their defence (sic) into their own hands, and the result can be easily apprehended."

August 18, 1849, the *Star* reported, "Government cancelled mail route from Corpus Christi to Laredo. Why!! . . . Local one established . . ."

And the following New York resolution did not help matters:

"Resolved, That the territory lying between the Nueces and the Rio Grande is the common property of the United States, and that our Senators and Representatives in Congress be requested to use their best efforts to preserve the same as such common property and protect it from the unfounded claims of the State of Texas, and prohibit the extension over it of the laws of Texas or the institution of domestic slavery."

Needless to say, Editor Peoples had some strong opinions to offer in regard to the "wiseacres" who introduced the resolution.

———

BAD TIMES

The Corpus Christi Star, published March 10, 1849, reported smallpox in Victoria, and Asiatic cholera in Brownsville, Matamoros, Rio Grande City and other military posts along the Rio Grande, but still none in Corpus Christi.

Smallpox was reported in Seguin on March 17, 1849. Also reported, was the beginning of a weekly stage line between San Antonio and Corpus Christi, and thirty New England boys arrived by ship en route to California.

Indian raiders entered Rio Grande City April 21, 1849, led by the notorious Roque, a Mexican who had been captured by the Comanches as a small boy and was, at this time, about 20 years old.

The following cholera report was published in the April 24 weekly paper: 34 of the 150 of the white population at Brazos Santiago dead, ½ of the population at Brownsville dead, ⅓ of the 300 at Brazos dead, and at Matamoros 300 died in one week. Colonel Hardee lost 20 of his command, Company 2 of the Second Dragoons, en route from Laredo to San Antonio.

On May 5, cholera was reported to be in San Antonio. Also on May 5, Lt. Bee of the newly reactivated Texas Rangers captured the notorious Comanche war leader, Roque; and Indians were reported to be on the Nueces.

A ranch owned by Colonel H. L. Kinney, the Rancho del Alazán, was attacked by Indians on May 19, 1849, much of the stock was driven off, and one herdsman was killed and three were wounded.

About 400 Indians were said to be in the war party along the Nueces. Thirty mustangers came to Colonel Kinney's ranch on the Nueces, "Barranco Blanco," and reported being attacked by Indians. They said four of their men were killed and their entire caballada driven off. Kinney hired the entire group to guard his ranch. He had been a heavy loser. Mr. Kinney invited Mr. Mann and other citizens to drive their caballadas to the strongly guarded Barranco Blanco Ranch for safety.

General Cazneau and Colonel Kinney were ordered by Governor Wood, as of June 1, 1849, to form a company of Rangers for protection of the frontier. The company was to consist of one hundred men.

By June 23, the company of Rangers was organized. The following officers were elected: Blackwell, Captain; Walker, First Lieutenant; Rankin, Second Lieutenant; Aikens, Third Lieutenant; C. W. Bryant, in charge of the Commissary and Quartermaster; and Dr. Swift, Surgeon.

1849—MORE UNITED STATES FORTS

On March 3, 1849, United States troops occupied the old Spanish fort at Laredo that had been garrisoned by Mexican soldiers from 1821 until 1846.

The United States called their encampment here Fort Crawford, but soon changed the name to Fort McIntosh, in honor of Colonel J. S. McIntosh who was mortally wounded at the Battle of Resaca de La Palma.

Fort McIntosh was abandoned in 1858, but was reoccupied in 1859. A new fort was built in 1868, one-half mile south of the old fort and was occupied continuously until 1946. At that time it was declared superfluous by the Federal Government and offered for sale. The City of Laredo bought it and turned it into a municipal park. Now it is the site of Laredo Junior College.

FORT DUNCAN — During the War with Mexico, Camp Eagle Pass was built nearly opposite the old Spanish Presidio

San Juan Bautista, a few miles south of present Eagle Pass. When Captain Sidney Burbank established Fort Duncan on March 27, 1849, Camp Eagle Pass was discontinued.

Confederate troops took over Fort Duncan on March 20, 1861, and used it continuously during the Civil War. Federal troops did not reoccupy it until 1868. They abandoned it again in 1883, but regarrisoned it in 1889, and maintained it until after World War II.

While Pancho Villa and other raiders were active along the Mexican border, National Guardsmen occupied Fort Duncan. The Great Goat War of San José was fought during this time and the Guardsmen participated in it, joining the Texas Rangers.

Fort Duncan has again become known as Camp Eagle Pass, officially. Caretakers are keeping the extensive stables in fair condition, along with the other buildings, so that it can be occupied with a minimum of time and effort, if need be.

CAMPS DRUM AND BUGLE — Camps Drum and Bugle should really have been called "Camps Grumble and Bumble." The Fourth Artillery was ordered to build Camp Drum opposite the Mexican town of Guerrero, then capital of Tamaulipas, late in 1851.

Hardly three weeks later, the Second United States Dragoons arrived on a nearby hill with orders to establish Camp Bugle. Quite a controversy resulted between the commanding officers. Finally, they appealed to higher "brass," and were ordered to combine their camps into one and to name it Camp Drum. After all of this noise and trouble and expense, Camp Drum was ordered abandoned before the end of 1852.

AT CAPITANEÑO

The fifteen young Comanche braves hiding in the ravine back of the well at Capitaneño Rancho had proven themselves. They had successfully raided at Laredo, Camargo, Roma, Mier, and at several ranches along both sides of the Lower Rio Grande. But this time they were on a different kind of mission.

Roque, the leader of the group, had been the pride of the tribal chieftain since he had been captured at the age of four and carried—fighting every inch of the way—from his parents' burning rancho to the Comanche raiders' camp.

For more than a year now, Roque had ridden with war parties and had become one of the most dreaded and notorious of the Comanche raiders. The Chief had called to Roque above the din of battle during each raid so all would know who the quick, strong youth was.

At Mier, the Chief had been wounded in the leg and it would not heal. Soon now Roque would be Chief and he must choose a mate. He looked with disdain at the Indian girls he knew, but he had seen a girl just the right age to steal whom he desired for a mate.

He had seen her first with her family in Laredo, while he was spying—about a month earlier. That was the day his party had taken the officers' horses from the stables at Fort Mc-Intosh. Since then, he had seen her four times at her home, unknown to her, while he was trying to figure out a way to capture her. These times, he had been dressed as a Mexican farmer and had ridden a plodding burro past her father's forted Capitaneño Rancho, which was about twenty miles southeast of Laredo.

Roque had learned that the twelve-year-old girl usually went to the well alone about the middle of the morning. The well was in the middle of a motte of live oaks and partly hidden from all directions. He also learned that a group on horseback could follow the dry creek bed from the southwest to the back of the motte of oaks and remain unseen by occupants in the ranch house and in the cotton field. This was important, for early May was cotton chopping time. Also, the sandy creek bed would muffle the sound of the horses' feet.

About eleven o'clock on the morning of May 7, 1849, María walked gracefully to the well, balancing a clay water jar on her head. She could manage the heavy oaken well-bucket because a small donkey (burro) furnished the power. A strong maguey rope was threaded through the hand-carved wooden *carrillo* (pulley) that was attached to the crossbeam above the well. Two strong posts supported the beam. One end of the rope was tied to the bucket handle and the other to the burro.

Just as María dropped the bucket into the well, she was seized and held from behind by an Indian brave, while Roque tied a rope around her waist and lifted her upon a horse. The other end of the rope was tied around the horse's neck. Roque warned María in good Spanish that if she jumped or fell off, she would be dragged.

Before the Comanches were beyond hearing distance with

their captive, she managed a piercing scream, and the cotton choppers caught a glimpse of the Indians racing toward the west. María's father was informed of the happening, and he and the farm workers quickly formed a posse and rode in pursuit.

Apparently the Indians' horses were tiring, for the posse was about to overtake them at the Magueyitos Rancho, which was not far from Old Rancho de Dolores. However, the Comanches had a fresh remuda waiting for them here, with extra horses for loot and captives.

Roque and his braves were being so hard-pressed that there was no time to transfer María to a fresh horse. Roque left her unharmed, but still tied to the horse, when he quickly leaped onto a fresh one from the remuda and raced away.

Within a couple of minutes, her father had untied her and she was riding safely with the posse toward home. This time, though, the pace was much more leisurely.

ROQUE MAURICIO RETURNS

In 1833, Roque Mauricio was a Mexican boy about four years old living near Camargo, Mexico. His parents lived on a small ranch and owned some sheep and other livestock. Early one morning the Comanches swooped down from the mountains and across the valley and down the river, plundering and killing. Roque's parents were killed and their home burned. But when Roque fought like a little demon, the Indian Chief decided to keep him for his own son. He would make a fine brave one day.

So Roque was taken to the Comanche camp some distance away. He proved to be intelligent and daring. By the time he was about twenty years old, he was made a Comanche War Captain. Soon he was notorious throughout northeastern Mexico. On April 21, 1849, Roque led a group of Comanches into Rio Grande City. They made their way quickly into the stables of Ringgold Barracks and rode off with all the horses belonging to the officers stationed there.

Several Mexicans living in the vicinity formed a posse and managed to crowd the Indians so hard that they recovered a few of the horses for the Army.

A week later, Lieutenant Hamilton P. Bee of the Texas Rangers, scouting with a few of his men, saw some Indians riding near Laredo and attempted to reach them, but were unable to get within rifle range. They chased the Indians toward some men led by Captain H. Clay Davis a few miles away, who managed to kill two of the Indians and capture several horses and mules the Indians were herding.

One of the dead Indians was wearing clothes that had belonged to a Mexican cartman of Mier named Welch. A week or so earlier, Welch and his family had been found on the prairie murdered. His oxen had been killed and his goods scattered. Several bolts of cloth were found blowing about the prairie, and caught on bushes. Some were even wrapped about tree limbs, with ends of the cloth waving frantically.

As Clay Davis and his party neared the town, they spotted a lone Indian lurking about. When he realized he had been seen, he ran into the town, hoping to hide. However, the men managed to capture him. They were surprised to learn that he was the notorious Roque Mauricio, the captive Mexican boy.

The Rangers were able to persuade Roque to renounce his affinity with the Comanches, and to avoid punishment by joining them. He proved invaluable many times.

Early in the morning of May 29, 1850, a group of Rangers under Captain Rip Ford were returning to their camp at San Antonio Viejo, and serving as escort and guide to half a dozen men from Ringgold Barracks who were in charge of a detail of pack mules. These men had accompanied the Rangers northward earlier, parting at Fort Merrill for Corpus Christi while the Rangers continued to San Antonio. The pack mules were carrying 100 dragoon pistols—one-shot and inferior to the revolvers carried by the Rangers—and several boxes of cartridges. The men and Rangers had rendezvoused at Fort Merrill for the return trip.

About 10 o'clock, they came across a fresh Indian trail. Roque and another Ranger were sent ahead as spies, with the others following at a more leisurely pace. The spies soon sighted the Indians camped in a mesquite motte on an elevation along the north bank of Amargosa Creek, near the Ranch headquarters.

Roque signaled the Rangers, who raced toward the Indians, but were seen before they came within rifle range. The Comanches did not stand to receive the charge, but galloped hastily out of camp, heading in a northeasterly direction toward Agua Dulce Creek. The Rangers turned quickly in pursuit.

Captain Ford noticed that the Indians made signals whenever they passed over high ground. Captain Ford asked Roque what these signals meant. Roque replied that the Indians had men waiting ahead, and were telling them to come forward.

This meant trouble for the Rangers' rear guard. Ford sent Roque to have the rear guard move forward as quickly as possible. Seeing Roque dash off at full speed toward the rear, the Indians assumed the Rangers were panicking, so they held their ground.

Suddenly, they found themselves crowded. The rear guard came up and hit them in the flank. . . . Only one Ranger, William Gillespie, received mortal injuries, and these were due to the ill-natured horse he was riding.

He had been warned by Rip Ford of the beast's nature, but had prided himself on his ability to handle horses, and thought he could handle him. Just as Gillespie pulled the trigger of his Colt revolver to finish a wounded Indian he had seen move, his horse shied. This caused the bullet to miss the Indian and be spent harmlessly in the ground. Reacting instantly, the Comanche shot him in the side with an arrow, which penetrated his liver and left lung.

Several Indians were killed and wounded. The Chief and a young warrior dismounted and gave their horses to some of their injured men. When another horse became available, the Chief quickly mounted him, riding like mad to join his warriors who had suddenly deserted the battlefield.

Ranger David Steele pursued and, at 125 yards, shot the Chief back of the ear with a rifle ball. The dead Chief was Otto Cuero.

The young warrior who had dismounted with the Chief had failed to get another mount, and had hidden himself in a nearby clump of brush on the caliche hill that had been the battlefield. During the fight, he had been hit in the groin by a rifle ball that was nearly spent, for it penetrated the flesh but did not pierce the bone. Roque spotted the young warrior, spoke to him in his native Comanche language, and persuaded him to surrender. He assured the young warrior that his life would be spared.

The captive was Carne Muerto, the reputed 18-year-old son of the celebrated Comanche Chieftain Santana.

Roque treated Carne Muerto's wound, using "Comanche medicine." It proved so effective that the captive was able to ride with the Rangers as they continued their journey to Camp San Antonio Viejo.

ROQUE AND CARNE MUERTO

Following the Amargosa-Agua Dulce Creek fight with the Comanches, the Rangers made a litter for badly wounded Captain Bill Gillespie in order to transport him as comfortably as possible.

It was during this time that Roque Mauricio saw Carne Muerto hiding in a nearby clump of bushes and spoke to him in his native Comanche, assuring him that his life would be spared if he surrendered peaceably. So he surrendered without further ado. He was wounded in three places, but the most severe was in the groin where a rifle ball had penetrated. Although the Indians' loss had been four killed, including Comanche Chief Otto Cuero, and seven wounded, the Indians had managed to retrieve all except the Chief and Carne Muerto. The Rangers had suffered only two wounded, including Captain Gillespie.

As quickly as possible, the Rangers began their trip toward Captain John J. Grumble's camp that was about ten miles away, on Agua Dulce Creek. But within a couple of miles, Gillespie weakened, so the Rangers stopped. It was now about dusk, so they decided to make camp. Gillespie died in about an hour.

Roque again treated Carne Muerto's wounds, using Comanche medicine.

At dawn the next morning, the Rangers continued their journey to Captain Grumble's camp, using a mule to carry Captain Gillespies body. During all this time, Carne Muerto appeared unconcerned.

Soon after the Rangers arrived at the camp, they began preparations for Gillespie's funeral. On a nearby rise, some three or four men started digging the grave, while others brought out rifles to be fired in salute.

Carne Muerto watched the proceedings with increasing alarm. Soon tears began coursing down his cheeks. He thought the preparations were being made for his execution, in payment for Captain Gillespie's life.

After a 36-hour rest, the Rangers renewed their journey to San Antonio Viejo. The remarkable powers of the "Comanche Medicine" allowed Carne Muerto to ride horseback along with the Rangers, with scarcely a wince. And he continued to recover rapidly.

Although the Rangers had badly crippled the Comanches, they knew the Indians would soon return in an effort to free Carne Muerto.

The next day, the Rangers took Carne Muerto to Fort McIntosh for safe-keeping. They were going on a planned scouting trip to Webb County, so simply took him along. It was very little out of their way to leave him at the fort in Laredo. All of the company except a few camp guards under command of Lt. Hightower accompanied Captain Ford.

RANGERS' AND INDIANS' FIGHT CLOSELY CONTESTED

Shortly after the first group of Rangers had been formed by Colonel Kinney and General Cazneau in April of 1849, Governor Wood had reactivated the Rangers on a statewide basis, and Colonel "Rip" Ford was sent to the Llanos Mesteñas.

Several companies were under his command, with substations at strategic locations. Texas Ranger companies were smaller than other military groups of like strength, for they operated on the supposition that one Ranger could hold his own with 20 Indians.

Rip Ford chose San Antonio Viejo, located between Randado and Cuevitos in present Jim Hogg County, as his first headquarters. It was 45 miles overland from Ringgold Barracks and about 70 from Laredo, because the terrain was very rough in much of this vicinity.

A large stock raiser had had his ranch quarters here during the early 1800's, but had been driven off by Indians. Several large wells and stone watering troughs in the midst of a motte of oaks made this an ideal camping ground.

Following the previously mentioned Amargosa Battle, Ford and his men returned to San Antonio Viejo with their prisoner, Carne Muerto, Comanche Chief Santana's son. But Ford took Carne Muerto on into Fort McIntosh within a couple of days and turned him over to Captain Sidney Burbank.

A few days later, the Comanches attacked Camp San Antonio Viejo in an attempt to get Carne Muerto. Most of the company was Indian scouting with Ford in Webb County. Just a few had been left with Lt. Hightower on duty as camp guards.

The camp was under siege for two days, but the Rangers

had plenty of food and water and were ably commanded by Highsmith. None of the camp guards were killed, and they so defended the camp that the Indians were unable to rush it. Someone reported the attack, and troops of the First United States Infantry Regiment commanded by Captain J. J. LaMotte of Ringgold Barracks marched to their assistance. Of course the Indians were gone, riding their horses, before the infantry arrived. But they may have stayed around another day or two had they not been aware of the infantry approaching.

The Rangers had to scout the entire Llanos Mesteñas region between the Rio Grande and the Nueces, for the United States did not put any forts in the hinterlands of this region. So that, other than the armed citizens themselves, this area had no protection from roving bands of Indians and outlaws other than the Texas Rangers.

MORE RANGER AND INDIAN FIGHTS

Late in the summer of 1850, Camp San Antonio Viejo was abandoned, and Captain Rip Ford established his headquarters at Los Ojuelos in present Webb County.

This move was decided because of the increased trade between Corpus Christi and Laredo. Slow-moving Mexican carts were used to transport much of the goods, and the load was frequently very valuable. This commerce accelerated the occupation and development of the Llanos Mesteñas.

Camp Los Ojuelos was on the main road between Corpus Christi and Laredo, about 40 miles east of Laredo. It was also between two main traveled Indian trails, and had been a favorite camping resort of the Indians. Plenty of water, grass, and wood were available.

One of the most closely contested fights ever to occur between Texas Rangers and a group of Indians was fought on the Laredo-San Antonio Road a few miles south of the Nueces River, near Lagarto Creek.

Lt. Ed Burleson had been ordered to deliver the Comanche prisoner, Carne Muerto, from Fort McIntosh, where Captain Ford had taken him for safe-keeping, to San Antonio. From Fort Sam Houston in San Antonio, he was returned to his own people.

Shortly after the Rangers had crossed the Nueces on their return to Camp Los Ojuelos from San Antonio, they saw three

73

Indians on horseback. Burleson took eight of his men and gave chase, ordering the rest to continue toward camp.

After racing a couple of miles, the Indians stopped and prepared to fight. Then the Rangers saw eleven others on foot. About fifty yards from the Indian line, the Rangers opened fire. Then through some mistake, Burleson's men thought he signaled for them to dismount, so they did. At once the Indians rushed them and a terrible hand-to-hand encounter took place.

There was no time to maneuver. Each man fought for his life. They were on an open prairie, with no trees or ravines— just grass. Their only cover was the horses, which were what the Indians wanted.

After a few minutes, the Rangers managed to beat off the Indians, after killing more than half of them. Two Rangers were killed, Baker Barton and William Lackey. Jim Carr was very badly injured, but recovered.

About a month later, the Rangers were through this battlefield again, and picked up more than 200 arrows in an area less than one quarter of an acre.

After the fight was over, the Rangers saw a train of Mexican carts traveling toward San Antonio. The three Indians had been watching the cart train so intently they had failed to see the Rangers coming from the other direction until they were almost on them.

The cartmen were so thankful. They felt as if Divine Providence had interceded for them.

Finally, after two years of Indian depredations along the Lower Nueces, the Federal government got around to establishing a fort on the Nueces. But it was not much of a fort and it was not always garrisoned. No officers wanted to be stationed here because of its distance from any city. Also, infantrymen were sent here, and they were not very effective in pursuit of the mounted Indians.

Fort Merrill was established February 26, 1850, by Captain S. M. Plummer, in command of the First United States Infantry. It was named in honor of Captain Hamilton W. Merrill, Brevet Major of the Second Dragoons, for gallantry under fire during the Mexican War.

The location chosen for Fort Merrill was near the old Lagarto Crossing of the Nueces, in present Live Oak County. This crossing had been used by the Spaniards a century and a half earlier.

Oak logs were used for the lower sides of the buildings, for oak abounded in the vicinity at that time. Weatherboard was used for the upper part of the buildings and for floors.

Fort Merrill was permanently abandoned December 1, 1855, with Indians still committing depredations throughout the area.

PABLO PEREZ, PROMINENT PIONEER

With Corpus Christi coming into its own as an important Texas port in 1850—partly because of the yellow fever and Asiatic cholera that had been raging intermittently in Brownsville, Matamoros, Galveston, Port La Vaca and other ports of the Texas coast, as well as some inland cities, since 1849—trade was flourishing. Streams of Mexican carts and long wagons pulled by oxen and mules were crisscrossing the Mustang Plains on the inland trade routes to and from the rich landlocked North Mexican States.

The dependable springs that helped feed San Diego Creek, which were within the present city limits of San Diego of Duval County, had furnished water for "civilized" travelers and their beasts since before the Escandón era when the route between La Bahía (Goliad) and Mier, Tamaulipas, Mexico by way of the Lagarto Crossing of the Nueces was established.

Ostensibly, the Mier Municipality extended to the Nueces River, claiming parts of the land areas of present Starr, Jim Hogg, Brooks, Duval, Jim Wells, and Live Oak Counties. Settlement was just getting well under way, however, when the Mexican Revolution broke out, causing the removal of Spanish presidial soldiers, thus allowing the hostile Indians to return.

Shortly before the outbreak of the Revolution in 1809, Julián Flores and his son, Ventura, had tentatively received their grants, "San Diego de Arriba" and "San Diego de Abajo," and had had them surveyed. Their lands followed a mutual southwestward boundary for about fifteen miles, from Gato Creek to the springs on the San Diego Creek, before parting. From here, Julian's lands extended to the west and Ventura's to the east. That the Flores families did make improvements is shown by the fact they received their deeds in 1812. This was one of the requisites for receiving deeded lands.

Pablo Perez was born in Mier on May 12, 1812. He grew to manhood here and watched the growth of the rich trade, much of it contraband, through Mier.

75

In 1848, Colonel Kinney of Corpus Christi established an "easy-to-follow route" from Corpus Christi to Laredo by fastening a plow to the end of a wagon, turning the turf. This route closely followed San Diego Creek from its juncture with Chiltipin Creek to the present west city limits of San Diego before turning southward.

About this time, Pablo Perez bought property along the north banks of San Diego Creek from Ventura Flores. Here he built several rock houses and brought in several families. This settlement was known as Perezville for a couple of years, but became known officially in 1852 as San Diego when it got a post office.

In 1850, Pablo Perez had married Vicente Barrera, the only daughter of Manuel Barrera, who owned the thriving Amargosa Rancho. Amargosa was to the northeast of San Diego, and also on the Mier-Goliad Road. The Amargosa Ranch was but a small part of the extensive "La Tinaja de Lara" grant that Manuel Barrera had received title to in 1836.

Indians and outlaws, mostly from strongholds in the Sierra Madre Oriental Mountains of northern Mexico, began raiding the Llanos Mesteñas region after the United States soldiers and the Texas Rangers were mustered out following the Mexican War. Isolated ranchers suffered the most, losing their stock and often their lives. Amargosa Rancho residents were among those returning to Mexico for safety.

Several men, apparently connected with Civil War planning activities, took over Amargosa Ranch in 1852. In 1854, Pablo Perez was instrumental in getting Felix von Blucher to survey La Tinaja de Lara grant. Von Blucher was the first official surveyor of San Patricio District, which included the entire Llanos Mesteñas region during the Republic and early statehood days. When Texas became a state in 1846, the area between the Nueces and the Rio Grande became Nueces County. Von Blucher not only knew this entire very well, but he was also a man of integrity.

During the 1850's, Pablo Perez established two other ranches on the Tinaja de Lara grant, but had trouble getting clear titles, so he disposed of them. They were Los Reales Ranch in the south part of the grant on the Rescada Enmedia (Middle Resaca), and El Muertecíto Ranch along Muerto Creek, about half way between the Amargosa and Los Reales Ranches.

The heirs and assignees of Manuel Barrera, at the instigation of Pablo Perez, finally brought suit in 1860 (with the passage of a law that gave them a chance to win their suit) to regain title to and occupancy of their land. This suit, recorded as "Hamilton P. Bee vs. The State of Texas," was heard by Judge Edmund J. Davis, Judge of the 12th District officiating in the 16th District.

Although Judge Davis ordered the land returned to the heirs of Manuel Barrera, with certain stipulations, there is no record showing the Amargosa Ranch in their possession until after the close of the Civil War.

In 1867, Perez bought a large tract of the Charco de Los Preseños grant along San Fernando Creek from Fabriano Zambrano. This was a portion of the Agostadero de San Fernando grant originally deeded to Marcelino Lopez. Pablo Perez later sold some of this land to N. G. Collins, who founded the short-lived town of Collins.

Pablo and Vicente Perez became the parents of four fine sons (and two or three daughters, but the record is not clear concerning his daughters), each of whom did his part in developing the Mustang Plains. These sons were Anastacio, Manuel, Abraham, and Roman. Of the four, Abraham seems to have most nearly followed in his father's footsteps.

Doña Vicente de Perez died February 21, 1876, and was interred in the San Diego Cemetery. At this time, San Diego was the largest place between Laredo and Corpus Christi and had the only place of public worship between these two towns. Father Claude Jaillet was the lone priest in these hinterlands and conducted the funeral services.

For added proof of ownership as well as for tax purposes, Pablo Perez filed an inventory of the property his wife had left him. Added to his own extensive holdings, this inventory proved him to be a very wealthy man.

Pablo Perez died May 29, 1892, and was buried in the San Diego Cemetery a short distance from the grave of Vicente, his wife. Both their graves are still protected by similar wrought-iron fences, and the engraving on both headstones is still discernible.

BIG CHARLIE AND BALL HIGGINS

Speaking of horsey characters, the Llanos Mesteñas has had its share—both noble and vicious.

Texas Ranger Baker Barton's favorite saddle horse, Big Charlie, was a big bay about sixteen hands high. He could carry his rider comfortably at a brisk walk for several hours. Barton rode Big Charlie down from San Antonio to Laredo when he first bought him. And he really learned to respect him on this trip.

Twice, Big Charlie stood perfectly still on command—allowing Barton to shoot a coiled rattler that probably would have struck the horse in the flank had he not responded instantly.

Big Charlie was with Barton three or four years before they parted company. They had been through several outlaw and Indian skirmishes and along several trails together. They had gone with Lieutenant Ed Burleson to San Antonio to deliver an important Indian captive to the United States Army and were returning to their camp at Los Ojuelos when the final break occurred.

They had just crossed the Nueces River at the crossing about twenty-five miles southwest of present Cotulla when the Rangers, about a dozen altogether, spied three Comanches on horseback. Burleson took six or eight Rangers with him to pursue the Indians, and told the others to go on up the road to a good spot and make camp. . . . "We'll be along as soon as we dispose of these Indians."

After streaking across the prairie about three miles, the Indians suddenly stopped. They had led the Rangers to a group of eleven Indians on foot, who suddenly rose above the two-foot grass and shot their arrows almost point-blank at the Rangers, hitting one in the shoulder. Quite a hand-to-hand battle ensued. The Rangers shot over their saddles and under the bellies of the horses, which the Indians were desperately trying to get without injuring.

Baker Barton dismounted to reload his rifle, standing by his loyal horse, Big Charlie. Three arrows pierced him and he grabbed the saddlehorn—and died on his feet. In a matter of minutes, the fight was over. When the first Ranger reached Baker, Big Charlie still had not moved. Baker's convulsed hands were still clutching the saddle horn. Big Charlie had done all he could do to help.

Then there was Ball Higgins—a magnificent black stallion that John Salmon (Rip) Ford had bought in 1847 at Austin. A stockman named Higgins had recently moved onto a survey about fifty miles west of Austin and needed money, so he brought the stallion where he could be seen and sold.

Rip Ford rode Ball Higgins to Corpus Christi and on down Padre Island to Brazos Santiágo, from where Ford and Ball Higgins took a boat to Vera Cruz. There they joined Col. onel John Coffee (Jack) Hays' First Regiment of Texas Volunteers. Ford was made an adjutant and was put in charge of a spy regiment.

Ball Higgins and Ford made names for themselves at Monterréy and in Mexico City, and returned to Austin together. However, Ford was the only one for whom Ball Higgins had any affection—or maybe, it was just grudging admiration.

When Rip Ford was made a Captain in the Texas Rangers late in 1849 and stationed in the Llanos Mesteñas region, he brought Ball Higgins with him and made him a part of the Ranger remuda, to be ridden by any Ranger who might need a fresh horse. Apparently, Ball Higgins resented this and became increasingly ill-tempered. Ford had enjoyed the endurance and beauty of the horse, but had known not to trust him too far. He warned the Rangers that Ball Higgins was capable of vicious tricks and to watch him. Later, Ball Higgins was guilty of causing the death of one of the Rangers.

Lt. William Gillespie chose Ball Higgins as his mount on May 29, 1850. The Rangers were accompanying a squad of five soldiers from Fort Merrill on the Nueces in southern Live Oak County to Fort McIntosh at Laredo. The soldiers were transporting 100 dragoon (one-shot) pistols and several boxes of cartridges for them by pack mules.

On this particular morning—the first out from Fort Merrill—the Rangers intercepted a fresh Indian trail, followed it, and engaged in a fierce running battle with a group of Comanches between the Amargosa and Agua Dulce Creeks. The Rangers were firing at the Indians while pursuing them at top speed, and one of the Indians fell from his horse. He had been shot through the body twice and his neck once and was thought to be dead. As Gillespie on Ball Higgins passed the fallen Indian, he thought he saw the Indian move; so he reined Ball Higgins and aimed at the Indian with his revolver. Just as he touched the trigger, Ball Higgins jumped to one side, causing the shot to miss the Indian. Instantly, the wounded Indian let fly an arrow, which hit Gillespie in the side and penetrated his liver and left lung. He died eight hours later.

COUNTIES CREATED BETWEEN 1852-1857

About a third of Cameron County and a bit of Starr County, a total of 1541 square miles, were used to create Hidalgo County in 1852. Its first county seat was near present Hidalgo, but was called Edinburg.

José de Escandón had established a settlement here in 1750, which the settlers had named La Habitación. John Young, a Scotch immigrant, acquired extensive holdings in and around the settlement in 1852 and changed the name to Edinburg. However, the capricious Rio Grande made the original site of La Habitación a part of its bed during heavy flooding in the 1930's.

Hidalgo County was named for Miguel Hidalgo y Costilla, a native Mexican who was ordained a priest in 1779, at the age of 26. His parish for many years was the mission at Old Dolores, which was established east of the Rio Grande at the mouth of Dolores Creek about seventeen miles south of Laredo. Father Hidalgo had worked here faithfully, teaching his humble parishioners improved methods of agriculture and various kinds of industries. He smarted, along with his parishioners, at the unjust taxation and exploitation suffered at the hands of the arrogant Spanish government and church rulers.

On September 16, 1810, Hidalgo and a hundred of his parishioners seized the prison at Dolores, freeing those they thought were unjustly imprisoned. This was a revolt against both the Spaniards and their Creole lackeys. After a small measure of success, Hidalgo was defeated by the Spanish Army. Some of his bandwagon followers betrayed him into Spanish hands and, after being degraded from the priesthood, he was shot as a traitor during the late summer of 1811.

Encinal, Maverick, and Live Oak Counties were created by order of the Legislature in 1856.

Live oaks grew in profusion along the Frio and Nueces Rivers and in the sandy land east and northeast of Laredo, so two of these counties were named for these beautiful trees—one taking the Spanish name and the other the English.

Encinal County was created out of the present eastern extension of Webb County. The town of Encinal, a couple of miles south of the present town, was to have been the county seat. Year after year passed and no resident took the initiative in getting the county organized; so, on March 12, 1899, the Legislature abolished the area as a county and reincorporated it into Webb County.

Live Oak County was created from Nueces and San Patricio Counties. The Nueces County lines were re-surveyed at this time and a few minor changes other than at its north border line were made, also. Soon after its creation, the Irish settlers organized Live Oak County at a public meeting held in Gussettville. Oakville, near the junction of the Frio and the Nueces Rivers, was named the first county seat. The Oakville townsite had been donated by Thomas Wilson for this purpose. In 1919, just after the new courthouse was built, the county seat was moved to George West because of local politics. The old well-built courthouse is still standing at Oakville (1968), which almost became a ghost town. But during the early 1960's, Highway 9, connecting Corpus Christi more directly with San Antonio and Austin, was made a main route, and Oakville is recovering its former importance, for Highway 9 passes by the courthouse and through the middle of the old townsite.

Although Maverick County was created from Kinney County in 1856, it was not organized until 1871. It was named for Samuel A. Maverick, one of the Bexar representatives to the Convention of 1836 and a signer of the Declaration of Independence at Washington-on-the-Brazos.

Sam Maverick, who died in 1870, had built his home at the present intersection of North Alamo and Houston Streets, overlooking the Alamo. Many of his friends—Irish, Latins, Americans, Germans, but all Texans—had been killed in the Alamo. Had he not been in Alabama getting married, he probably would have been with them. Maverick was mayor of San Antonio from January 8, 1839 until January 8, 1840. In 1842, he was captured by a band of Adrian Woll's Mexican force in San Antonio and taken to Mexico and put in prison. Through the efforts of Waddy Thompson, United States Minister to Mexico, Maverick was released in 1843.

Eagle Pass was named the county seat of Maverick County in 1871. It was laid out as a townsite by John Twohig in 1850 at El Paso del Aguila, so called because of the many eagles flying over the Rio Grande at this point. Fort Duncan, about two miles to the north, had been established early in 1849. Eagle Pass was a river-crossing of the Rio Grande on a main emigrant trail through North Mexico to California during the

Gold Rush—at which time Texas got rid of many unsavory characters.

Bee County was created from parts of San Patricio, Goliad, Live Oak, Refugio, and Karnes Counties late in 1857. Beeville-on-Medio Creek, where the county's first post office was established in 1857, was the first county seat. In 1860, the county seat was moved to Maryville—later renamed Beeville-on-the-Poesta. Bee County was named for Barnard E. Bee, a former governor of South Carolina. Bee came to Texas in 1836 and served as the Secretary of the Treasury and State in the "ad interim" government under David G. Burnet. He was one of the three commissioners who accompanied Antonio Lopez de Santa Anna to Washington, D. C. In the Republic of Texas, Bee served as Secretary of War under Sam Houston, and as Secretary of State under Mirabeau B. Lamar.

Bee was against the annexation of Texas to the United States. Soon after Texas was annexed on February 19, 1846, Bernard Bee returned to South Carolina and he never did come back to Texas.

THE YEAR 1852

In several ways, the year 1852 was a memorable year for the Llanos Mesteñas, which was becoming the Mustang Plains with an increasing number of English-speaking settlers.

The long-dreamed-of trade between Corpus Christi and Chihuahua over the road opened by General Cazneau and Colonel Kinney in 1849 had become a reality. Trade was also flourishing along the Lower Rio Grande Military Road to Chihuahua from the port at Brazos Santiago, now called Port Isabel. And at the mystery-shrouded landing halfway between, spoken of as Smugglers' Pass but never referred to directly in the newspapers, tax-free goods were bringing fortunes to shadowy traders. Texas Rangers were providing travelers and traders with much-needed protection from Indians and outlaws—with a show of assistance from the generally inept United States Infantry.

In 1852, the first large group of European immigrants landed in Corpus Christi. Heretofore, Indianola (called Karlshaven by German immigrants) and Galveston had been the only ports of entry. English, Scotch, Irish, and German colonists were on this first immigrant ship. Soon, other immigrant ships were arriving from Europe with passengers from Poland, Czechoslovakia, and France as well as the already mentioned countries.

These new citizens settled along the south bank of the Nueces at first, across the river from the Irish of McGloin's and McMullen's Colony. Among descendants of these first "south of the Nueces" European colonists still living here in 1968 are Halsey Wright, Miss Josephine Price, Mrs. R. R. Reynolds, Felix Hobbs, N. O. and Harry Adams, Richard Miller, Mrs. F. G. Miller, Mrs. Goode Wier, John and R. G. Almond. The Blucher, Bluntzer, Holbein, Gilpin, Sutherland, and Wade families are among other descendants. They are numerous.

Another type of invasion also began in 1852. A group of men new to the Mustang Plains visited the courthouse in Corpus Christi and studied the available maps of Nueces County, which until 1848 had included the entire area between the Nueces and the Rio Grande from the coast to the Laredo-San Antonio Road, a part of El Camino Real ordered blazed by the King of Spain in 1690 and well traveled since the mid-1700's.

These men soon moved onto the Amargosa Ranch—after an "Indian" raid and fear of others forced the owner-occupants to flee to Mier, Tamaulipas, Mexico—their former home. Thusly, Amargosa Ranch entered the smuggling scene and remained a part of the upper "cotton road" during the Civil War. Not until 1868 did any of the heirs of Manuel Barrera, original owner, again come into possession of the ranch.

Pablo Perez, wealthy Mier citizen who had married Manuel Barrera's daughter, moved into South Texas and led in the building of a small settlement, known as Perezville, along San Diego Creek. The settlement thrived, and in 1852 was designated a Post Office known as San Diego. For several decades, San Diego was the largest town between Corpus Christi and Laredo.

Fort Ewell was established in 1852 to aid in the protection of trade along Cazneau's Road. It was built near the south bank of the Nueces River in present La Salle County, near a main river crossing of the Comanches.

Mustangers, as ruthless as the Comanches and Tonkawas, were building more stockades throughout the prairies. The United States Army was a large buyer of horses, for they were learning that foot soldiers could not overcome the Indians.

The Mustang Plains was a busy cosmopolitan region in 1852.

In 1852, there were neither long, low-lying smoke clouds nor smog hovering menacingly above or shrouding the beautiful port and bay of Corpus Christi. The flour-white bluffs were a welcome sight to the passengers aboard ship from England, France, Germany, Poland, and Czechoslovakia, who were terminating their 50-day trip from London.

Among these passengers was an English family consisting of the parents and two boys—five and six years of age. When the parents succumbed to Ruben Holbein's glowing praises of the Mustang Plains and agreed to emigrate to Texas, they did not realize the primitive conditions and dangers facing them on this frontier.

All goods were hauled overland by oxen—from a single ox pulling a creaking Mexican cart to a train consisting of many huge wagons, each pulled by eight or ten yoke of oxen. There were no bridges, so if the streams should be at flood stage, the travelers merely camped on high ground near the crossing until the water receded.

Corpus Christi, Nuecestown, Laredo and Brownsville were the only places attempting to maintain schools. Their curriculm was said to be simple, with "less attention being given to the cultivation of the memory and more to the development of the reasoning faculties."

A hundred acres of fine fertile land was often sold for the price of a fine pair of boots. In some places in the Mustang Plains, "Motts Land" (land with groves of trees, usually oak), was often sold for ten to fifteen cents per acre. Even so, few people wanted to buy land here. There were several reasons for this. Most of the region was public land, unfenced and its use was free. Land was taxed if you owned it. Indian and Mexican raids frequently terrorized ranchers and isolated communities. Almost every full moon, these raiders stole great herds of cattle and horses and drove them into Mexico.

Great droves of mustangs, deer, elk, and longhorns wandered freely about on the plains, and countless paths criss-crossed the area. A Mr. Dwyer took the wrong turn one day while returning to Corpus Christi from San Antonio and followed a mustang path instead of the proper "road" to Corpus Christi in the Agua Dulce vicinity, and was lost for two weeks.

If a man attempted to make a living by farming, he was considered weak-minded and fit only for a lunatic asylum.

It was impossible to obtain lumber, so houses were built of logs hauled from the Nueces River bottom, or of pickets (small tree trunks and large limbs, also called jacales) from the area creeks and swamps, or of caliche blocks that hardened almost like concrete. Lightweight willow poles were used for the roofs, and leaves of the palmetto that grew mostly in the San Patricio area for thatch.

Longhorns were used for work animals or oxen. Steers were "broke to the yoke" when young, if they were good natured and a bit wider or heavier than average; and they proved to be very satisfactory. They were generally healthy, strong, long-winded, and could live on cactus if its thorns were singed off in the camp fire. Also, they were seldom bothered by ticks.

A PAIR OF REAL PIONEERS

Six-year-old William Adams and his five-year-old brother, Robert, were brought to Corpus Christi from England by their parents in 1852. Here, south of the Nueces, they grew to manhood. Few Americans lived along the Nueces in 1852. After the soldiers were mustered out following their return from the Mexican War, quite a few remained along the Rio Grande. However, the California "Gold Rush" enticed many of these and other Texans westward—but not the Adams family.

The boys received the best education available locally, until the beginning of the Civil War which caused schools to close for lack of personnel and interest.

By 1862, the exporting of cotton through Mexico had become big business. Nearly all cotton exported from Tennessee, Louisiana, Arkansas, and Texas at this time crossed the Nueces River south of San Patricio and followed the old Spanish La Bahía Road southward through Banquete, and the old Santa Gertrudis Camp, and Santa Rosa southward on across the Rio Grande into Matamoros. Here, the road led eastward to the Civil War city of Bagdad, Mexico near the mouth of the Rio Grande.

William and Robert Adams, though only teenagers, got into the act, using a large Mexican-style cart drawn by four yoke of oxen. They loaded the cotton, which had been baled by a mule-powered gin capable of ginning four bales of cotton a day, onto their "carreta" at the Santa Gertrudis Camp, which was about two and one-half miles west of the site of the first King Ranch house (which was built after the Civil War). At Bagdad, the brothers picked up a load of European manufactured goods for their return trip. They hauled for two years.

When the Federals captured Brownsville and moved into Fort Brown, the cotton road shifted to the west. Mier became the main port of entry into Mexico while the Union soldiers and their hired "partisans" raided Laredo and the Lower Rio Grande Valley. This area was experiencing a severe drouth during the last two years of the War, and the Rio Grande was easy to ford in the Mier vicinity.

In 1864, William Adams contracted to haul cotton from Laredo to Bagdad. He crossed over to the Mexican side of the river at various crossings, depending on the location of the Union patrols. After delivering his cotton, Adams returned to Matamoros. Once he boarded the ferry and crossed over into Brownsville with his empty cart. While in Brownsville, he loaded his cart with machinery destined for a cotton factory in Waco, and resolutely returned to Laredo.

After the War, the two brothers decided to form a partnership and go into the sheep-raising business. They chose public land along the Barbon Creek, where, probably unknown to them, the Spaniards had mined silver and had fought a losing battle against the Coastal Indians a century earlier.

1867 was a memorable year for the Adams brothers. Besides farming their partnership land, they both married.

William Adams married Sarah Dodson, daughter of Archelaus B. Dodson, a veteran of the Texas Revolution, and Sarah Bradley Dodson, designer of the first tri-color Lone Star flag of Texas. Robert Adams married Loreno McWhorter, daughter of a Texan patriot who went with General Somerville to the Rio Grande and returned with him.

THE RANGE WAS UNFENCED AND FREE

Both William and Robert Adams, who had married in 1867, lived near the Casa Blanca Fort ruins a short distance west of present Sandia, where soldiers and settlers had lived intermittently since the Spanish Escandón era.

86

Shortly before their marriages, they had formed a partnership to engage in the sheep business. The range along the nearby Barbon Creek was unfenced and free, so their only initial expense was for the sheep and their care.

In 1869, the Adams Brothers sold a large flock of fat muttons to Messrs. Little and Shand at the top price of $2.00 per head, on the range. The sheep had to be driven to Denison for shipment to the slaughter pens in Chicago, for this was the nearest railroad terminal to that market.

Robert Adams had to accompany the sheep drive to San Antonio in order to get the money, because the buyers were afraid of being robbed in the Nueces River vicinity northwest of the range. The buyers paid off with Spanish doubloons and American half-dollars.

After proving to themselves that they could make money raising sheep, the brothers decided to pre-empt 160 acres each along Tecolote Creek. The pre-emptions were adjoining. The creek was so named because the trees growing along its banks were thickly populated with owls. The brothers operated their land as a single ranch, and chose the Spanish name for owl as the name for their ranch. Thus, the Tecolote Ranch was begun by William and Robert Adams in 1869. It is still owned and occupied by descendants of Robert Adams.

Before they could move their families to the ranch, houses had to be built. There were no lumber yards nearer than Corpus Christi, and the cost of hauling the lumber would exceed the cost of the lumber. Since the brothers had very little money, they decided that each would be responsible for building his own house on his own pre-emption. Their first houses were similar—typical pioneer log cabins.

Tall mesquite trees grew along Lagarto Creek. They cut down enough to build the walls of their houses. Each, driving his own yoke of oxen, dragged his logs to his homesite. Willow trees grew in profusion along the Nueces River on the west banks in certain areas where the banks were low. The brothers hitched a yoke of oxen to each of their carts and hauled enough of the lightweight willow poles to roof their cabins. For thatch, they drove to the sandy ground around San Patricio and filled their carts with leaves from the palmettos that grew there so abundantly.

The Adams brothers paid strict and intelligent attention to their business of raising sheep, and within a few years they

87

were the owners of several thousand head of the best sheep in the State.

In 1875, 200,000 head of cattle were sent from this region south of the Nueces to Kansas. Captain Richard King of the Santa Gertrudis Ranch had furnished 60,000 head of these.

So in 1878, the Adams brothers decided to fence their land and begin a career as breeders of fine cattle, along with their sheep business. They fenced their land with posts bought near San Diego for 15¢ apiece. Each mile of fencing cost them an average of $630.00.

TECOLÓTE RANCH ONE OF FIRST TO BRING IN BLOODED CATTLE

After the Adams brothers fenced in their Tecolóte (Owl) Ranch at a cost of $630.00 per mile, they imported some pure-bred Durham bulls to improve their stock. They were among the first ranchers in South Texas to do so.

Texas Longhorn range steers rarely weighed over 800 pounds. They were long-legged, long-horned, long-winded, wonderful racers, and apt to be just about any color imagined. Although they had long backbones, they usually lacked depth and body width. But their strength, general good health and lack of trouble with fever ticks were very good qualities. It is to be remembered that at this time, they were still being broke to the yoke, so that speed and strength were desirable qualities.

Seventy-five per cent of their first imported purebred cattle died within a short time with so-called "Texas fever." However, the next year the Adams brothers imported a few more bulls. Through careful, diligent effort, in 1884 they sent their first beeves to market that weighed 1250 pounds on arrival at their destination in St. Louis.

Most local residents thought the Adams brothers had lost their minds when, in 1888, they bought the Maximo Farias Grant, "Los Preseños de Arriba," consisting of two leagues of land, for $3.00 an acre. Parts of San Diego and San Fernando Creeks east of Alice formed its south boundary; from east to west, it extended approximately from Highway 44 bridge over San Fernando Creek to Texas Boulevard extended. The grant was about twice as long as wide.

Before 1920, most of the land in the Farias Grant had been sold for $40.00 or more an acre.

In 1891, William Adams bought a large ranch about five miles south of Alice and made it his home, leaving the Tecolóte Ranch to Robert. The two brothers terminated their partnership in 1893.

Robert and Loreno (McWhorter) Adams were the parents of five sons and three daughters whom they reared on the Tecolóte Ranch. The parents built a small one-room ranch school, and here their children and the Almond and Wright children attended elementary school. Both the ranch house and school, which replaced the first log cabin home, were built of hand-cut caliche blocks.

Although both William and Robert Adams were good judges of livestock, Robert was considered one of the best judges of both cattle and sheep in the entire Southwest.

Soon after William Adams moved to his new ranch, he became a County Commissioner of Nueces County and was a Commissioner for 16 years. When Jim Wells County was created by the Legislature in 1911, William Adams was appointed Chairman of the Commissioners to Organize Jim Wells County. Thus, he was Judge of Unorganized Jim Wells County. Although his office was temporary, this made him Jim Wells County's first Judge.

Six children survived William and Sarah Adams, and now several of their children's children are living in and contributing to the growth and betterment of the Mustang Plains.

When 74 years old, William Adams was devoting more time to business than most men half his age. He was managing his ranch and farm interests, was President of the Alice Cotton Oil Company, and was Vice-President of two other companies—the South Texas Cattle Loan Company and the Alice Broom Corn Drying Company.

———

SCHOOLS COME TO THE LLANOS MESTEÑAS

Two very important "firsts" happened in the Llanos Mesteñas region in regard to education.

The first Protestant Mission School to be opened for Spanish-speaking children of Mexican background was started in Brownsville by Miss Melinda Rankin in the spring of 1852. This was the Presbyterian Mission School for Girls. Eventually, Miss Rankin carried her missionary work on into Monterrey, Mexico—opening the first Protestant school in Mexico.

Strangely, or perhaps to meet competition, the first Roman Catholic school to be opened was also for girls. The very first branch of the Order of the Incarnate Word, whose avowed objective is the education of youth, to be established in the Western Hemisphere was started in Brownsville in 1853.

Both of the above schools had very humble beginnings, and were faced with inadequate financial resources. However, the nuns had much more local help than did Miss Rankin, so they had an adequate school built by the end of the year.

The yellow fever epidemic of 1858 and the Cortina raiders of 1859 proved to be no respecter of schools. Both schools were forced to close during the height of each ravage. The Catholic School barely continued to function during the Civil War, but the Presbyterian School was forced to close because Miss Rankin was a Yankee—from New England.

In 1865, the Presbyterian Mission School opened in a nice new building. By this time, the Catholic School had grown. Both the Convent and the school building were enlarged, but the hurricane of 1867 utterly demolished the school's new addition and ruined the new building. However, the astute nuns rebuilt their school, with help from the Oblate Fathers and local citizens, and were granted a state charter in 1885. Among those enrolled were Protestant and Jewish girls as well as Catholic.

Wealthy ranchers had, for years, sent their children to boarding schools after two or three years of private tutoring. Area "colleges," actually of high school and junior college level, were opened in San Patricio, Laredo, Brownsville, Lagarto, and Corpus Christi before and immediately following the Civil War. Community schools had been established by this time in San Diego, Nuecestown, and a few other places.

Winnifred Gordan Sutherland, known as "The Sage of Bluntzer," began teaching about 1872. His first school was at Concepción in Duval County. He taught in various schools throughout the Mustang Plains—from along the south bank of the Nueces to the north bank of the Rio Grande. He left the school at Nuecestown to teach at the new school at Amargosa in 1877. In 1890, he was teaching at the school in Collins, which had diminished considerably that year because a school was started in Alice. The first school in Collins had been taught by Mr. Oscar Staples.

The first school in Alice, while it was still called Kleberg and had no post office, was begun in 1888 in the second story of the Becham Place. This had been moved over from Collins and served as a boarding house for men working on the San Antonio-Aransas Pass Railway, and as a stage stop.

The proprietor was Mr. Becham's widowed daughter, Mrs. Walker, who later married a Mr. Sedwick. So the place is also referred to as "the old Sedwick House."

This first school was a private school with only eight or nine pupils in attendance. Miss Mary Woods was the teacher.

In 1890, a school board of trustees was elected in the growing town of Alice, who, with the backing of the people of the town, built a two-story four-room frame building between Second and Third Streets facing Adams Street. Miss Mary Woods became the first teacher of the elementary grades there. The first principal was a Professor Baxter.

Alice's first brick school building was the Hobbs Building, at the corner of Third and Reynolds. It was built in 1905.

In the Orange Grove area, George Reynolds built a house and a one-room school building nearby on his Ventana Ranch in 1867. Both were built of hand-cut caliche blocks. Both are still standing, restored and well cared for by Mrs. Randolf R. Reynolds, present occupant. Mr. George Reynolds had six sons and two daughters for whom he hired a governess to teach in this school.

The first school in the present Alfred area was about a mile from the little town, called Driscoll before the railroad came through, at the William Adams Tecolote Ranch as early as 1874. Professor Sutherland taught at this school for several years, also.

After finishing at their respective local schools, the majority of the pupils in the present Jim Wells County area attended Goliad College before 1886, while it was open.

In the Palito Blanco area, the first school was a Nueces County school taught by a Louis Clark about 1880. The first community school was built in 1889 by the county. It was approximately 600 feet west of the present Palito Blanco School. A Luis Pueblo of Mexico taught English to the community children. The nearby community schools of Loma Alta and La Bandera later consolidated with the Palito Blanco school. At the present time, the Palito Blanco and Ben Bolt schools are consolidated.

FORT EWELL

Fort Ewell was established on May 18, 1852 near the south bank of the Nueces River in present La Salle County—about 60 miles northeast of Laredo and about eight miles from present Artesia Wells. It was named in honor of Captain Richard Stoddert Ewell, a captain of the dragoons in the United States Army. The first buildings were of wood, temporary, and erected by the troops.

In 1853, a commissary storehouse, a block of small shops, and two sets of company quarters were built of caliche blocks.

This location was selected because it was near a main crossing of the Comanches and was at the San Antonio-Laredo crossing of the Nueces River. The Army considered this location necessary in order to protect travel along this route and for added protection of nearby settlers. The site was poorly chosen, however, because it was surrounded by a salt marsh which made the soil unfit for the growing of vegetables and fruit trees.

Even though the Indian danger was very great, the Army abandoned Fort Ewell October 3, 1854 because of its unpopular location. No officers wanted to be stationed there.

Early settlers of the upper and middle Nueces River Valley were raided by Apaches, Comanches, and Kiowas until about 1860. Later, Mexicans and Indians from northern Mexico, joined and even led by renegade whites, raided this section from strongholds in the mountains of northern Mexico.

Fort Ewell—because of its remoteness from large settlements, nearness to Mexico, and mid-river location—became a rendezvous for raiders. The deserted buildings provided protection from the weather and storage for stolen goods.

During the Civil War, settlers along the middle and upper Nueces Valley were not bothered much by raiders because of military activity and travel through the region; but afterwards and until the end of the 1870's they were particularly hard hit.

The last recorded raid emanating from Fort Ewell took place in 1878. It was on such a large scale and was so frightful and received such nationwide publicity that both the State and National governments took instant notice.

TRAINING GROUND FOR CIVIL WAR LEADERS

Ulysses S. Grant's initiation into the Llanos Mesteñas was

by way of a dunking in Corpus Christi Bay in 1845, when he was a lieutenant in General Zachary Taylor's Army.

The pass into Corpus Christi Bay was too shallow for the large troopship to enter, so it anchored in the Gulf and a light steamer was pressed into service to transport troops ashore.

When Lt. Grant was ready to go ashore from the steamer, all the nearby sailors were busy, so he decided to work the pulleys himself. In doing so, he inadvertently took a firm hold on the center rope—and fell head first into the bay.

Between 1848 and 1852, eleven officers were stationed at Ringgold Barracks, near Rio Grande City. Of these eleven officers, seven became Generals in the Civil War. . This ratio was probably about average for all the frontier forts.

Of these seven from Ringgold Barracks, the only one to be in the Union Army was Brigadier General Gabriel Rene Paul. Those becoming Generals in the Confederate Army were Brigadier General Robert Selden Garrett, who was killed at Carricks Ford, Virginia on July 13, 1861; Assistant Adjutant General E. A. Palfrey, General Dabney Herndon Maury, General E. Kirby Smith, Major General J. H. Forney, and Major General C. M. Wilcox, all of whom served from 1861 until 1865.

Jefferson Davis, destined to become President of the Confederacy, was an officer with General Zachary Taylor's troops on the Rio Grande in 1846-'47. Had it not been for Colonel Davis' well-drilled First Mississippi Infantry on February 22, 1847, the outcome of the attack at Buena Vista against Taylor's reduced forces would probably have been quite different.

Edmund J. Davis, who served in the Mustang Plains as deputy collector of customs at Laredo and as district attorney and district judge of the 12th District from 1850 until the outbreak of the Civil War, became an ardent Unionist and the extremely unpopular Reconstruction Governor of Texas.

He joined the Union Army as colonel of the First Texas Cavalry, which consisted mostly of Unionists who had escaped into Mexico, and worked his way up to brigadier general.

In March of 1864, Davis led 200 Unionists against Laredo, but they were not successful in occupying the city. However, he was successful in one foray against Texas—his group destroyed the salt works at El Sal del Rey.

1857

The year 1857 proved to be especially turbulent, not only

93

locally but statewide and nationally and, specifically in regard to this area, internationally.

A severe money panic which hurt business in the manufacturing North, but did not seriously affect agricultural Texas, caused further division between the North and the South. Since the economy of the South was based on agriculture, the Southern members of Congress were able to block a tariff bill which was designed to help Northern business—but would hurt the South.

The Supreme Court widened the breach by declaring the Compromise of 1850, in the Dred Scott decision, to be illegal. This opened all the states and territories to slavery. Now, the South was jubilant and the North angry.

The Cart War, with international complications, affected friendly relations with Mexico. Many Texans, including the Rangers and the people of the frontier, had slight respect for the Army posts along the Rio Grande because of their slowness of action in regard to Indian and outlaw raids. But when the United States military freighting contracts were awarded to Mexican cartmen in preference to native Texans, those who were underbid by the Mexicans really got riled.

San Antonio was the main supply depot for the frontier forts. Most of the cargo was shipped by water to the port at Indianola, now a ghost town, and hauled overland from there to San Antonio. Fighting began here between the Mexicans and Texans. The Mexican cartmen bid the contracts at such ridiculously low prices that the Texans simply could not compete and maintain a decent standard of living.

Mexican freighters also hauled cargo to the forts along the Rio Grande from the supply depot in San Antonio. Several of these supply trains were attacked by teamsters from north of the Nueces. A few cartmen were killed and their freight and carts were ruined. This took place on the roads between San Antonio and Eagle Pass and Laredo. The road from San Antonio split south of the Nueces, with one leading to Eagle Pass and the other to Laredo.

The killing of José Antonio Delgado, a Mexican citizen, in Karnes County precipitated government action. The killing was protested by the Mexican minister in Washington, D. C. He claimed that 70 or more other Mexican nationals had also been killed in such fights.

94

When Governor Pease learned that General David Twiggs at San Antonio had been forced to send convoys of soldiers to protect United States goods from destruction by competing freighters, he asked for a company of Texas Rangers to police the roads. However, before the Rangers arrived, area citizens had taken matters into their own hands and had cleared the Llanos Mesteñas of these culprits who had come from other parts of Texas. You see, some of these freighters were financed by men living in this region.

Indian raids along the Nueces Valley began again in October of 1857 with increased vigor. And, at strategic points along and below the Nueces, more strangers began moving onto ranches left vacant by owners who had been killed or frightened away by raiders.

Some people said these raiders were law enforcement officers or were encouraged by them. Many probably were.

COSMOPOLITAN GROUP OF 1858

Zapata County, located in a controversial region, was named for a controversial figure. There must have been two Colonel Antonio Zapatas, because some sources say that he was a Mexican Revolutionary figure, an Indian fighter, and a supporter of Mexico in the Texas Revolution. Other sources state that Colonel Antonio Zapata was a highly respected rancher, Indian fighter, and a friend of the Texans.

Zapata County was organized soon after it was created in 1858, and Carrizo was named the county seat. Near the end of the 19th Century, Carrizo was renamed Zapata. It has a very interesting history dating from 1770.

By the turn of the 18th Century, a massive structure had been built at Carrizo. Later, Texas Rangers "Rip" Ford and Santos Benavides, and American military personnel, were stationed here or chased outlaws nearby.

An 1853 description of this structure opposite Guerrero (formerly known as Revilla) dwells on its massiveness. The describer suggests its use by the United States Army as a base. Its high massive walls were described as suitably built to sustain heavy field artillery. As with other Spanish-built forts and haciendas, it had parapet walls with loopholes or portholes

95

for "musketry." A United States Army camp was nearby at this time.

During the Civil War, Colonel Santos Benavídes was here with his Frontier Regiment group for several months.

Carrizo was second in population only to Matamoros in cities along the Rio Grande in 1853. Besides the fort, there were 250 stone houses and numerous jacales, with 3,000 residents.

McMullen County was created in 1858 from Live Oak County, but was not organized until 1862. Dog Town was named its county seat. Within a short time this county organization had to be abandoned because of outlawry and lack of settlers.

Dog Town was so named because the local inhabitants used dogs to round up livestock subsisting in the brush. And, according to many old-timers living south of the Nueces River, to waylay unwary travelers.

A group of A. & M. students, descendants of Spanish and Mexican land grant recipients, were returning home for the holidays one pleasant December day during the 1870's when they were ambushed at the Nueces River crossing in the vicinity of Dog Town and killed. The route between San Antonio and Laredo was considered reasonably safe by early travelers—if they managed to get past the Frio and Nueces River crossings.

Several old-timers who lived deep in the Llanos Mesteñas recalled that "everyone thought those ambushers in the Dog Town area were members of a well-known family consisting of a father and several sons"—but this was never proven.

By 1877, quite a few new families had moved into the area, and vigilante groups were formed who drove out the criminal element and organized the county. Dog Town was then named Tilden, for Samuel J. Tilden who was the 1876 Democratic candidate for President of the United States.

Duval County was created in 1858 and organized in 1876. It was named for the early South Texas ranchers Burr H., John C., and Thomas H. Duval. Part of Nueces County, with a bit of Live Oak and Starr Counties added when county lines were surveyed, furnished its acreage. San Diego, the largest settlement between Corpus Christi and Laredo, was named the county seat.

Settlement began along San Diego Creek in the present Duval County area during the early 1800's after Julian and Ventura Flores were issued the Spanish Land Grant, "San

Diego." The road from Mier to La Bahía (Goliad) passed through the present San Diego city limits.

A trading post was opened in San Diego as early as 1852. General Cazneau and Colonel Kinney marked a wagon-train route from Corpus Christi to Laredo in 1849 that led through San Diego. The Dix Brothers, Surveyors, had opened an office in San Diego by 1854. The Texas-Mexican Railway reached San Diego from Corpus Christi in 1879. By 1880, the population numbered a thousand; a bank, a newspaper, and a church were functioning.

La Salle County was created from an area that had been a part of the McMullen-McGloin original grant.

When the First Congress of the Republic of Texas extended San Patricio County southward to the Rio Grande, about one-third of the western part of the original municipality of San Patricio became a part of Bexar County. By the time La Salle County was organized, its lands were taken from Bexar and Webb Counties.

The Webb-Bexar County boundary line was not clearly defined until 1880, when La Salle County was finally organized. When created by the Legislature, the county was designated as being named for the tragic far-seeing Rene Robert Cavalier, Sieur de la Salle. The most populous community in the county in 1880 was La Salle, which had mushroomed around abandoned Fort Ewell.

In 1882, Cotulla (first called Twohig) became the county seat and La Salle soon became a ghost town. Several Polish immigrants settled in the area, and Cotulla was named for one of them, Joe Cotulla.

Dimmit County was created in 1858 from parts of Maverick, Webb, Bexar, and Uvalde Counties. Like La Salle County, it was not organized until 1880, and its boundaries were not clearly defined until that time.

Mexican settlements, made in 1834 along Las Moras Creek and the Nueces River, failed because of Indian hostility. The first attempted settlement from the United States was by a colony of Negroes from Nacogdoches soon after Texas joined the Union. This settlement also failed, for the same reason.

The first permanent settlement was made in 1865 at Carrizo Springs by families from Goliad, Frio, and Atascosa Counties. Other settlements were soon made on nearby creeks.

Dimmitt County was named for Philip Dimitt, but was misspelled in the legislative statute creating the county. Philip Dimitt came to Texas from Kentucky in 1822 at the age of twenty-one, and became a well-known frontier trader. In 1828, he married Maria Louisa Lazo and became a naturalized Mexican citizen. He received title to one and one-fourth leagues of land east of LaVaca Bay in 1835. Here he established Dimitt's Landing, a trading post. He maintained a small company of men here to protect his trading post, which had been designated a place of deposit for government stores.

In 1841, Dimitt and three friends were building a store near Corpus Christi Bay when they were seized by Mexican soldiers. They were told that they were being taken to Mexico City to be shot, along with others in custody. Several of the Texans managed to escape in Saltillo. The Mexican captors announced that Dimitt would be shot within a specified period of time if the escapees did not return. It is presumed that Philip Dimitt committed suicide to save the others, for he managed to be killed in a public place.

_____

CORTINA RAIDS

Juan Nepomuceno Cortina, Mexican born but a great-grandson of José Salvador de la Garza who had received the Espiritu Santo grant from the King of Spain in 1782, resented the encroachment of Americans along the Rio Grande. The main reason for this was because the City of Brownsville and Fort Brown summarily occupied without permission and, in the case of Fort Brown, without compensation for more than forty years, about 15,000 acres of this grant. This resentment grew into depravity; by 1850, Cortina was indicted for murder. He already had a reputation for petty thievery and horse-stealing.

Cortina organized his first border raids in 1857, but was repulsed by Texas Rangers promptly sent to the Rio Grande by Governor Sam Houston.

On July 13, 1859, when City Marshal Robert Shears arrested and reputedly roughly treated a former servant of his, Cortina demanded the release of the prisoner. Shears threatened to shoot Cortina if he interfered, whereupon Cortina shot twice without warning. One shot wounded Shears in the shoulder. Cortina then took the rescued prisoner upon his horse with him and galloped out of town at the head of his group of about forty followers.

About four o'clock in the morning of September 18, 1859, Cortina and a group of mounted men—variously estimated to number from 40 to 80—entered Brownsville. Soon they began shooting and yelling, "Vivo Cheno Cortina" and "Mueran los Gringos"! Thus awakening the population to the realization that the city was in Cortina's possession. Cortina had posted sentinels on main street corners and armed men were riding the streets. Cortina loudly announced that he had no intention of harming any Mexicans or foreigners, he just intended to kill the Americans!

Cortina established his headquarters in Fort Brown, which was temporarily deserted.

After killing the jailer and a constable, Cortina's men broke open the Brownsville jail and liberated the prisoners—who joined the invaders. Cortina then shot and killed Mr. William Neale's son who was still in bed, and sent two men to find Adolphus Glavecke (ex-scout for General Taylor's Army and prominent citizen and constable), the wounded city marshal, and several other prominent citizens.

Not until December 27 was Cortina chased from Brownsville and defeated.

Texas Ranger Santos Benavides, who later became a brigadier general in the Confederate Army, and Lt. Robert E. Lee, who became Commander-in-Chief of the Confederate forces, combined their efforts and rid the Lower Rio Grande Valley of Cortina and his henchmen.

SANTOS BENAVIDES

Santos Benavides was a grandson of the Honorable Thomas Sanchez, founder of the city of Laredo in 1755. Santos was born and reared in Laredo. He was a superb horseman and a gentleman. Also, a former mayor of Laredo.

After about a decade of intermittent service helping to protect the frontier from Indian and outlaw raids, Benavides offered his services to the Confederacy early in 1861.

Governor Edward Clark commissioned him a Captain in the Confederate States of America, and authorized him to raise a company of Rangers to help protect the frontier.

Captain Benavides soon had his Ranger company ready and reported to Colonel "Rip" John Salmon Ford, who was Commander of the 2nd Cavalry Regiment of Texas and in charge of home defense in South Texas. Colonel Ford of the Cavalry and Colonel P. N. Luckett of the Infantry remained in charge of this region from February 15, 1861, when the Confederates took over the United States posts, until January 29, 1863, when General Hamilton P. Bee arrived to take charge.

Colonel Ford ordered Captain Benavides to join Captain Donelson's Company in protecting the vicinity between the Rio Grande and Fort Ewell. It is assumed that Captain Donelson's Company was infantry.

Benavides was stationed at Carrizo, which became known later as Zapata. Raiders had for several years crossed the Rio Grande in this vicinity, gathering at Guerrero, capital of Tamaulipas during the early 1850's, and crossing about where the Falcon Dam now stands.

Cortina and Ochoa, notorious Mexican outlaws, were known to be in this vicinity in command of a large group of partisans (Union soldiers and sympathizers) and highwaymen.

In May of 1861, Cortina, with a force of about 70 well-armed men, crossed the Rio Grande from Guerrero at a point about four miles above Benavides' camp. Only thirty-six men were in camp at that time; the others were on patrol. Nevertheless, the Rangers attacked, surprising the raiders and catching them in a cross-fire. Lieutenant Atanacio Vidaurri, also from Laredo and a friend of Benavides, led a few Rangers and managed to get in front of the raiders, making the initial attack especially virulent. Several raiders were killed. The others were completely routed and driven back across the Rio Grande.

Captain Santos Benavides' Company of Rangers proved to be so successful in their vigilance and in their encounters with Mexican raiders and partisans that these troublesome groups soon rerouted their forays farther down the Rio Grande.

Captain Benavides and his Company of Rangers withdrew from Carrizo on October 29, 1861, moving southward to intercept the raiders at their new points of entry.

---

100 YEARS AGO

The people of Texas were being pushed around by a "radical minority," whose philosophy was "revenge." These radicals had gotten in control of the Federal Government and were giving President Andrew Johnson, who was trying to see that the South was treated justly, a bad time.

These radicals had also infiltered Texas, as well as elsewhere, and had managed to undermine State laws controlling vagrancy, apprenticeship, and labor, and were in control of the Federal agency called "The Freedmen's Bureau." Working through this agency, they did all they could to discredit Governor James Webb Throckmorton, an able and well-liked man who tried to cooperate with the Federal Government but insisted on upholding the dignity and rights of Texas.

These radicals were also in control of the Army, so that it was impossible to get frontier protection. For the carpet-bagging Freedmen's Bureau insisted that the presence of the Army was necessary in the cities to protect the "union" men from the "rebels."

On March 2, 1867, these radicals managed to get the First Reconstruction Act passed over President Johnson's veto.

The State's outstanding "ultra-radical" was the scalawag Edmund Jackson Davis of our own Mustang Plains—from Corpus Christi but a native of Florida. Davis had been a practicing lawyer in Laredo, Brownsville and Corpus Christi, and a judge of District 12 of the Lower Rio Grande Valley.

He was considered an excellent judge. Why had he turned against his neighbors and electorate in such an acrimonious way? According to one report, Judge Davis offered his services to the Confederate Army as a Captain, but was summarily turned down because of his lack of military training and experience. Others attributed his actions to the fact that he was defeated in the election of members to the Secession Convention.

At any rate, he had joined the Union Army and had led an attack against Laredo, but it had failed. Later, his "partisans" attacked and destroyed El Sal del Rey salt works.

Following the War, Davis did become a delegate to the Constitutional Convention of 1866 and was its president in 1868-'69. As a member and leader in this convention made up of scalawags and carpetbaggers, Davis advocated disfranchisement of all former Confederates, unrestricted Negro suffrage, and the division of Texas into three states.

On February 13, 1867, the Convention of 1866-'67 had voted almost unanimously that "neither slavery nor involuntary servitude, except as a punishment for crime, should exist in Texas and that freedmen should be protected in their rights of person and property. . . . Freedmen should be prosecuted in the courts under the same rules as obtained for whites."

In February of 1868, out of a total vote in Texas of 56,129, 40,750 voters were Negroes. However, 52,964 registered voters did not vote; of those who did not vote, 11,730 were Negroes. The election was in favor of holding the Constitutional Convention of 1869, which proved to be wasteful, costly, and unproductive.

Davis was elected Governor of Texas in an election directed by the United States Military Commander General Philip Sheridan, and ruled in true dictatorial fashion for the next four years. He imposed martial law, substituted State Police for the Texas Rangers, appointed local civil officers throughout Texas who should have been elected, and allowed military courts to take the place of trial by jury. Rioting and temporary reigns of terror characterized his term of office. It took the "Tax-Payers Convention"—called a "convention of soreheads" by the Davis clan—to get the Texas government again into the hands of Texans who were decent, law-abiding citizens.

EPIDEMICS

Reoccurring epidemics of yellow fever, along with yearly outbreaks of malaria and dengue, harassed the Texas coast and other low-lying marshy areas. Yellow fever was so debilitating, so repulsive in its last stages, and caused so many deaths that it was especially dreaded. Constant rumors of yellow fever saved the Texas coast from more extensive invasion by the Union forces during the Civil War. The first epidemic found recorded in this area was at Matamoros in 1843. It had become an important port and was receiving ships from tropical Mexico and South America.

Yellow fever is primarily a tropical disease, transmitted by various types of mosquitoes—as are malaria and dengue fevers.

In 1881, Carlos J. Finlay in Cuba announced the conclusion that the common mosquito transmitted the disease, after having bitten a person or animal with the disease and receiving the virus. Later systematic experiments conducted by the Yellow Fever Commission of the United States Army in Cuba proved this conclusion to be true.

Particularly severe epidemics occurred in the Mustang Plains during the late summers and falls of 1849, 1858-'59, 1867, and 1882. A quarantine station was built on Padre Island in 1882 across from Point Isabel (now called Port Isabel) and one was also built on the south end of St. Joseph's Island.

Certain existing conditions recorded in the Mercer Log, Number 1, which was written during July and August of 1866, in the light of our present knowledge, help explain these epidemics.

On July 22nd, the horses came up entirely covered with mosquitoes. Because of a lack of wood and help, few fences were built. If horses were needed the following day, they were roped when they came to the barn for their feed, and staked nearby to graze during the night. But with the mosquitoes biting so fiercely, it was almost impossible to keep a horse staked. The Mercers attempted this when the mosquitoes were in such swarms and lost a horse.

They built a smoke to drive off the mosquitoes, but the horse, named Rebels, managed to get his rope in the fire and burned it. He jumped and jerked around so in fighting the mosquitoes that he broke the rope where it had been burned and ran off. By the last of August, he still had not been found.

On July 23rd, the suffering of the cattle, along with that of the people "and all," was mentioned. Mr. Mercer stated that he had never known the mosquitoes to bite for so long a time.

On July 29th, he noted that the mosquitoes were not so bad and that all were able to get a good night's sleep.

But a new generation must have developed. The entry for August 10th stated that the mosquitoes were so bad that "we had to make a smoke for the horses and ourselves, too.' (A smoke was a bonfire made with wood that burned slowly and made a great deal of smoke.)

The August 27th entry stated, "Mosquitoes are powerful bad now mind I tell you."

Great epidemics of yellow fever have occurred in Barcelona, New Orleans, New York, Philadelphia, Paris and other great cities, brought in by ships from the tropics and spread by local mosquitoes.

A young man died in Corpus Christi the latter part of November, 1866, two days after his arrival by boat from Indianola. His death was definitely attributed to yellow fever. He had recently left Paris, France, for New York. At New York, he embarked on a ship for Galveston, the trip taking about two weeks. He probably picked up the virus in the vicinity of Galveston, allowing about a two-week incubation period. There were doubtless others, whose deaths were not recorded as due to yellow fever, who brought in the virus.

103

The 1867 yellow fever epidemic was at its height during August, in the Mustang Plains. On his way from San Diego to Corpus Christi, Father Jaillet (the lone priest in the hinterlands area at that time), recorded four deaths at Los Preseños. He also recorded that he met several wagons carrying the dead out of town for burial.

When he arrived in Corpus Christi, he saw several bodies lying in the streets, and people crying and calling for doctors.

Two of the four Catholic priests in Corpus Christi died of the disease, and another was stricken but recovered. Those who did recover remained immune to the dreadful disease.

The legend persists among the few remaining old-timers that Father Gonnard, one of the two priests who died, became so overcome with grief at the pain and desolation he witnessed, that he offered his life to God to stop the epidemic. Of course the truth of this cannot be proven, but Father Gonnard's death was the last to be recorded in 1867 as due to yellow fever.

WELLS: BARREL AND HORSE-DUG

Barrel and horse-dug wells were numerous throughout the Mustang Plains during early pioneer days and well into the last quarter of the Nineteenth Century. These were possible because of the high water table.

Most Mexican ranches and settlements had these wells, usually as auxiliary wells. Los Preseños, a Mexican settlement officially mapped from 1831 until 1878 when the post office was moved across San Fernando Creek to the new town of Collins on the newly extended Texas-Mexican Railway, contained several such wells.

Barrels were plentiful in those days, for nearly all kinds of food were shipped in them, as well as nails and other small items of hardware. Should travelers be forced to camp some distance from a river, creek, spring, or well, they would look for the lowest nearby spot of soil. Here they would dig a hole two or three feet deep, knock out the ends of a barrel, and sink it into the hole. The sides of the barrel acted as a casing, holding back the dirt and keeping the water clear. For water would soon gather in the bottom of the barrel and probably fill it.

Barrel wells were often used during dry summer months at favorite picnic grounds. These were usually in dry creek beds where there was a level sandy spot in the midst of a motte of trees. One favorite place near the Nueces River was shaded by the bridge that spanned the steep banks of a creek that fed the Nueces in rainy weather, and by a large oak near the road.

Horse-dug wells were much longer lasting. Although these were usually only ten or fifteen feet deep, about four feet wide, and eight to ten feet long, sometimes they were deeper. When they were deeper, they had to be longer, because the horse had to pull the scoop or fresno out of the well at an angle that was not too sharp. These wells also used a well-sweep, which consisted of a long tapering pole that was swung on a pivot and was attached to one end of the top of the well casing, or attached to a heavy post at one end of the well. The well-bucket was suspended from the tapered end of the pole.

These were referred to as "horse-dug" by the early settlers because Spanish and Mexican ranchers had dug them, using the mustang to pull the fresno, long before other settlers had come into the Mustang Plains. The small, wiry mustang could stop and "turn on a dime," and was the best available power.

Before the San Antonio-Aransas Pass Railroad was built into this region and before the city of Alice began, a horse-dug well was in use on Latta Creek near present Aransas Street. This well furnished water for the narrow-gauge Tex-Mex engines on their way to San Diego and Laredo or to Collins, Banquete and on to Corpus Christi. Several native Mexican families lived nearby in jacales, for this was a part of José María Garcia's Mexican land grant, "La Vaca."

An especially large horse-dug well was at present Alfred, then called Driscoll. "Uncle Willie" Wright remembered it as being in existence for several years during his boyhood and youth, and said that it was the largest he ever saw. It was about forty feet deep, four feet wide, and eighteen feet long. The upper part of it was rock lined, with the rock extending about four feet above the ground, forming a strong wall around the well. A heavy oaken bucket hung from the well-sweep, and generally two men were needed to bring up the large, heavy wooden bucket full of water.

DON JESÚS DE LA GARZA

Jesús María de la Garza—generally known as Don Jesús— was proud of his right to the Spanish title, "Don."

He was born January 12, 1845 in Villa Garcia, a small settlement in the shadows of the Sierra del Fraile, near Monterréy, Nuevo León, Mexico.

Not much is known of the childhood of Don Jesús, other than the fact that he received a liberal arts education, probably attending secondary school and college in Monterréy. He was a scholarly person, preferring to read rather than to engage in the popular local sport of "bronco-busting."

About 1870, Don Jesús married Obdulia Garza of Doctor Cross, a village near the eastern boundary of Nuevo León not far from Camargo, which was a leading port of entry to the States of North Mexico during the 19th Century. The couple came to the United States by way of Clay Davis (Rio Grande City), where they remained for a short time before moving to San Diego of Duval County, Texas, about 1873.

Indians were still raiding the San Diego vicinity from time to time, and mustangs were running wild in large herds—some of them magnficent animals. The chief sport and money-making pastime of the area was corralling mustangs. Doña Obdulia often chided Don Jesús, calling him lazy, for never taking part in this sport. But Don Jesús thought his five-foot, two-inch frame stood little chance against a wild mustang—besides, he would rather read. She would rather he read, too.

Father Peter Bard—Padre Pedro—San Diego parish priest from 1877 until 1920, had an excellent library. Most of the books were written in Spanish, but several were in French, German, and in English. Don Jesús read every book in Father Bard's library.

To make a living, Don Jesús taught Spanish privately in nearby Santa Cruz until 1904 when he moved to Alice. He continued his classes in Alice.

The De La Garzas had no children of their own, but they had adopted a year-old niece, Guadalupe Garza of San Diego, and had reared her as their own. She had grown to womanhood and had married Trínidad Salazar. Her namesake, Miss Guadalupe Salazar, and the other Salazar children never knew their real grandmother. Their Aunt Obdulia was always "Grandmother" to them, and Don Jesús was "Grandfather."

When they moved to Alice, the De La Garzas bought "the old Mills place." It adjoined the property that Trínidad Salazar had bought, built his house on, and moved into in 1899, which was the reason why the De La Garzas moved to Alice.

About a year later, Don Jesús taught at a private school in Runge for several months, coming home weekends on the San Antonio-Aransas Pass Railway. Miss Salazar said she remembers that he always brought home quite a bit of fruit and vegetables from Runge.

Don Jesús built a fruit stand about 1906, where he sold pottery, herbs, patent medicine, ice cream, pilón, and other candies.

Doña Obdulia died October 9, 1908 and is buried in the Old Collins Cemetery.

Don Jesús carried his age well. A favorite saying of his was, "I will dance with my great-grandchildren on my one-hundredth birthday." But he did not quite make it.

Soon after this picture was made in 1934,* Don Jesús became ill and moved from his home, where he had lived alone since the death of his wife, to a bedroom (there must have been seven) in the Trinidad Salazar home.

Two years later, he seemed to be dying from an obstruction in his intestines. Dr. P. S. Joseph of Alice and Dr. J. G. Garcia of San Diego (father-in-law of Hector Lopez of Alice) operated on him on a table in his bedroom. They were afraid to move him. This operation would give him a hundred-to-one chance to live.

Don Jesús survived the operation and lived two more years. However, he walked very little any more because of the pain it caused him. On October 29, 1938, Don Jesús María de la Garza died and was buried by the side of his wife in the Old Collins Cemetery east of Alice, Texas.

During the 1920's, Don Jesús wrote and had published an historical novel written in Spanish, *Adventuras de Un Medico*. The story takes place in Monterrey, Mexico beginning in 1845.

*In picture section at front of book.

OLD BLUE

Outstanding characteristics were a part of the makeup of most of those living on the Mustang Plains before the railroads eliminated this frontier. These characteristics were not limited to humans. Quite a few animals, and even some trees possessed them in some form.

There was "Old Blue," for instance. Although his horns hang in the West Texas State College at Canyon—claimed by the Panhandle-Plains Historical Society—Old Blue was a native of the Mustang Plains.

The "Moro" (as vaqueros called such a blue-colored calf) Longhorn was born on a small ranch along the south banks of the Nueces River in 1870. Before long, he was a ranch favorite. Because of his rather unusual color, he was noticed; but he was remembered because he preferred to hobnob with people and horses. He grew to be large and heavy, so he was broken to the yoke while a yearling.

The moro was sold to John S. Chisum, the almost-legendary stockman, when he was three years old. Chisum was building a herd to drive north in the spring. When the October moon shone full, Comanches visited the Chisum spread, drove off several horses, and shot an arrow into the blue longhorn's flank. He never forgot the smell of an Indian; this added greatly to his value. Indians were never able to surprise herds led by him, for he always detected their advance spies.

In the spring of 1874, the moro was among the large herd of cattle that Chisum sold to Charles Goodnight out in West Texas. Goodnight took the herd to Colorado, where he planned to establish a ranch. The moro placed himself at the head of the herd, and there he remained all the way to Colorado. It was on this trip that the moro earned his name, "Old Blue."

The ranching venture in Colorado did not pan out for Charles Goodnight because of drouth, so he took his herd to good pasture in Canada—with Old Blue leading. Nothing spooked Old Blue, but he did become stubborn if he smelled Indians and insisted on changing directions—or would stop walking and shake his head vigorously.

In 1876, Goodnight established his JA Ranch in the Palo Duro Canyon. He brought 1600 head of cattle from Canada to stock it. Old Blue brought the cattle in safely.

Goodnight was ready to drive his first herd to market in 1878, so he bought a bell for Old Blue. It took the blue Longhorn no time at all to get used to his bell, for he was immensely proud of it and seemed to realize what it was for.

On this first trip to market, Old Blue set the pattern he was to follow during the ten or twelve trips he led herds from the JA Ranch to Dodge City. At night when it was time to bed down the cattle, one of the cowboys would fasten the bell-clapper so it would not sound. The following morning when it was time to resume the journey, Old Blue would amble over to one of the mounted cowboys to have his bell-clapper freed.

Old Blue refused ever to bed down with the cattle that followed him. When camp was made, he wandered around like a pet dog, begging handouts and nudging a favorite wrangler, perhaps hoping to be petted and to have his huge head scratched. Before turning in, one of the cowboys would hobble Old Blue so he could graze with the horses.

After delivering the cattle to market, Old Blue really enjoyed the return trip with the men and horses, and had no trouble keeping up with them. He even ate with the horses and liked their food.

Although he was often referred to as a "Judas," because he led other cattle to market, somehow it did not seem bad in Old Blue. Probably, because he seemed not to consider himself a member of the cattle family, but more of a horse or a human. Old Blue only *led* the cattle herd, he never hobnobbed with any of them. He could have thought of himself as a buffalo— once he brought two back to the JA Ranch. This was not entirely his idea, though.

On Old Blue's trip home after taking his last herd to Dodge City, he brought a pair of buffaloes from the Canadian River. The buffalo pair was yoked to Old Blue, one on either side, because Colonel Goodnight wanted to build a herd of them, for he realized they were facing extinction. And Old Blue brought them home, with the cowboys tagging along.

This was a tiring trip for Old Blue. He knew every campsite along the trail, and he did not pass very many each day before resting. When he stopped, the wranglers did not argue, even though it might be mid-afternoon.

When they finally made it back to the JA Ranch, Old Blue was retired and allowed to roam the range at will. Several drovers tried to buy Old Blue for use as a lead ox, but Colonel Goodnight refused to sell him. Old Blue died when he was twenty years old.

———

ARANSAS COUNTY ONCE PART OF REFUGIO COUNTY

A most interesting part of original Refugio County became Aransas County in 1871. It was named for an old Spanish-Mexican fort that once guarded the entrance into Copano Bay. The Spaniards called the fort "Aranzazu." The settlement that grew up around it was also called Aranzazu. Mary Austin Holley wrote about it in her book, *Texas, Observations, Historical,*

Geographical, and Descriptive, that was published in 1833. The Spaniards called a tribe of Indians living in the vicinity "Aransuas," and named the Aransas Bay for them.

The north arm of Aransas Bay, now called St. Charles Bay, was called "Laguna del Bergantin" by the Spaniards. For unnumbered generations, the Karankawa Indians used these shores for camping grounds. Evidences of a prehistoric cannibalistic civilization have been discovered in the area.

Bergantine Creek is a marshy continuation of the Bay into the prairie to the north. Early Texas colonists are said to have named the creek this because they found a Spanish barkentine stranded far out on the prairie where a savage hurricane had blown it. According to legend, the ship was carrying the payroll for the San Antonio and Goliad garrisons. Early colonists stripped it of its metal and timbers, but did not find the gold.

St. Joseph's Island fits Cabeza de Vaca's description of the island on which he was shipwrecked. Many historians consider it as his landing place in Texas in 1528, rather than Galveston. Diego Ortíz Parrilla explored it and named it Culebra (Snake) Island in 1766.

Irish immigrants to Power's and Hewetson's Colony in 1834 were stranded on St. Joseph's Island when their ship was unable to negotiate the pass. Two hundred and fifty of them died there of the cholera.

Following the Texas Revolution, several Texas cattlemen and seamen established homes on the southern tip of St. Joseph's Island. Aransas became a prosperous port—until invaded and destroyed by the United States Navy during the Civil War in 1862.

Three miles above Goose Island State Park is the present tourist mecca and Republic of Texas established town of Lamar. It was originally called Point Lookout, and had been a Comanche Indian rendezvous. Irish members of the Powers and Hewetson Grant settled there in 1838 and named it for President Mirabeau B. Lamar. During the Civil War, it was partly destroyed. Since 1915, Rockport has been its post office.

James C. Fulton, a native of Philadelphia, came to Texas in 1837. He married the daughter of Provisional Governor Henry Smith in 1840, and became Collector of Customs for the Aransas District. He and Henry Smith formed a real estate company and located bay-front sites on the shores of Aransas, Cópano, Nueces, and Corpus Christi Bays. Fulton moved with his family to Baltimore in 1846 so his children could attend school.

In 1867, Fulton returned to Texas and got into the cattle business. The town of Fulton, known as Aransas City from 1890 until 1900, was named for James C. Fulton. It is best known for the Fulton Mansion, which took four years to build. Partially restored to its original elegance during the 1950's, it has been a target of vandals and thieving souvenir seekers, and is once again a weather-beaten old house (1966).

When built, it followed the general lines of elegant French houses of the era. From its French mansard roof and cupola, down through its three stories and into its basement, it was the last word. It had central heating, carbide lights, a bathroom on each bedroom floor, and a powder room on the first floor. Bathrooms on the second and third floors were furnished with hot water from a sun-heated tank in the cupola. The furnace, cooling room, kitchen, and wine cellar were in the basement. Heat from the furnace was vented to fireplaces in each room, resplendent with marble mantles and Italian tile.

Ships from France brought carpets, scrolled door handles and latches, chandeliers, Italian tiles, and other furnishings. The ships landed in Aransas Bay, and the furnishings were hauled directly to the mansion.

Fulton's sister and her family occupied the second floor. The third floor was occupied by Fulton and his immediate family. The cupola was above a storage room on the third floor that was said to contain a secret stairway.

Fultons study occupied the cupola, from which could be seen all of Cópano Bay, and Aransas Bay to the sand dunes of the Gulf Islands—if binoculars were used. He kept his money in the cupola, where on stormy nights, some say, he is still to be seen counting his money. Should you venture close enough, you might hear him climbing his secret stairs.

PHILIP POPE PRICE

Among the many who have been influential in the development of the Mustang Plains, especially of the hinterland, were three men—natives of widely separated areas. These three, one a commissioner and county organizer, one a judge, and the third a county superintendent, were allied politically and are to be commended especially for their integrity and competent handling of public affairs during their many years of service.

Of the three, perhaps Philip Pope Price helped bring the most culture and happiness into the lives of individuals through his school teaching and his sight-improvement crusade.

Philip Pope Price was born and educated in Warrenton, North Carolina—graduating from the small college there when but seventeen years old. Upon his graduation, he applied for a position at Goliad College, and was accepted. He came to Texas and began his teaching career in 1867. At Goliad College, which drew most of its students from the area south of the San Antonio River, Price taught Latin and Greek.

After teaching at Goliad College a few years, Price began to study law. He resigned his teaching position at Goliad, and taught for a few years at Gonzales. While here, he passed the State Bar Examination. However, his law practice was only incidental, for his eyesight became very poor. He decided to study optometry, which proved to be of special interest to him. While pursuing this course of study, Price taught in Nordheim and in Yorktown. He completed his study of optometry near the close of the century and moved to Duval County.

Realizing that he could not make an adequate living here as an optometrist, Price taught school, and, in his spare time, traveled throughout the Mustang Plains fitting and delivering spectacles. In his role as teacher, he was able to see the great need for eyesight improvement and to recognize the ignorance that prevailed in regard to optometry. He was indeed a needed missionary here in this field at this time.

In 1903, Price married Elizabeth Almond, the daughter of Mr. and Mrs. Joseph Almond, children of English immigrants and owners of a large ranch about eight miles north of Alice. They became parents of one child, a daughter, whom they named Josephine.

Price continued his teaching in Duval County and his optometry crusade for two or three years, then established the Price Farm and Ranch out of a portion of the Joseph Almond Estate. He brought better farming and ranching methods into this region, and shared his improved seeds and stock with neighbors.

In 1914, he was elected Jim Wells County Commissioner of Precinct 2; but when he ran for county judge in the 1916 election, he was defeated. He returned to his teaching career and taught in the neighboring ranch school at Old Amargosa until

1924. After he became County Superintendent, he was able to establish El Carro Common School District, which included Old Amargosa.

From 1927 until 1935, Price was Jim Wells County School Superintendent. He did an excellent job, and established at least two common school districts. By this time, his daughter, Josephine, had finished college and had taught in Austin a year. She was ready to return to South Texas, so she began teaching in Jim Wells County and Price retired as county superintendent.

Philip Pope Price died at his ranch home on August 31, 1943.

LA MOTA DE OLMOS

"On the waters of the Santa Gertrudis in the valley of the Anaquas . . .", begin the lilting phrases of the deed to survey Number 9, located in south-central Duval County. Francisco Bazan, a native of Nuevo Leon, Mexico, bought this 160-acre tract from the State of Texas in 1871. Reconstruction Governor E. J. Davis and Jacob Kuechler, Commissioner of the General Land Office, signed the deed.

Near the center of the survey, a motte of elms marked the source of La Mota Creek—and furnished the name for the ranch, "La Mota de Olmos." Many of the trees are still there, along with additional younger ones. These shade a small sandy canyon, which has been the picnic grounds for five generations of Bazans.

La Mota Creek empties its occasional waters into La Bandera Creek, which in turn empties its waters into the Anaquas, a tributary of the Santa Gertrudis Creek. During dry weather, the Bazans and other early settlers used these creek beds for roads. The sand was not very deep and was much easier on the oxen's and horses' hooves than much of the prairie. The creek beds were also cooler, for any trees that existed in the area were along the creeks.

Francisco's brother, Pedro, helped develop the ranch. By 1876, the brothers had built a forted ranch house. This was very necessary, because the Comanches were raiding in Llanos Mesteñas, joined by Kiowas and other tribes of northern Mexico. A tribe of Comanches maintained camping grounds at a spring in the vicinity of present Freer, and were in the habit of raiding nearby ranches. The Piedras Pintas Ranch, nearby to

113

the northwest of La Mota de Olmos, would send a rider to warn the Bazans when Comanches were in the area.

The Bazan brothers used 640 hand-cut 18"x18"x24" caliche blocks, called sillars, to build their forted ranch house. Its 14-foot high walls are still standing, with only one bad crack and that near its chimney. Well preserved four-by-six inch rafters of cypress hold up its sagging roof, which is now (1968) broken through near the chimney-end of its forty-foot long walls. The fort is twenty feet wide, with a fireplace at one end and double doors at the other.

The fireplace is the size of a single sillar, proof that cooking usually was done elsewhere. The chimney does not extend beyond or even to the top of the wall. Instead, it slopes to the side of the wall one sillar below the top, and there is the flue opening safely above the roof within the parapet walls.

This is one of the few caliche forted ranch houses of this region built with keystone blocks over all its original windows and doors.

La Mota de Olmos Ranch is still owned, managed, and used by descendants of Francisco and Pedro Bazan. The present owners are Mr. and Mrs. Roman Escobar of San Diego. Mrs. Escobar is the former Hermelinda Bazan, daughter of Juan Bazan (Saenz) and granddaughter of Francisco Bazan, the original owner.

Mrs. Escobar's father once spent, along with the rest of the family, an entire week in the enclosure above the roof when he was a small boy. Comanches were gathering in the area and a raid was expected momentarily. This time, however, La Mota Ranch was spared. On several other occasions, La Mota de Olmos and the neighboring Pintas Piedras Ranch were raided and lost many fine horses to the Comanches. A bit of the original corral remains. Its posts were set in a double row, joined by wire, with the space between filled with thorny brush and cactus.

In the spring of 1904, an attractive second ranch home was built. Its walls are also of sillars, but its roof is sloping and has overhanging eaves. It faces the east, shadowed by a big columned porch along three-fourths of its length.

Juan Bazan brought his bride here a few years later, and here they reared their family, one of whom was Mrs. Escobar, who, with her husband, continued to live on the ranch for several years. Their first two children were born here. The oldest, a little girl, lies buried in the ranch cemetery that is about a quarter of a mile from the ranch house. But the first to be buried in the ranch cemetery was one of the ranch hands.

Back in 1904, when the family moved into the new house, the old fort became the first school. Six families lived in the immediate neighborhood at this time and sent their children to the old fort school. In 1906, the ranch settlements of Casa Las Anaquas and Papalote* joined with La Mota de Olmos to form a common school district. They built a wooden school building large enough to house forty pupils. It had a bell tower with a bell to announce "school time." It also announced church time once a month, for Father Bard, "Padre Pedro," called regularly at La Mota de Olmos for many years—long before the schoolhouse was built.

Some teachers at La Mota School were: Miss Daisy Tinney, daughter of the owner of Las Piedras Pintas Ranch; Miss Antonia Garcia of Benavides; and, the last teacher, Miss Zulema Garcia (Valadez). The school was permanently closed in 1953.

Except for weekends and holidays, La Mota de Olmos is almost deserted. However, the ranch is stocked, and early mornings and evenings the cattle gather around the old well for water and to be fed by the Escobars and their nephews, the Garcias, who also run some stock on the ranch.

*Windmill.

"UNCLE WILLIE" — W. T. WRIGHT, SR.

Uncle Willie Wright, in reviewing his life from a 90-year vantage point a few years ago, had difficulty deciding which of his career roles—as a cowboy extraordinary, as a peacemaker and executor, or as a politician—had given him the greatest satisfaction.

William Thomas Wright was born of English immigrant parents at Old Nuecestown on June 4, 1869. Two years later, his father, T. C. Wright, homesteaded 7,000 acres of public land in the present Alfred area. In 1877, he built a fine two-story residence which became the meeting place for the first Episcopal congregation in the present Jim Wells County area. Later, when the San Antonio-Aransas Pass Railway built near the Wright residence, T. C. Wright became postmaster of the station stop named Driscoll. W. T. Wright grew to manhood in this Christian home.

115

When Uncle Willie was a small boy, the nearest school was two miles away on the neighboring Robert Adams "Tecolote" (Owl) Ranch. He attended grammar school there. When he was fifteen years old, he went to Goliad College. However, he attended just two years, from 1884 until 1886, because a tornado destroyed the "college" building in the summer of 1886 and it was not rebuilt.

He returned to Driscoll Station to work for his father as a cowboy, where he had grown up and learned to handle livestock. Soon, he began to deliver cattle by contract from ranchers to buyers. From Victoria alone, Wright moved more than 30,000 head—some as far as Monroe, Louisiana. His cattle never stampeded. This fact gave him a great deal of satisfaction.

Mr. Wright said that his cattle never stampeded because he and his cowboys handled the cattle quietly. His cowboys never popped their whips or shouted, but communicated with each other through a series of signs. Also, they would sing if the cattle seemed restless. This would soothe them.

When he was a boy, W. T. Wright had seen and had vowed to buy the El Carro Ranch some day. In 1898 he had the opportunity. Then he moved the small house that was near the creek to the top of the hill where he had visioned it. With his bride, the former Miss Bertha Halsey, and his small daughter by a previous marriage, he moved into his new home on October 18, 1899.

"Uncle Willie" and "Miss Bertha" became the parents of six children, all of whom were christened in the Episcopal Church of the Advent in Alice.

In 1907, Mr. Wright was asked to divide the 12,063 head of cattle belonging to the N. G. Collins estate among the feuding heirs. He felt that this was a major accomplishment. It was one from which he derived much satisfaction, for he not only divided the cattle in a manner agreeable to the heirs, but brought about an end to their feuding.

Until Jim Wells County was created and organized in 1911, its area was a part of Nueces County. Uncle Willie was a Commissioner of Nueces County from 1905 until 1911. He was chosen to be one of the committee of five to organize Jim Wells County, which was created by the Legislature on February 3, 1911. Following the election of May 6, 1911, organized Jim Wells County had the City of Alice for its county seat. Wright ran for constable, but was defeated. In January of 1919, he became Commissioner of Precinct Number 2, and held this office until January, 1947.

Mr. and Mrs. Wright lived long enough to celebrate their 60th wedding anniversary, with both in reasonably good health. About the last year of his life, Mr. Wright was in poor health. He had to have his leg amputated, so was unable to move about as he always had before, but he recovered well enough to return home. On January 5, 1965, almost exactly seven months after his 95th birthday, W. T. Wright died peaceably in his sleep.

RANGERS, RUMORS, AND OUTLAWS

Quite a few happenings and attitudes present in the Coastal Bend now are strongly reminiscent of those during 1874. For one thing, the Texas Rangers were being strongly criticized by certain groups and their dupes.

On October 10, 1874, a company of about forty Texas Rangers under Captain Wallace came into Corpus Christi. Many of the townspeople gave them the cold-shoulder, accusing them of pushing innocent people around and "strong-arming" others unnecessarily.

The Rangers had come into the area because ranchers had requested them. Cattle and horse thieves were making raids into the area again, and several ranchers and their families and workers had been tortured and a few murdered, as well as several hundred head of livestock stolen.

The editor of *The Nueces Valley* newspaper had the courage to write an editorial upholding the Rangers. He said that rather than injuring others, the Rangers were generally the aggrieved ones; that they attempted arrests, if at all possible, without physical injury so the law could take its course. The editor ended his editorial with this sentence, "We think this statement is due Captain Wallace."

Some of those involved in a robbery and attempted murder about a month later were among those responsible for spreading rumors against the Texas Rangers.

The H. Blain and Brothers store of Los Olmos was on the Brownsville-Corpus Christi Road, several miles from any neighboring ranchers. It was a welcome sight to travelers on this long, miserable, dusty route. Blain's Store was also near the less-traveled east-west route that, in times past, had been a connecting link of "Smugglers' Pass."

117

Shortly after sunset on Thursday evening, November 5, 1874, as Mr. George Blain, store manager, and Roman Barrera, clerk, were preparing to close the store for the night, a group of about forty horsemen rode up.

About half a dozen of the men came into the store passing by Mr. Blain, who was standing by the door preparing to close it. One of the men suddenly grabbed Blain, pinning his arms back while another went through his pockets and removed his small pocket pistol. Barrera recognized one of the men and said, "Cosme, what is the meaning of this?"

The one addressed as Cosme cursed Barrera and told him to shut-up and pointed his pistol at him. "Get over by the door. Outside. Down on your knees," he ordered. "And don't look any place but down at the ground unless you want to be killed."

About 12 other prisoners who had been brought from nearby ranches were herded over near Barrera and forced to kneel by him in the lantern light. Two or three bandits remained outside with their guns trained on the kneeling men. Several others were stationed along the road to avoid being surprised by a posse of Rangers stationed in the area.

The rest of the bandits began ransacking the store. Mr. Blain recognized two of the men. They were Alberto Garza of Matamoros, and a character referred to as "El Tejous" of Brownsville.

Garza, who seemed to be the leader, held his gun at Blain's head and forced him to open the safe. Usually, money was taken to Corpus Christi to the bank on Fridays, but that morning the hack bringing mail had brought a large sum of gold to Blain from Mexico in payment for wool and hides he had had delivered to Camargo. Mr. Henry Blain had decided to accompany the hack on to Corpus Christi and to ride horseback, letting the gold and his week's accumulation of specie ride in the hack. So only $50.00 was in the safe.

Just as the bandits discovered there was no gold in the safe, there was a sudden noise outside. They rushed to the door to see what was happening.

The small company of Rangers under the command of Stephen B. Burleson had quietly approached through the sandy field and rushed the bandits. It was dark by this time, with no moon. The Rangers had to act quickly to save the lives of those captured by the bandits. The bandits could not see them,

118

so they jumped on their horses and fled, exchanging a few shots with the Rangers.

At daybreak, the Rangers started tracking the bandits, and learned that they had passed through Carrizo and were in Guerrero, Mexico.

In reporting the incident, Mr. Blain said that he owed his life to Ysidro Garza, who had just ridden up to the store from his small ranch about four miles away. Garza was letting his horse drink from the water trough back of the store when he heard the horsemen coming. He remained in the shadows, then mounted his horse and raced across the field for the Rangers' Camp as soon as his suspicions that the riders were bandits were verified.

Blain and the other prisoners who had recognized some of the men probably would have been killed and the others tortured, if help had not arrived promptly.

You can be very sure these people who owed their lives to the prompt arrival of the Rangers helped dispel the vicious rumors. Some of the area men who had so loudly denounced the Texas Rangers were no longer seen on the streets of Corpus Christi, for now there were witnesses who had the courage to testify.

MISS RUTH DODSON, RECORDER OF DON PEDRITO'S LIFE AND CURES

Had it not been for Miss Ruth Dodson, it is doubtful if very much authentic information concerning Don Pedrito Jaramillo would have been recorded. As a matter of fact, the story of his life and the stories of his amazing cures would have been, in all probability, lost or considered just another imaginative Mexican legend.

Ruth Dodson wrote her book about Don Pedrito entirely in Spanish and even had it published by a Spanish publisher. It was copyrighted in 1934. However, the copyright is not printed in the books, but is handwritten.

She chose the title *Don Pedrito—"Curandero,"* for her book, which was rather small, containing only 155 pages. Los Talleres De La Casa Editoria Lozano of San Antonio was publisher.

Miss Dodson translated her book into English and sent the manuscript to The Texas Folklore Society who published it, along with some other Mexican tales, in 1951 under the title of

The Healer of Los Olmos and Other Mexican Lore. It was edited by Wilson M. Hudson and has a preface by J. Frank Dobie. A facsimile edition was published in 1966, both by The Southern Methodist University Press.

Miss Dodson wrote other stories for The Texas Folklore Society, and published a small volume of traditional history. She also wrote articles that were published in *The Frontier Times*, in *The Southwest Review*, and in J. Frank Dobie's newspaper column.

J. Frank Dobie relied on Ruth Dodson extensively as a source for many of his tales regarding the vicinity along and south of the Nueces. Her first-hand knowledge and close observations made her the outstanding authority of her time in regard to this region. Her knowledge of both Spanish and English, and of the people who spoke these languages, gave her an insight and an overall view that could not be matched.

None of Ruth Dodson's ancestors arrived in Texas later than 1839, and several members of her family tree were among those coming to Texas with Stephen F. Austin and living in his first colony.

Ruth Dodson was born in Nueces County on September 3, 1876 at her father's Perdido (Lost) Ranch. And here at the ranch school she received all but two years of her formal schooling. One year she attended Lagarto "College"—probably the second grade and during 1883 and 1884. Her last year of formal study was at the public high school in Corpus Christi in 1893.

Growing up on the ranch as she did, Ruth Dodson's only constant early playmates were her eight brothers and sisters and the children of the Mexican ranch hands. She loved these Spanish-speaking people and learned their language, becoming truly bilingual. She knew their customs and beliefs as well as those of her own people.

Ruth Dodson enjoyed the company of children. From 1901 until 1909, she kept open house for her nieces and nephews.

Other than on the Perdido Ranch, Miss Dodson lived in both Mathis and Corpus Christi. She was well known in Alice, for she visited here frequently with her niece, Edith Garrett (Mrs. McGehee) Word, Sr. She was living in Corpus Christi when she died on July 19, 1963.

Miss Ruth Dodson is buried in the Mathis Cemetery in San Patricio County. Other than her name, her gravestone shows only the years of her birth and of her death. Mrs. Word said that she thought this was so because Miss Dodson chose, ordered, and paid for her grave marker before she died. She knew the year of her death, but not the month and the day—so she only had years engraved. It looked better this way.

DON PEDRITO JARAMILLO

Don Pedrito Jaramillo—the Faith Healer to the Mexican people of South Texas and Northeast Mexico and to quite a few others who saw the results of some of his works and who believed—received his power to heal from God, to whom he gave the credit.

His gift of healing had already been bestowed on him before he came to Texas in 1881 from Guadalajaro, Jalisco, Mexico. The terrible scar on his face was truly his healing trademark, for he received his power to heal when he was cured of the pain from his fractured nose and cheekbone.

He was herding some sheep when he was brushed off his running horse by a tree limb and fell on rough bark of the tree trunk, and his nose and cheekbone bore the brunt of his fall. Jaramillo lay unconscious for two or three days under the tree. After he regained consciousness, he returned to the ranch where he worked, but continued to suffer intense pain. Finally, he went out to a pool in the woods and lay for quite a while with his face in the cool mud at its edge. After repeating this treatment for three days, he was healed. In the night, a voice told him he had received the gift of healing and to heal his master, who was sick.

His master followed his prescription to take a tepid bath daily for three days, and was healed. Soon after this, Jaramillo came to South Texas, and settled on the Los Olmos Ranch about halfway between Corpus Christi and Brownsville. The only doctor in the Mustang Plains hinterlands at this time lived in San Diego.

Don Pedrito treated only his close neighbors at first, but soon began visiting ranches in an ever-widening circle, until he had visited nearly all ranches south of the Nueces. He either walked or rode a horse on these visits of mercy until about the turn of the century, then he rode a donkey, but he made fewer and fewer trips. As his fame spread, he stayed home more and treated those who came to him. And there was almost a constant stream of callers.

121

Money as such had no attraction for Don Pedrito. He did not charge for his services, but people gave him donations. He had a barrel in his yard, and whenever anyone wanted to pay him, he told them to just put whatever they wanted to give into the barrel.

He kept a storehouse full of staple groceries to feed those in need. Canned tomatoes were among his favorite prescriptions. He often provided what he prescribed to those who were unable to buy.

Don Pedrito's dress was as individualistic as were his habits. He usually wore the dress of the Mexican peasant, over which he wore a leather vest like cowboys usually wore, and a hat. He is said to have gone barefooted some, but usually wore heavy work shoes on his trips to the ranches.

Severiano Barrera was his foster son to whom he left all of his worldly goods. And his foster son sold the use of Don Pedrito's name and picture to Fernando Tijerina of Laredo to use as his trademark for the boxes of herbs he still sells—60 years after Don Pedrito's death.

Don Pedrito Jaramillo died July 3, 1907 and is buried in the old Los Olmos Ranch cemetery. A visit to this small cemetery near Falfurrias and the singular white open mausoleum,— a tiny white concrete-block house with a door and one window and made very warm by the many constantly burning votive candles,—is an interesting experience. Hundreds of people still visit Don Pedrito's resting place annually.

———

BELL, WELL, AND CURANDERO PROTEGÉ

San Jose is a community too small to be included on most road maps, but a roadside marker on a lonely stretch of newly-finished State 2295 that connects the counties of Webb, Zapata, Jim Hogg, and the southern part of Duval more directly with A. & I. University in Kingsville announces its existence. Other than a house or two, all that San José seems to consist of is a modest church with the surprising name of Saint Joseph's Catholic Church—in English. This is an example of the delightful cosmopolitanism of Llanos Mesteñas.

The bell, mounted on a five-foot metal tower at the side of the church, calls the faithful to worship, and the small statue in front seems to bid "Welcome." Both the statue and the bell were gifts to the church. The bell is especially significant in this case, for its former home was the bell tower of the schoolhouse at La Mota de Olmos.

The old forted ranch house that served as a fort during Indian and outlaw raiding days, then for a couple of years as a school house, continued its service for almost half a century as a general store. Ruins of some of the smaller homes that once housed La Mota residents are camouflaged in the surrounding brush—known only to a few.

Before paved roads and school buses took the school children to the consolidated school at Benavides, the activity of La Mota community centered around the General Store, the school, the corral, and the well. Before the old fort became available, a much less pretentious building served as a small store or commissary for families of the ranch workers. The bell called the villagers together—in case of trouble or to announce the time for scheduled meetings.

Beyond the old corral, the well now sustains a windmill. It was not always so. A deep well was necessary to insure safe water for drinking, as well as an adequate supply. The well-casing is made of caliche blocks like the old fort, and was probably built at the same time. It forms a twelve-foot square, three sillars high, around the well above the ground.

During the early days, a small mule treaded a beaten path, back and forth, at the end of a long rope threaded through a carrillo. A large oaken bucket was fastened to the other end of the rope. The "carrillo" was the hand-made wooden pulley, also of oak, that allowed the bucket to be raised and lowered.

The windmill is anchored to heavy boards securely fastened to the upper casing.

Less than twenty-five miles from La Mota de Olmos lived the legendary faith healer (curandero) of Los Llanos de Las Mesteñas, Sr. Pedro Jaramillo—affectionately called "Don Pedrito." He lived on land given to him that bordered Los Olmos Creek to the east of Falfurrias, in the north part of Brooks County.

His rebuilt tomb—once destroyed by vandals—is a shrine to many natives of South Texas and northern Mexico. Many persons are reported to have asked him to bestow his powers of healing upon themselves or on someone else. His reply was always that his power to heal was God-given and that he had no power to do so.

What is not generally known, though, is that his power of

healing—at least to some extent—was bestowed upon another, also named Pedro.

One day Pedro Bazan, the young brother of the first owner of Los Olmos Ranch, was working in the field when he saw a man riding a furiously running horse toward the field. Straightening from his weed chopping, he watched the rider curiously. He did not recognize the rider as being anyone he knew, but he thought something seemed to be wrong with him. The stranger rode the horse up the row toward Pedro, not stopping until he reached him, but calling to him in Spanish, asking if he were Pedro Bazan Saenz.

When Pedro answered affirmatively, the man continued, "Don Pedrito told me to see you. That you will make the cure. I am very faint. A rattlesnake has bitten my foot." And he extended a badly swollen foot.

Although Pedro Bazan Saenz (Spanish usage often included the mothers maiden name after the father's surname) had had no previous warning or knowledge that he was to become the protegé of Don Pedrito, he suddenly knew what to do.

He led the horse to a tree near the house, and told the man to wait a few minutes. Pedro went into the ranch house. Presently, he came from the back of the house carrying a shovel and a small box.

Then he helped the man from the horse and to lean against the tree. With the shovel, he dug a hole in the ground about a foot in diameter and eighteen inches deep. From the box, he took a dozen eggs, cracked them and emptied them into the hole. He had the man put his bitten foot into the eggs in the hole and hold it there for a few minutes.

When Pedro Bazan told the man to take his foot out of the hole and wash it, the pain and swelling left his foot and leg and the bite was completely cured.

Pedro Bazan Saenz was twenty-six years old at this time. From time to time, Don Pedrito continued to send people to Pedro Bazan to be cured, and Pedro began to spend quite a bit of time with Don Pedrito and became known among the local residents as Don Pedrito's protegé. However, Pedro Bazan did not begin to make calls or heal anyone completely on his own until after Don Pedrito's death on July 3, 1907.

Then Pedro Bazan continued as a healer until he died at the age of 74, on March 21, 1934.

Possibly many cures that Pedro Bazan affected have been

attributed to Don Pedrito, or even disbelieved because of the time the cure was purported to have been made, because of the similarity of their names.

TRINIDAD SALAZAR

Trinidad Salazar was truly a self-made man, whose motto, "El derecho al respecto ajeno es la paz," is remembered in the lives of his children. He was born in Ciudad Jimenez, Tamaulipas, Mexico on April 16, 1862. When very young, he was orphaned and had no real home. He came to Texas when a youth, in hopes of finding a better life.

Pablo Perez, prominent rancher whose wife, Vicente Barrera, inherited the Amargosa Rancho about 1852, befriended him. By 1880, Salazar was wool and hide buyer for the ranch. He was thrifty and frugal with his money.

In 1886, he married Adalaida Bazan of Santa Cruz, a small community about 25 miles southwest of present Alice, and opened his first store in that community.

When the first San Antonio-Aransas Pass Railroad train arrived at its southern terminal point, which was at its intersection with the narrow-gauge Texas-Mexican Railway, Trinidad Salazar was on it. He was returning from San Antonio with a quantity of goods he had bought for his store in Santa Cruz. But he found a number of people living near the railroad intersection, with no store to serve them.

He loaded his cart, and while he was doing so, he had so many requests to sell goods that he returned the next week with goods from his Santa Cruz store and sold from a cart two days a week for a couple of years. During this time, in 1890, his wife died, leaving him with three small daughters.

In 1894, he married Guadalupe Garza of San Diego. He sold his store in Santa Cruz in 1896 and, later in 1896, he bought the Lichtenstein Hotel which was on the corner of First and Aransas Streets in Alice. On the first floor of the former hotel, he opened a general merchandise store; onto the second floor, he moved his family. One daughter, Beatrice (Mrs. Jesús Lopez), was born here.

A heavy rain along the watershed of San Diego Creek in 1898 caused a flash-flood in Alice—with the sun shining! The water was so deep on Aransas Street that it entered the Salazar Store. This caused Mr. Salazar to look for a better location.

He built a frame house on much higher ground and moved his family into it in December of 1899. This home, somewhat altered, is still lived in by members of the Salazar family. It is on present Prospect Street.

Business was good, so Mr. Salazar decided to move his store to a better location and expand. He had made plans to do this as soon as possible when he built his home.

Nearby, where the Rio Theater and Ralph's Foodland Market now stand on present South Reynolds, Salazar opened his huge new store in 1904. Here, everything from thread to buggies and groceries to coffins was sold—from a stock valued at $75,000.00, which was a very large sum in those days.

The first two telephones in Alice were put into the T. Salazar Store and home. This was done while Mrs. Salazar was visiting her folks. She had never seen a telephone, so when she returned from her visit, she was curious about the little black box with the mouthpiece that was on the wall.

"That is for you to whistle into to let me know when dinner is ready," her husband told her.

When dinner was ready, Mrs. Salazar did just that. But Mr. Salazar did not come to dinner. Finally, she sent one of the children to get him. "Why didn't you do as I told you?" he asked. "I did," was the firm reply. "I not only whistled several times, I shouted, too." How Mr. Salazar laughed! Then he showed her how to use the telephone.

This has remained a favorite family joke.

Extremely interested in his children having a better education than he had been able to get, Mr. Salazar was largely responsible for getting the Nayer Elementary School built.

He was civic-minded and charitable in other respects, too. He was instrumental in getting the first bridge across Latta Creek that is a few blocks south of and parallel to Front Street. The creek bed was generally wet and muddy, and often had water in it.

Quite a few squatters lived in the low-lying "Transporte" area near the intersection of the railroads. With every heavy rain, they were flooded and forced from their homes. Mr. Salazar furnished lodgings for these unfortunate people as often and for as long as was necessary.

The T. Salazar Elementary School in South Alice is named for him because of his interest in education and for his many charitable acts.

Also a memorial to Trinidad Salazar and his gracious wife is their family. Thirteen children, six girls and seven boys were born, eleven of whom grew to adulthood. Six are living in Alice, two in Laredo, and two in Rio Grande City. All finished high school and all but two of the girls went on to college or to commercial school. Three are teachers, one is a salesman, one a stenographer, three are housewives, and the others are in the business world.

Six or seven of T. Salazars great-grandchildren are now attending the T. Salazar School. One is being taught there by his grandmother, Mrs. Zoila Salazar Vela (1967).

RAILROADS COME TO THE MUSTANG PLAINS

Railroads came to Llanos Mesteñas a few years earlier than they probably would have otherwise, because of the French and General Philip Sheridan. The French planned to take over Mexico and the United States still believed in the Monroe Doctrine, so General Sheridan was sent to Brazos Island to establish a military camp as a show of strength to discourage Maximilian in his undertaking. Ironically, instead of becoming the hero who saved Mexico from the French, Sheridan became the loser in getting the victorious Mexicans to spare Maximilian's life.

Sheridan had been using railroads for some time, so he heartily disliked the idea of having to move his cargo overland using wagons and carts and ox teams. He probably did not have any soldiers who could handle ox teams, anyway.

Just about the first thing General Sheridan did after arriving at Brazos Santiago Pass on June 23, 1865, was to have a railroad built down Brazos Island from the pass, across Boca Chica to a landing at the White Ranch on the Rio Grande. This little railroad was eighteen miles long and served his camp well. As a matter of fact, it remained in use about five years.

This region's second railroad was built not far away and was 22½ miles long. On November 1, 1870, the Rio Grande Railroad Company was organized for the purpose of connecting Brownsville with the nearest seaport, which was Point (now called Port) Isabel. It was a narrow-gauge railroad and was in full operation by the beginning of 1872. However, when the owners began charging exorbitant prices to haul cargo to Brownsville and Matamoros, some local men reorganized the old "Fast Freight" transportation line of wagons pulled by oxen and charged very reasonable rates.

The railroad bed was destroyed by floods in 1873 and again in 1875. A hurricane in 1880 destroyed a lighter (vessel used to bring cargo from ocean-going vessels too large to negotiate the pass) belonging to the railroad and damaged the railroad. Other floods in 1888 and in 1892 carried away parts of the track and roadbed. Although the repairs were costly—estimated to be $100,000 the first ten years—the railroad did a $120,000 gross annual business from 1875 to 1878, which were the most profitable years. After the yellow fever epidemic hit Brownsville in 1882, the estimated yearly gross business dropped to about $60,000 for the next ten years.

THE TEXAS-MEXICAN RAILWAY

On Thanksgiving Day, 1875, a gold (coated) spike (stolen that night) was driven by Colonel Uriah Lott signifying the beginning of the construction of the railway connecting the "two great ports" of Corpus Christi and Laredo. The Corpus Christi, San Diego, and Rio Grande Narrow Gauge Railway was chartered March 18, 1875 to nine residents of Corpus Christi, three of San Diego, three of Laredo, and two of Galveston.

The railroad was built to Banquete, a distance of twenty-five miles, before the company ran out of money. On January 1, 1876, the first train ran. The railroad was not extended any farther until Richard King and Mifflin Kenedy furnished financial assistance to allow the road to be built to San Diego by 1879.

N. G. Collins also helped by buying about one-half of the Las Preseñas Mexican Grant that was subdivided among the heirs of the original owners in 1878. Mr. Collins laid out a townsite and gave the railroad one-half of his townsite to build through the town of Collins, a distance of about forty miles from Corpus Christi. By this time, the railroad also had forty sections of land.

June 30, 1881, a new charter was granted to allow extension of the railway to Laredo. The Mexican National Railroad had controlling interest and the name was changed to the Texas-Mexican Railway. By November, 1881,—a distance of 162 miles,— the Texas-Mexican Railway reached Laredo. The International and Great Northern Railroad reached Laredo at about the same time, coming in from San Antonio.

THE S. A. A. P.

The San Antonio and Aransas Pass Railway was chartered in 1885. It bypassed Lagarto and forked at Mathis, with one branch proceeding on to Aransas Pass, bypassing San Patricio. The other branch crossed the Nueces at Sandia and proceeded in a southwesterly direction, bypassing Collins and intercepting the Tex-Mex Railroad at the watering station about three miles to the west.

Here, the town of Kleberg began, but its name was soon changed to Alice to satisfy the postal authorities. Not until 1894 did the S. A. A. P. continue southward, and then only as far as Falfurrias. Area residents called it "the SAP."

THE ST. L., B. & M. RY.

The Lower Rio Grande Valley, south of Laredo, was without a railroad connecting it with the rest of Texas until the St. Louis, Brownsville & Mexican Railway through the King Ranch was completed in 1904. The city of Kingsville was established to house the general offices of the railroad. Here the roundhouse and machine shops for the St. Louis, Brownsville & Mexican Railway were also built.

With the coming of the railroads, vast lands were made easily accessible and the Mustang Plains were no longer, as considered by the Americans and Mexicans generally, a frontier. Now, with a much easier way of life open, settlers flocked to the region.

The horses and cattle that had roamed wild for so long, along with the burros and elk, were rapidly and wastefully disposed of. The miles and miles of beautiful grass and their spring introduction of myriads of colorful flowers, were burned, plowed up, and over-grazed so that thorny shrubs soon replaced much of it.

The springs and streams dried up. The coastal bend region that was known as Los Llanos de Las Mesteñas during the Spanish and the Mexican eras and as the Mustang Plains until about the turn of the present century, became known as "The Brush Country."

RAID OF 1878

The Mexican and Indian raid of 1878 was the last extensive

raid suffered by the settlers of this region between the Nueces and the Rio Grande. Similar raids had occurred in 1870, 1872, and in 1875, along with several others on a smaller scale. Earlier, settlers of this region had been raided by Apaches, Kiowas, and Comanches of Texas—after the loathsome Karankawas had been dispatched about 1830—but since the Civil War, they were victims of raids emanating from strongholds in northern Mexico.

This 1878 raid was led by a renegade white man with blonde hair. Mr. W. T. Wright, who was a small boy hardly ten years old at the time, said that he saw the raiders with the yellow-haired man in the lead. But the raiders did not see him because he was hiding in tall grass.

From their rendezvous at Fort Ewell, the bandits followed a well-traveled road to the Toribio Ranch about 36 miles to the southeast, in the north part of Duval County. Here they stole or destroyed everything they found of any value and killed the chief shepherd of the ranch owner T. W. Gillette. The shepherd's name was Vicente Robledo. They also killed another worker named Tomas Zunega.

The raiders had divided into three groups when leaving Fort Ewell, so they had their advance guard, their center, and their rear guard. Their center consisted of their main or largest group.

From the Toribio, these groups followed separate paths in order to attack a larger number of herdsmen and small ranches.

The main group went to the Charco Escondido (Hidden Pond) Ranch where they killed the son of the ranch owner and a friend. These two happened to be the only ones at the ranch house when the bandits arrived.

After leaving the Toribio Ranch, the other two groups met at the Solidad Ranch, killed three people, and drove off all the horses they could find in the neighborhood. The Indians took charge of the horses, and, along with the rest of the raiders, joined the main group at the Charco Escondido. From here, the raiders left in small groups continuing their eastward journey.

Converging at the Amargosa Ranch, the raiders were able to drive off all their ranch horses. Continuing on to the next two ranches, which belonged to the Prices and the Wrights, the raiders were able to get all of their horses also.

The raiders were coming into a more heavily populated area in the vicinity of present Alfred, then called Driscoll, so were in danger of meeting with armed resistance. They turned back, partly retracing their raiding route, and rode all the way back into Mexico without meeting any army or cavalry units.

Apparently, the Indians hid all or a part of the horses some place in the vicinity of Driscoll, because several of the stolen horses were sold at a livestock auction that was held in Corpus Christi not long after the raid.

According to several sources, none of the original owners were able to get their horses back. The few who happened to be in Corpus Christi the day of the sale and who saw their horses, did not have their bills of sale with them. They were unable to prove ownership on the spot and could not get the sheriff to stop the sale. However, they were able to alert state and national authorities and the public to their plight so that such wide-scale raiding never occurred again.

This Indian raid is a vivid example of what settlers along the south side of the Nueces River suffered repeatedly after the United States Army abandoned Fort Ewell.

Immediately following this raid, the Committee of People of this area wrote an address and sent it to the Secretary of State of the United States. Copies of the address were sent to the Governor of Texas, the President of the United States, and to leading newspapers and magazines throughout the country. The address was signed by the County Judge of Nueces County, the Judge of the Twenty-fifth District, the Mayor of Corpus Christi, and several prominent ranchers and citizens of the Lower Nueces Valley. Several signed affidavits of witnesses were included.

Below is a part of the address:

> ". . . The raiding party stopped at Fort Ewell, La Salle County, an abandoned government post on the Nueces River. The entire band seemed to have converged here and used it as headquarters.
>
> It has long been one of the chief objective points for concentration of Indians when on frontier raids. Exits are made, generally, from this vicinity, whether they take an upper or lower line of departure. There should be—and this is the voice of all our people—a post here and a company of cavalry ready for instant use. . . ."

The address continued, describing the raiders, (Mexicans and Indians led by a blonde white man); the path which was taken (the raiders had been followed at a distance by a rancher, who signed an affidavit, and some of his workers); including the names of those murdered by the raiders and where they were killed.

The rancher who had followed the raiders had sent a courier to San Diego where a company of United States Cavalry had recently arrived, and another courier to Fort McIntosh at Laredo.

Although the raiders were at no time more than sixty miles from a United States Government Post and came as near as fifteen miles, the men following the raiders received no assistance from either the Cavalry at San Diego or the Army at Fort McIntosh.

The command at Fort McIntosh received the message the night of the nineteenth, but made no movement to help until four o'clock on the afternoon of the twentieth.

The Cavalry at San Diego made no effort to help. Their excuse? They were new in the area and did not know where to go.

The Governor of Texas immediately sent a company of Rangers to the area.

The federal government sent Lieutenant John Bullis in command of a company of colored infantry troops within a few weeks. They maintained a camp on the east prong of Carrizo Creek, about eight miles southwest of Carrizo Springs in present Dimmit County. The campsite was about two miles from the Charles Vivian Ranch that had been attacked by two hundred Indians in 1870.

SAN CAJO, LOS PICACHOS, AND LOMO ALTO

San Cajo is shown on nearly all of the early maps of the Llanos Mesteñas area because the Kinney-Cazneau trade route from Corpus Christi to Castroville, opened in 1849, passed near it. Prior to that, San Cajo had served the Spanish explorers and travelers for over a century as a landmark on their way from Laredo to La Bahía (Goliad). The Spanish explorers named the long, thin chalk-white hill "San Cajo"—because, to them it looked like a bleached shinbone rising above the prairie.

It is now mostly covered with chaparral and parts of it have been used for building and paving purposes. Over two hundred years of natural erosion have also helped alter its appearance since it was first viewed and named by the Spaniards. It remained mostly free of chaparral into the Twentieth Century. About two miles west of San Cajo, the Spaniards had lined a deep spring with rock, making a well about six feet square. Whether an hacienda or an early fort was here is not known, but this square well was used by the mid-Nineteenth Century traders who traveled this route, as well as by Texas Rangers, sheep herders, Indians and outlaws. It was rimmed by a few trees, twelve or fifteen feet away, from which the ground sloped down to the edge of the lined well.

Early one morning during the late '80's, a cowboy was returning to a nearby ranch from a trip to Corpus Christi and arrived at the well soon after sunrise. He had been irritated because he and his horse had been unable to make it to the well the night before because of weariness. Both he and his horse were very thirsty.

As they neared the trees marking the depression leading to the well, the horse suddenly stopped and snorted in alarm. The cowboy could see or hear nothing. Thinking there must be a puma lurking in the area and that his horse suddenly caught the puma's scent, the cowboy urged his horse on to the well. But their thirst was to go unslaked.

There, toppled into the water glinting red in the sunlight, was a horse with his saddle and bridle still on—dead. He had been shot.

Not knowing whether whoever was responsible for the deed was still about, the cowboy and his horse left pronto.

Later, he was to learn that an area rancher, a man named Ed Gray, had been shot and killed at the well.

Sometime later, a group of Mexicans consisting of men, women and children numbering thirteen in all, were found killed and thrown into the well. They had been to San Antonio and were returning home, camping here for the night.

After this, people gave the well a very wide berth and followed a road some distance to the south.

San Cajo is east of present Freer and to the northwest of San Diego in northeast Duval County. It is part of a fault that extends from below Freer diagonally to the west side of the big bend in the lower Nueces River. This helps explain why Freer is an oil town.

LOS PICACHOS

Along the fault about twelve or fifteen miles northwest of San Cajo, metamorphic rock bubbled and pushed through to form a hill whose summit is still not covered with grass or chaparral. Doubtless, this lone rock hill in a chain of grass and chaparral-covered caliche hills and mesas was as surprising to the early Spanish explorers as it is to its present-day viewers. Its bare rock stubs reach a bit higher than the surrounding caliche hills and mesas, so the Spaniards named the hill "Los Picachos" (The Peaks or The Summits). English-speaking settlers referred to it as "Picacho Hill" or "Painted Hill."

Much of the rock, especially on the north side, is covered with bright orange, soft green, and black lichens. This, coupled with the black, varied reds, violets, and light grays of the rock itself, gives the hill a painted look.

The Indian name long ago merged with the Spanish, so whatever they called it is lost—but proof of their use of it as a factory is very much in evidence. Chips, discarded imperfect arrowheads and other Indian weapons and tools are mound high about its base and among its rocks. Early settlers say these were really extensive fifty or sixty years ago.

A gravel road past a pumping oil well leads to the foot of the exposed rock, about halfway up the hill. A short distance, perhaps twenty feet up, is a gaping cave about four feet high and six feet wide. It is shallow, and tall rock beams allow the sunlight and the rain to filter through.

The winding path leads upward from the road, around past the cave, through rocks and on up to a flat top rimmed with jutting rocks. This is a split-level top—part of it is about four feet higher than the rest. Windblown dust has lodged among the crevices and some grasses and small plants are growing. The rocks are not all flint; some are lava-type and some look like baked clay.

LOMO ALTO

About two miles northwest of Picacho Hill is a divided mesa that was named "Lomo Alto" by the early Spaniards. It is nearly as high as Picacho, but because of its greater circumference at the top it is noticed from a greater distance. Its level top contains about three hundred acres of excellent grazing land, but only one path leads to it.

Mr. Adolf Moos says that he knows of only one person to ride a horse up this path. And he was a cowboy astride a sure-footed mustang.

State Highway 173 from San Antonio to Freer, through

Tilden, passes very near Lomo Alto and about a mile and a half west of Picacho Hill. However, Los Picachos does not present its most spectacular side to the highway. Its only distinguishing feature from this distance and direction is its multiple-pointed summit.

PEÑA STATION

Peña Station was located at the hub-site of the Llanos Mesteñas, which was the trade area that had been opened by Escandón's Nuevo Santander colonizing enterprise in 1749. It was at the crossroads of the San Antonio-Mier and Camargo, Tamaulipas, Mexico freight and stage route and of "Smugglers' Pass" that led from Penascal (Baffin) Bay to Laredo and to San Juan Bautista Presidio. The Smugglers' Pass route divided near Los Ojuelos, with one road leading west to Laredo and the other continuing northwest to San Juan Bautista, which was across the river from present Eagle Pass. El Mezquite Rancho had been the original crossroads station.

Just when Peña Station was first built is a moot question. Some old-timers say that they remember hearing their fathers say that it was in existence long before the Civil War. Others say that it was not started until during or after the War. One thing is known, however: that Peña Station was a well-known place by 1879.

The Texas-Mexican Railway Company bought out the Corpus Christi-San Diego and Rio Grande Narrow Gauge Railroad Company that had built to San Diego by early 1879 and secured a new charter. This charter provided for completing the line to Laredo and for extending it to the Sabine River, as well as to El Paso. Branch lines were to go to Rockport, Peña, Aransas Pass, and other stations en route.

The line was completed to Laredo by 1881, but no branch lines were built. Instead, the railroad dipped southward from San Diego and joined the old freight wagon route that led from Corpus Christi and Peñascal, following the route from Realitos through Old Los Ángeles and into Laredo. Peña Station was located between Los Ángeles and Realitos. (Los Ángeles was a ranch settlement on the María Joséfa Cuellar "Caberero de Los Ángeles" grant.)

Peña was the halfway station between San Antonio and Ringgold Barracks, which had been built in 1848. Ringgold

Barracks was just south of Rio Grande City, formerly known as Clay Davis, gateway to the Mexican trade area along the San Juan River in the Mexican States of Tamaulipas and Nuevo León.

Soon after the railroad came past Peña's Station, W. R. Hebbron built a railroad station about a half-mile west of Peña's. As settlers moved into the area near the railroad, Hebbron's Station became known as Hebbronville, the official railroad station and post office, and Peña was no longer shown on maps. However, freight continued to be hauled by wagons and carts, which used Peña's Station well into the Twentieth Century.

The yellow fever epidemic of 1882 in Brownsville closed the port, and until the Mexican National Railroad completed its line to Matamoros in 1905, very little freight went through Brownsville.

Lazarro Peña was the name of the owner of the station remembered from about 1890 until 1920, known personally to many area early settlers. Records show that a Lazarro Peña bought several sections of land in 1875 along Pavilla Creek on the main and more direct route between San Diego and Laredo, which was on the first planned railroad route chartered between Corpus Christi and Laredo. Whether this was the same man is not known.

The remembered Lazarro Peña was a big fat jolly fellow who sold little more in his freight station than "Black Horse" tobacco, axle grease, sardines, and crackers. During the early 1900's, the station was a somewhat rundown clapboard building.

The road approaching Peña Station from either direction was sandy, so that the sounds made by the hooves of horses and other livestock approaching were muffled and could not be heard from a distance. The sounds of approaching wagon and cart wheels were also muffled, so that they were very near before one was aware of their presence. This gave the station an eerie setting, for all other stations in the region were on hard ground, caliche or clay or rock.

Travelers to and from the cities along the Rio Grande more frequently used the route through Peña Station (also called Peña's Station) because it was faster, due to the infrequent calls by ships to the port at Point Isabel or Brownsville between 1882 and 1905. The following recommended travel route from Washington, D.C., to Fort Brown was published in 1893. Fort Brown was an active place during these years.

"Come by ship to Corpus Christi. At Corpus Christi, board the Tex-Mex Train to Peña Station. At Peña, an, excellent stagecoach will take you to Rancho Davis (Rio Grande City) to the ferry on the Rio Grande.
"The ferry will take you a short distance down the San Juan River into Camargo, Mexico, where another stagecoach will take you to San Miguel, a distance of about 25 miles. Here you will entrain for Matamoros. The Matamoros Division of the Mexican National Railroad runs along the Mexican side of the Rio Grande through Reynosa to Matamoros. From here, another ferry will deposit you almost at the gates of Fort Brown."

AT OLD NUECESTOWN

During the 1880's, a family by the name of Elliott lived near Nuecestown, which was between Gallagher and Corpus Christi. Mr. Elliott worked for Captain Richard King. He participated in cattle drives, branded cattle, checked fences, and even acted as personal guard for the Captain on occasion. So that he was seldom at home except on Saturday nights and Sundays.

Windmills had come into the Mustang Plains by this time, and the Elliotts had joined the growing group of users. Mr. Elliott's necessary absences from home was the reason they bought a windmill as soon as they did, and were one of the first in Nuecestown to have one.

With a well, it was a simple thing to replace a frayed rope or a broken pulley or a leaking bucket. But with a windmill, when something went wrong, an expert had to be called in. Thereby hangs a tale of the affinity of experts, or of the superiority of professionalism over amateurism. An expert can always recognize a tyro.

The averment, "Don't fence me in," at that time included just about everything along with man—his hogs, cattle, chickens, horses, goats, ducks . . . in other words, the Elliot's hogs were not penned.

As were most wooden houses in those days, their house was built on log stilts two or three feet above the ground and was not enclosed at the base.

Also as with most people those days, the Elliots had several children. Their house was not overly large and did not contain closets. This made it harder to hide things from their children.

Apparently, Mrs. Elliot, living thusly, was not motivated to be very energetic. At any rate, the hogs and the chickens and the dogs were allowed absolute freedom in frequenting their favorite spots. And most of the time these were all under the house.

Captain King paid his help in tiny gold 50-cent pieces during these years. And not many years had elapsed since Nuecestown had been raided by a gang of outlaws. Mrs. Elliot was mortally afraid that another raid was imminent.

Also she reasoned, "Them banks is no safer. Nearly every week's paper tells about one bein' robbed summers. Either outlaws has broke in or one of the bankers hisself has run off with the money."

So the problem was to find a safe hiding place for the sorghum can in which they kept their gold, where neither children nor thieves could find it.

"Ah," she thought one cold day in January when the gold savings began to be enough to really worry about. "Under the house. Husband'll be havin' a right smart this Satiddy, and it's about time we hid it before the children start blabbin' about it if one of them finds it."

So Saturday night after the children were asleep, Mr. and Mrs. Elliot crawled under the house in the faint light of the last-quarter moon. They dug and dug, using two heavy soap-making spoons; and they buried the sorghum can between the third and fourth pilings in the second row from the front of the house—eight hand-spans from the third one.

Here for many weeks, but added to thrice, in seemingly undisturbed dirt, the sorghum can reposed.

On a hot day in June, soon after a stormy spell that left the weather unbearably hot and humid, the windmill broke down. It was several days before the repairman from Corpus Christi could come out to fix the windmill. The stormy weather had damaged several in the vicinity, and the Elliots just had to await their turn, for he was about the only one in the area who could repair it.

The repairman had arrived about eight o'clock, and by mid-afternoon he finally got the windmill to pumping water. He was plenty thirsty and looked around for something to drink

138

out of. There was the very thing—a gallon sorghum can with the lid on that the hogs had been rooting around.

He found the can to be very heavy. Using a piece of metal that was handy, he got the lid off. The can was more than half full of gold fifty-cent pieces!

Of course he knew that it belonged to the Elliots. Everyone knew that Mr. Elliot worked for Captain King and that Captain King paid his hired help in gold fifty-cent pieces. "But what in tarnation was it doin' out here?"

He hammered the lid back on the can and lugged it to the house to give to Mrs. Elliot. When he gave her the gold, he also gave her a talk about getting experts to take care of things.

"Now looka here," he said. "You wouldn't a got a carpenter to take care o' this windmill of yourn. Why turn all o' that money over to the hogs?"

The talk must have been convincing, for early the next morning Mrs. Elliot hitched up the horses, and, with the help of her older children, managed to get the sorghum can into the front of the buggy. She and the children drove straight to the bank in Corpus Christi and deposited the gold.

CATARINO GARZA, MASON-EDITOR-REVOLUTIONIST

"Just let a couple of the Rangers stand up and I'll prove that I wasn't using a knuckle-duster!" shouted the tall, slender man in court in Corpus Christi who was defending himself against a charge of aggravated assault with a deadly weapon. He had severely beaten a Texas Ranger and was accused of having worn brass knuckles.

This man was Catarino Erasmo Garza, the liberal editor of two weekly newspapers published in the Mustang Plains that were waging a battle against Don Porfirio Diaz, long-time President of Mexico, but more specifically against General José María Garza Galán, Governor of Coahuila. The year was 1890.

His editorials against and stories of injustices practiced by their hirelings and henchmen were beginning to needle the authorities of the Mexican Government, so they had protested that Texas and the United States were allowing their citizens to violate their neutrality laws. Now, the State and Federal lawmen began to needle Garza.

Garza was a striking figure—over six feet tall, fair-skinned, with blue eyes, and black hair and mustache. He was well-educated and quite an orator as well as a writer. He was reputed to be a very brilliant man.

On this particular occasion, Catarino held up a bullet between his thumb and forefinger, shouting, "Do you see this lead ball? Had it not been for my heavy watch chain and the angle the bullet happened to be traveling when it hit, I probably would not be alive to defend myself. I have witnesses to prove that I was in the barber chair leaning back being shaved when that Rinche fired this shot at me from the sidewalk. This bullet forced its way along my watch chain and finally became embedded in one of the links. Here is the chain, also."

After the bullet and chain had been examined as evidence, Garza continued, "When I left the barber shop, I found the Rinche that had fired the shot at me and beat him with my bare fists! Just let me show you what my bare fists can do!"

Although the Rangers contended that Garza had disposed of the knuckles, none offered to be a part of the demonstration. The Judge pronounced Garza, "Not guilty."

Garza was far from being without friends and influence. He was a thirty-second degree Mason and a respected member of the press.

Miss Amelia Perez, public school teacher in Alice, Texas and Catarino Garza's oldest grandchild, still has this bullet. Catarino's wife had it encased in gold and made into a fob as a present for Catarino. It is a cherished family possession.

No Ranger, however, seems to have recorded this incident in his memoirs.

Catarino Erasmo Garza was born on his parents' small hacienda near the outskirts of H. Matamoros, Tamaulipas, Mexico on November 25, 1859. His parents, Don Encarnación and Doña María de Jesús Rodriquez de la Garza, raised vegetables and fruit and ran a dairy on their hacienda. Catarino helped his parents with the work, and did not receive any formal schooling until he was ten years old.

A school was opened on the neighboring Rafael Vela Rancho, and Catarino was allowed to attend four hours daily. After school hours, he returned home to help his parents with the farm and dairy work.

Catarino exhibited a marked inclination toward learning, so he was invited to study under Señor José María Morales, a highly respected teacher, a man of vast culture, and an ex-curé. While studying under Morales, Garza also began military training. When he finished his course of study, he returned from Gualahuises, Nuevo León to Matamoros and enrolled in San Juan College. He also joined the National Guard, serving at the Port Plaza.

In 1885, Catarino Garza moved to Brownsville, Texas and began working for the Commercial Livestock Shipping Company. Because of his education, intelligence, charm, and command of language, Garza was sent as a delegate to the International Stockmen's Convention at St. Louis, Missouri in 1886. The Convention named him Secretary of the Mexican Department.

After the Convention, he returned to the Rio Grande—this time to Eagle Pass. From here, he traveled extensively in Mexico. Upon his return, he began publishing *El Comercio Mexicano*, a weekly newspaper directed especially toward the citizens of Piedras Negras, Mexico. Very soon, he began publishing a second weekly, *El Libre Pensador* (The Free Thinker), with El Señor Gabriel Botello, Mexican Vice-Consul, as its managing editor. The well-known writer, Adolfo Duclos also contributed to this weekly.

Mexican authorities took immediate notice and soon were threatening the Mexican population of both Piedras Negras and Eagle Pass with punishment if they bought or read either paper. Garza was prosecuted for criminal libel and jailed in Eagle Pass thirty-one days. All of his printing equipment and paper were confiscated. Botello posthaste destroyed all evidence linking him with Garza and moved to Corpus Christi.

On December 24, 1887, Garza contacted Botello, who secretly continued to work with him. Together, they helped nine refugees of the Diaz regime. At the house in the country a short distance above Corpus Christi where Garza and Botello were hiding the refugees, Garza resumed publication of *El Comercio Mexicano*. He began with the publication of Volume II, dated March of 1888. The periodical found its way into Mexico by devious routes.

Early in 1889, Catarino Garza moved into an old rock house west of Palito Blanco known as "the Old Steen Ranch House." Here he resumed publication of *El Libre Pensador*.

By now, Garza had broken completely with Diaz as well as with Galán, and both periodicals were highly inflammatory.

Señor Alejandro and Señora Estéfan C. Gonzalez lived in a comfortable home near the church in Palito Blanco; and they had a lovely daughter, Señorita Concepción. Catarino and Concepción fell in love with each other and were married in the church May 24, 1890. Within a short while, Alejandro Gonzalez died and Catarino and Concepción moved into the house with Sra. Gonzalez. Catarino printed his paper here, now, rather than at the Old Steen Place.

By 1891, Catarino Erasmo Garza was playing a vicious game of hide-and-seek with Mexican and United States authorities as well as with the Texas Rangers. For Don Porfirio Diaz wanted him out of the way!

According to most of the Mexican and United States authorities and to the Texas Rangers, Catarino Garza was merely a revolutionist who posed as an editor in order to inflame and recruit the idlers and malcontents of both sides of the Rio Grande, bringing added lawlessness to the Mustang Plains, particularly along the Rio Grande.

However, he was not considered so by much of the press— especially the Spanish language newspaper publishers north of the Rio Grande. They accepted Garza as a fellow editor, giving publicity to the many indignities suffered by the Mexican Indians and any others who criticized the regime of Don Porfirio at the hands of the "Cientificos." The Cientificos were those men appointed by Diaz to attend to minor details that were impossible for him to check personally. They worked together with some of the high officials, withholding many important matters from Diaz, in a scheme to crush out the lower Indian classes and acquire their real estate. Diaz refused to believe this.

Catarino Garza was well-liked socially and had many important and influential friends. He was well educated, cultured, and charming, and kept up his membership as a 32nd Degree Mason. However, after he became deeply involved with his revolutionary life outside the accepted law, he was not so well received. Many called him a fool. Others said that he was so intelligent and far-seeing that he could not remain true to himself if he refused to help put an end to the many indignities he knew were being perpetrated.

While Garza continued to publish his two Spanish language weekly newspapers, editing *El Libre Pensador* at his mother-in-law's home in Palito Blanco and *El Comercio Mexicano* near Corpus Christi, he began training recruits whom he called "Pronunciados."

Garza and his Pronunciados generally rendezvoused in an

old stone house between Palito Blanco and Benavides, but frequently met in other houses in the area to avoid detection. One of these was very near Benavides.

Early in 1890, General Francisco Ruiz Sandoval's revolution against Diaz failed and Sandoval was killed, along with several of his soldiers. Following this abortive attempt, Sandoval's men fled to Texas and joined the Pronunciados. Lawlessness increased along the Rio Grande, for the revolutionaries were training and were constantly being joined by others. And several of these were outlaws, merely using this as an excuse to come into this area.

Garza made his first overt revolutionary move on November 15, 1890. He crossed the Rio Grande near Carrizo (formerly Old Zapata and now inundated by the waters of Falcon Reservoir) and raided the small Mexican town of San Ignacio, some twenty miles west of the river. The Pronunciados killed several of the inhabitants and burned the buildings. According to Garza, this was land belonging to Mexican Indians that had been taken over by Cientificos.

Mexico sent a strong protest to Washington, charging that the neutrality laws accepted by the two countries were again being breached. The United States Secretary of State requested Texas Governor Lawrence Sullivan Ross, an ex-Ranger, to cooperate with the United States Army in apprehending the revolutionists.

Company F of the Texas Rangers under the command of Captain J. A. Brooks, and Company E with Captain J. S. McNeel in command were sent to the Mustang Plains immediately. The Third United States Cavalry stationed at Fort McIntosh in Laredo was alerted. Colonel A. P. Morrow, Commander, sent Cavalry Company C, under the command of a Captain Harding, to occupy the site of Old Camp Harney at Carrizo. The revolutionists soon ambushed one of their patrols and killed Corporal C. H. Edstrom.

After the murder of General and Dr. Ignacio Martinez of Laredo on February 3, 1891 because of an editorial he had written criticizing the Diaz regime and the "leeches who are his hirelings," Garza became still more involved. General Martinez had founded the Spanish language weekly newspaper, *El Mundo*, and was its editor. Following the murder of Martinez, Garza edited *El Mundo* for several weeks, along with his own two papers, until an editor could be hired.

143

Colonel Morrow, after learning that Catarino Garza's wife lived in Palito Blanco, sent a detachment of cavalry there to capture the revolutionist. They encamped in the area across the road from both the church and the Gonzalez house.

During the night a few days following their bivouac in Palito Blanco, a patrol reported that Garza had entered his home. Very early the next morning, a group of soldiers knocked on the front door and asked permission to search the house.

Señora Gonzalez, Catarino's tall, stately mother-in-law who had opened the door, stood proudly. She did not move from the doorway nor close the door while the soldiers were thoroughly searching her house. They did not find Garza.

But he was there—safely hidden from sight among the many floor-length petticoats under his mother-in-law's voluminous skirt.

Another story told by some early Palito Blanco residents is about Garza's escape later that same day. After the soldiers had returned to their camp across the way, Garza was seen to run from the house to his saddled and bridled horse that had been tied to a tree back of the house a short while before by his charming wife, leap upon it and race across the field. As several of the soldiers grabbed their rifles and prepared to fire, the officer in charge told the men, "Let him go." "Because," say the residents, "the officer was a Mason, too."

At dawn one morning in 1891, Captain Brooks and his Company of Rangers surprised a group of Pronunciados who were eating breakfast in the only motte of trees for miles around. The Rangers had seen the smoke of their campfire to the northeast and had filed up the sandy creekbed. The revolutionists' camp was about 25 miles northeast of Carrizo. They had a remuda of fresh horses saddled here.

The Rangers managed to get between these horses and Garza's men before they were seen. Then and there the nearest thing to a pitched battle that ever took place between the Rangers and the Pronunciados took place. However, Garza's men soon fled on their tired horses, because the Rangers were protected by the creek bank. The Rangers did not give chase. Instead, they enjoyed the bacon and eggs that had not yet been touched. After breakfast, they took the horses and turned them over to the United States Cavalry at Fort McIntosh.

Several running fights took place between Captain Brooks' Rangers and the revolutionists. Finally, Garza realized that his

144

fight in this area was futile. He managed to sail from Corpus Christi on the Union Americano to Key West, Florida. From there, he took a fog-bound ride with a rum-runner to Havana, Cuba. After a short while, he sailed to Costa Rica and remained in Puerto Limón for two years.

Garza is reported to have become involved in a revolution to overthrow the government of Colombia, and was killed, still fighting for the downtrodden. It is reported that his corpse was found on the plaza in Bocas del Toro following a brief encounter between revolutionists and Columbian nationalists. Catarino Garza was thirty-six years old at this time.

His wife had received weekly letters from him. Following this uprising, his wife received documentary evidence and personal belongings as proof of Catarino Garza's death. He left only one child, a beautiful daughter who grew up to marry Pancho Perez of Alice. Catarino Garza's wife, Concepción, did not live very long after receiving word of Catarino's death.

But a Palito Blanco resident who had lived all of his more than sixty-five years in the town of his birth, when questioned about Catarino Garza's death, shrugged his shoulders and said, "Maybe so. Did you ever see his picture? But he lived here at the home of his mother-in-law all the time he lived in Palito Blanco. I saw him many times. Excuse me, I must go now."

ALICE, NEE KLEBERG

When N. G. Collins and the San Antonio-Aransas Pass Railroad Company refused to breach the $1,000.00 gap between them, John B. Armstrong, Robert Kleberg, and Mifflin Kenedy incorporated the San Antonio and Aransas Pass Town Site Company to establish the town of Kleberg at the intersection of the S. A. A. P. and the Tex-Mex Railroads. With Mifflin Kenedy as president, the company bought 23,000 acres of land situated on the José María Garcia "La Vaca" Mexican Land Grant. Much of this land had already been condemned for the building of the Tex-Mex Railroad from Collins to San Diego, and now belonged to either the railroad company or to the State. F. B. Nayer and Frank Ellis were commissioned to sell the town lots.

George Hobbs and W. G. Sutherland are said to be the first persons to spend the night in the new town.

George Hobbs moved his store from Collins. It was the first store to be opened in the new town of Kleberg, but not the first building here. Hobbs bought lots five and six in Block Two, fronting on Aransas Street, which paralleled the SAP (as the San Antonio and Aransas Pass Railroad was usually referred to). Hobbs moved his two-story wooden frame building onto these lots. It was probably here that he and Sutherland spent that first night.

Other lots, numbering seven and eight in Block 14, fronting on San Diego Street, were bought by George Hobbs at the same time. This transaction took place August 30, 1888.

The first building to be erected in Kleberg was a small building at the SAP terminal to serve the dual purpose of a repair shop and tool house.

The Lichtenstein Hotel was built about the same time the George Hobbs Store was moved into town. It was on the corner of First and Aransas Streets on the north side of the street. An advertisement by The Lichtenstein Hotel was carried by the first newspaper published in Alice and for three or four years thereafter. The Lichtenstein family built this hotel to house railroad workers, travelers, and stockmen. In 1896, Trinidad Salazar bought the Lichtenstein Hotel for use as a general merchandise store. The Salazars used the upper story for a home.

Soon after George Hobbs moved his store to Kleberg, Mrs. E. D. Sidbury moved her lumber yard here. The first building moved from Collins into Kleberg had been the Becham House, which belonged to Mrs. Sidbury's father, Mr. Becham, and in which she made her home. Later, Mrs. Sidbury managed the place, which was used as a boarding house for railroad workers and travelers and, temporarily, for a private school in one of the upstairs rooms. The stage to and from Brownsville also stopped here for a while. Thus, the "Becham House" and the "Old Sidbury Place" is the same. The lumber yard was on the same block as the Becham House, but west of it, facing the Tex-Mex railroad tracks.

The post office remained at Collins in the Phil Hobbs Store until 1890. Phil Hobbs, who was the father of Mrs. Goode Wier and Philip Hobbs, both still living in Alice, was the postmaster of Collins. He had to come into Kleberg to get the mail from San Antonio and other points north, because it was brought by the SAP, and Kleberg people had to go to Collins for their mail.

Although permission to have a post office at Kleberg had been requested, it was denied because another town in Texas

146

was already named Kleberg. Also, Kleberg was too near Collins. So some Federal red tape had to be cut. Kleberg did not have a community school or a church or very many stores, but they did have a couple of hotels and eating places—and they were not allowed a post office. Proof was needed that Collins was fast fading into a ghost town, and that Kleberg was becoming rapidly more important. A name that was acceptable to the postal authorities also had to be chosen.

In 1889, George Hobbs, with the help of some friends, built a one-room schoolhouse near the location of the present Hobbs Building between Second and Third Streets. This building also served as the local Protestant Church building—mostly Methodists. Now Kleberg had a school house and a church building. About the same time, the church Father Bard had erected in Collins was moved into the present Alice area, about six blocks west of the old SAP Railroad station on Third Street. Now Kleberg had two churches. Several other buildings were moved over at this time, also. Then the report on the growth of Kleberg, along with the suggested name of "Alice" to replace the name of Kleberg was sent to the proper authorities. By late 1890, Alice had its post office and Collins had none.

Although the Trinidad Salazar General Merchandise Store was not officially opened in Alice until 1896, Mr. Salazar was a tradesman in Kleberg. He managed a store in the Santa Cruz community near Palito Blanco. When the first train entered Kleberg from San Antonio, Trinidad Salazar was on it with a large order of goods he had bought for his store in Santa Cruz. Several persistent customers appeared while he was loading the goods onto his oxen-powered cart.

Several Mexican families had been living in the area that had become the Tex-Mex watering station. A large horse-dug well was here. Traveling was quite a chore in those days, and several of these people needed supplies. It was to these people that Mr. Salazar made his first sales in present Alice. From this time until he bought the Lichtenstein Hotel and opened his store, he sold from his cart in Alice at least twice a month.

So, when the United States Post Office Department accepted the name of Alice to replace the name of Kleberg and removed the Collins Post Office and bestowed it on Alice, the town of Kleberg established by the San Antonio and Aransas Pass Town Site Company lost its maiden name—to become the town of Alice, Texas.

IN SHIFTING SANDS

By 1900, windmills were beginning to spin throughout the Mustang Plains. Ranchers and farmers were wanting them on all of their deep wells, whether newly dug or ancient Spanish dug and rock-lined. All large ranch homes and many town homes used windmills. In fact, early Alice had so many within its limits that it was known as "The Windmill Town."

An enterprising young man had been aware of this trend for some time and decided to cash in on it. Adolf Moos, at the age of seventeen, learned the fundamentals of well-digging on the Shafter Ranch. After working there for awhile, he moved south to Falfurrias where few windmills had been erected.

A Mr. Herring went with Mr. Moos as his helper, and they were kept quite busy. Generally, the business had been profitable, and their clients were well satisfied. However, the windmill at Sarita kept giving trouble.

Just at dawn one morning, a cowboy rode up in time to catch Mr. Moos and Mr. Herring as they were leaving to work near Concepción. He reported that the windmill at Sarita was losing water again and making an awful noise. Mr. Moos sent Mr. Herring on to Concepción alone, and went with the cowboy to Sarita.

Among other things, the lever that held the wheel still kept slipping, and neither Ed nor John Corkill, who were managing the ranch, knew how to stop the wheel. Mr. Moos explained how it could be held with a rope; and José, a mechanically inclined cowboy, offered to climb the windmill and stop the wheel.

This particular windmill was a sixteen-foot Eclipse. It was newly on the market with some innovations. But José was sure that he would have no trouble "tying-off" the windmill so Mr. Moos could repair it.

Apparently, José did not understand the directions. He attached the rope to something when he reached the platform, then took a firm grasp on one of the vanes of the turning wheel . . . and was thrown about sixty feet through the air.

Fortunately, he landed on a sand dune and slid about ten feet. He was not hurt, just scared a bit.

So much blowing sand in the immediate area was probably the cause of so much trouble with this Eclipse. The sand dune that José fell on had shifted into that spot recently. Very dry

ORIGINAL SITE OF
VILLA DE LAREDO
FOUNDED BY
TOMAS SANCHEZ
MAY 15 1755
BY ORDER OF
JOSE DE ESCANDON
COLONIZER OF
NUEVO SANTANDER

'Villa de Laredo' Monument

Capital of "The Republic of the Rio Grande," on 'Villa de Laredo' Plaza, near monument, in Laredo.

Casa Blanca of San Diego, built in 1852 (page 23).
View before owners began reconstruction, 1967, front.

Side, showing wide double-door, which allowed a cart pulled
by an ox to enter.

Newly whitewashed and remodeled front (February, 1968).

Side of fort still undergoing remodeling, with double-door closed in (February, 1968). Structure harmed by Hurricane Beulah.

Old Mexican cart, at Witte Museum in San Antonio.

Wheel detail of old Mexican cart.

Restored Casa Blanco, more recently often referred to as "Rancho Blanco," near Santa Maria in Cameron County (page 20).

Zachary Taylors headquarters in 1845-46 when reconnoitering along Lower Rio Grande. Not far from Santa Maria (page 55).

West side of fort, part occupied by Mrs. Aureliano Herrera, descendant of builder.

North side and front of fort, showing center lower part built in 1830 by Don Jesús Trevino, and higher corners of annex added in 1843 by his son-in-law, Don Blas María Uribe.

Fort San Ygnacio-Trevino, on banks of Rio Grande, just off Highway 83 in Lower Rio Grande Valley (see pages 28-29).

Inside northwest corner, also showing part of older section, and newer.

Roof detail, showing portholes for water draining; overlooking Rio Grande into Mexico.

Front doorway with sundial.

Detail of sundial, front.

Fort entrance with old sundial, placed on fort in 1951.

Guidon Store, served as settlement fort during Indian and outlaw raids of 1870's. Part of courtyard wall standing. Double
French doors at back wide enough to allow a wagon and team to
enter. On Teoroda and Mier Streets, facing Mier Street, which
was originally a part of Old Mier to Lagarto Crossing of Nueces
River Road. In San Diego.

St. Fransis de Paula, parish established in 1867. This church
built in 1908-09 by "Padre Pedro" Bard.

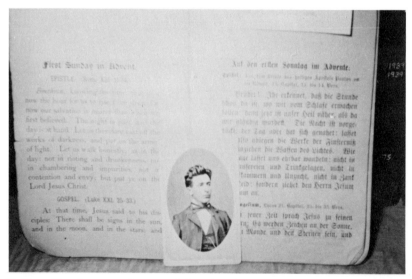

Father Bard soon after arriving in the Mustang Plains; pictured
in front of his English-German Bible. When the St. Fransis
de Pauls Church was dedicated, the services were conducted in
English, German, and Spanish.

Marker from first bridge to span the Nueces River. Bridge was
built by Grey White, completed in 1888. (See page 50.)

Ruins of early settlers stone cabin at edge of present Carrizo
Springs.

Old Tumlinson blockhouse in Carrizo Springs, used as a settlement fort during Indian raids.

Ruins of Camp Bullis below Carrizo Springs overlooking Carrizo Creek (1963).

THE MIER
EXPEDITION

A BODY OF TEXANS INTENT ON
INVADING MEXICO CAMPED HERE
ON DECEMBER 21, 1842 · AFTER
BEING MADE PRISONERS AT
SALADO, MEXICO, THEY DREW
BEANS, WHITE FOR LIFE IN PRISON,
BLACK FOR DEATH · 17 MEMBERS
OF THE EXPEDITION WERE SHOT
BY ORDER OF GENERAL SANTA
ANNA, MARCH 25, 1843

Erected by the State of Texas
1936

Monument near present Zapata on Highway 83.

Fort Duncan Monument, at Eagle Pass

Old bridge in Fort Duncan vicinity

Fort Merrill Monument, at site near south bank of Nueces River in present Live Oak County.

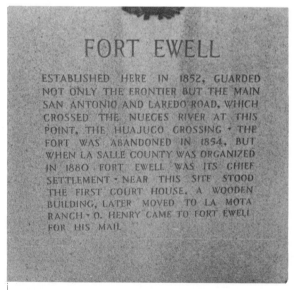

Fort Ewell Monument on south bank of Nueces River in southern LaSalle County.

Los Ojuelos, ruins of early trough built during Spanish or Mexican days.

House formerly occupied by Texas Rangers at Los Ojuelos.

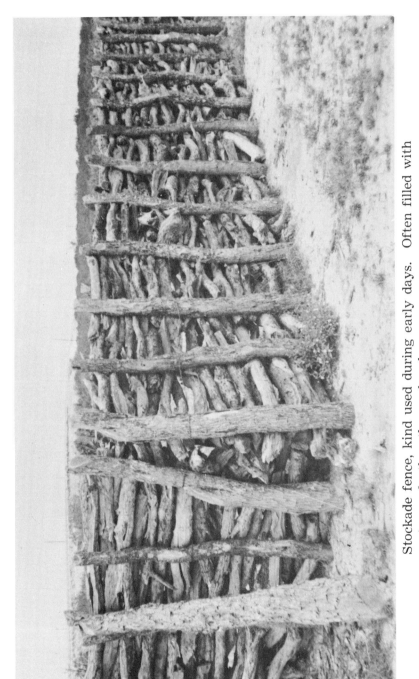

Stockade fence, kind used during early days. Often filled with cactus and other thorny brush.

Remaining houses at Old Amargosa, about nine miles north of Alice, showing parapet walls and portholes for both water drainage and musketry. Overlooking Amargosa Creek.

Old Cuevitas, ghost town north of Rio Grande City.

Former Fort Brown building, now renovated and a part of Southmost College of Brownsville.

Old sutler's building at Fort Clark

Only part of "Old" Fort Duncan extant, Eagle Pass.

Part of Ringgold Barracks, Rio Grande City

Parapet roof detail in Freer area, overlooking stockade, showing portholes for shooting through and for drainage.

Pablo Perez grave in San Diego

La Mota Fort: Old fort, with stockade in background. Hurricane Beulah blew down part of roof and walls.

Detail, showing keystone doorway.   This was one of few stone forts in area using this type of building.

La Mota Schoolhouse, built 1904, with old fort in background.

Present nearby community of San Jose, showing Saint Joseph's
Church with bell from old school.

Burial place of Don Pedrito Jaramillo

Front door detail of mausoleum

Picture of Catarino Garza

Picture of ranchhouse east of Benavides, reported to have been used frequently by Garza and his Pronunciados.

Where early newspaper was published and early school was held; built to specifications of Eulalio Velasquez. Still standing in Alice.

Philip Pope Price, early professor, optometrist, and scientific farmer and rancher.

Old Collins town picture

W. T. "Uncle Willie" Wright, Sr.

T. Salazar Store pictures

Don Jesús Store pictures

Judge Robert Roland Mullen

"Uncle Jim" Dobie Ranchhouse near Nueces River

Old Collins school picture

THE STATE OF TEXAS,

COUNTY OF BEXAR.

Know all Men by these Presents,

That **The San Antonio and Aransas Pass Town Site Company,** a corporation existing under the laws of the State of Texas, acting herein by its_____President,_____ *Mifflin Kenedy,*_____

for and in consideration of the sum of_____

_____ *Six hundred*_____DOLLARS,

to said Company in hand paid by_____ *George Hobbs*_____

the receipt of which is hereby acknowledged, have GRANTED, SOLD AND CONVEYED, and by these presents do GRANT, SELL, CONVEY AND DELIVER unto the said_____

_____ *George Hobbs*_____

of the County of_____ *Nueces*_____and State of_____ *Texas*_____, all the right, title and interest of the said THE SAN ANTONIO AND ARANSAS PASS TOWN SITE COMPANY in and to *three* certain tracts parcels or pieces of land lying and being in the State of Texas and County of_____ *Nueces*_____

and described as follows, to wit:

_____ *Lots Nos. Five (5) and Six (6) in Block No. Two (2) situated in the Town of Kleberg; said lots fronting each fifty (50) feet on Aransas Street and running back between paral lel lines on South Second Street, one hundred and thirty feet (130')._____ Lots Nos. Seven (7) and Eight (8) in Block No. Fourteen (14) situated in the Town of Kleberg; said lots fronting each fifty (50) feet on San Diego Street, and running back between parallel lines on King Street to the Alley; for further identification of the property above conveyed, reference is made to the plan of the Town of Kleberg, recorded in the records of Nueces County, Texas, in Volume S. pp. 266.*_____

To Have and to Hold the above described premises, together with all and singular the rights and appurtenances thereto belonging unto the said_____ *George Hobbs, his*_____

heirs and assigns, *forever.* And the said THE SAN ANTONIO AND ARANSAS PASS TOWN SITE COMPANY does hereby bind itself to *Warrant and Forever Defend,* all and singular, the said premises unto the said *George Hobbs, his*_____heirs and assigns, against every person whomsoever lawfully claiming or to claim the same, or any part thereof, by, through, or under it, the said Town Site Company._____

In Witness Whereof, the said Town Site Company has hereunto subscribed by its_____President, *Mifflin Kenedy*_____, and caused its official Seal to be affixed in San Antonio, this _____30 the_____ day of_____ *August*_____ A. D. 18 88._____

M. Kenedy

Prest. S A & A P Town Site Co

Attest:

Reagan Houston,

_____*Secretary.*

Deed to lot sold in old Kleberg

Sketch of Longhorn by Lorena Jones

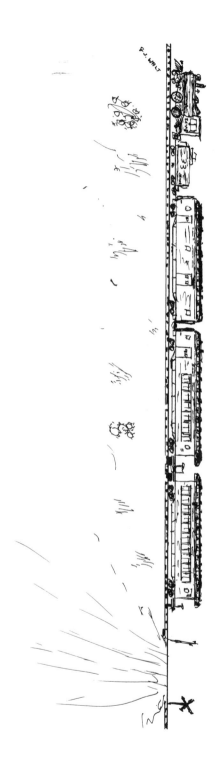

Sketch of S.A.A.P. train as remembered by George Walt

Perez grandchildren, and Seana and Julia McCoy and Halsey Wright, taken at old Amargosa Ranch.

Phil Hobbs Store in Alice about 1906

weather and constantly blowing winds, with many sand-devils, caused this shifting.

Static electricity had a heavy buildup here. Not long after Mr. Moos repaired the windmill, John Corkill was killed by a bolt of lightning as he was walking toward the well for a drink. He had been riding hard, so he had left his horse nearby to graze and cool off before drinking. The horse was unharmed.

During these years, ranchers in the shifting sands belt had a difficult time keeping their cattle penned. It seems that the wind-directed sand-devils would pick up sand dunes and delight in dropping them on fences. The heavy early morning dews would tighten the sand so the cows could walk over the fence. (Early morning was the only time the wind was still.)

One place the sand shifted so bad that three rows of fences had to be built, one atop the other.

And well-diggers had to be mighty careful, too. But in Mr. Moos' case, the sands shifted to his aid.

That summer, a cut-rate crew came into Falfurrias and underbid the Moos Well Digging Company so much that they beat him out of digging five wells real fast. He thought sure his business was ruined.

But the sand covered up three of those wells before they were paid for, and the well-diggers couldn't collect any money because they couldn't even find the wells. So they left town.

(Author's note: Mr. Moos said that everything he said may not be absolutely true, but he would guarantee that it would be interesting.)

———

EULALIO VELAZQUEZ—MAN OF VARIED TALENTS

Eulalio Velazquez, a man of varied talents, lived in Alice from 1903 until the middle of 1914. He established and published Alice's first completely Spanish newspaper, El Cosmopolito for about ten years. He probably contributed more toward the cultural, moral, and economic improvement of the Mexican-American citizens of Alice and of the immediate surrounding area than anyone else of his time.

On February 12, 1868, Eulalio Velazquez was born in San Pedro de Roma, now named Miguel Aleman, which is located about halfway between Mier and Camargo, Mexico. About 1890, he graduated from the Baylor School of Business in Waco.

149

He also studied agriculture, and read extensively in both English and Spanish.

About 1895, he married Miss Balbina Gongora of Roma, Texas. The couple lived in Laredo for a short while before moving to Alice.

In addition to his newspaper, Velazquez published progressive articles relating to business and economics, agriculture, health, and the arts. He was a gentleman of culture and integrity, well liked and respected by both the Latin and Anglo residents.

The enterprising Velazquez also taught a private school in Spanish for boys and girls. This school was held on the second floor above his printing shop. Here he also offered some night courses in both agriculture and business. Astounding as it may seem, he also found time to serve several Alice businesses as their accountant.

Velazquez published *El Cosmopolito* on the ground floor of the two-story building that is still standing at the corner of Flores and South Reynolds Streets in Alice (1968). Velazquez had this building constructed to his own specifications in 1903.

In 1914, he moved with his family to Kingsville, but remained there only a few months before moving to Eagle Pass. There he opened a printing shop, where he published another weekly newspaper until 1920.

In partnership with his older sons, Velazquez opened a publishing house in the state capital of Chihuahua, Chihuahua, Mexico. After a few years they sold this business and moved to Querétaro, on the south-central highlands north of Mexico City. Here, again in partnership with his sons, he opened another publishing house. However, they remained here only a short time before moving to the beautiful city of Orizaba, in the mountains of the western part of the state of Vera Cruz.

Here the men established another publishing house, which is still owned by his sons, the Velazquez Brothers.

Eulalio Velazquez died in Orizaba on September 18, 1941. His wife, Señora Balbina Gongora de Velazquez, his sons, Mauro, Elias, and Esau, and his daughters, Christina, Ofelia and Eloise all reside in Orizaba, as of 1967.

Miss Juanita Velazquez, his niece, lives in Alice on Hill Street. She is justly proud of the legacy of independence and service her uncle has left her in the city of Alice, and elsewhere.

J. FRANK DOBIE, ALICE GRADUATE

The Llanos Mesteñas has hosted some very interesting people. Some have achieved worldwide fame, and some have gained only notoriety; others, just as interesting and just as wonderful, have lived their lives here without benefit of much ado.

A native of whom Live Oak and Jim Wells Counties, Alice, the entire State of Texas, and most literate Americans are justly proud and admire a great deal is James Frank Dobie. Alice, for example, does not want folks to forget that Dobie lived here for two years, during 1904 through 1906, attended and was a graduate of the Alice High School. His eight-member graduating class of 1906 was the first to receive diplomas from Alice's first brick school, referred to as "The Hobbs Building." Dobie was salutatorian of the class.

After graduating from the Alice High School, Dobie attended Southwestern University at Georgetown, where he earned his B.A. degree in 1910. He must have had wonderful professors at Southwestern, for it was here that he learned to love poetry and good literature. Continuing his college career, he received his M.A. degree from Columbia University in 1916.

For a short while, Dobie taught English at Southwestern, and then at Oklahoma Agricultural and Mechanical College. He began teaching at the University of Texas, but the First World War involved the United States, and Dobie became a lieutenant in the 116th Field Artillery and was soon sent to France.

After the war, Dobie resumed his teaching career at the University. In 1921, he took a year's leave of absence in order to manage the James M. (his Uncle Jim's) Dobie Ranch, consisting of 250,000 acres, along the Nueces River. Here he lived among the Mexican vaqueros and learned about native ranch traditions and folklore. This ranch was near the Perdido Ranch, owned by Ruth Dodson's father.

After Dobie's return to the University of Texas in 1922, he became editor of the Texas Folklore Society. In 1933, he became a full professor at the University. His course, "Life and Literature of the Southwest," soon became one of the University's most popular.

During the late 1930's, he traveled in Mexico and the Southwest gathering information for his books. Grants from the Laura Spelman Rockefeller and the Guggenheim Memorial Foundations financed these travels.

As an upholder of freedom and men's rights, J. Frank Dobie is remembered and admired, as well as for his outstanding writings. His informal title, "The Maverick Professor," suited him well and he was proud of it. Dobie sanctioned academic freedom, even when it meant loss of his position at the University. Because of this courage and individuality, he is described as "unmistakably Texan as a Longhorn steer."

Dobie used a picture of the Paisano, also called Chaparral Cock and Roadrunner, as his "trademark." He usually depicted it as running. He had a large collection of pictures, pins, carvings, and such of this interesting bird.

Dobie's study of and passion for literature were instrumental in his raising his writings to the rank of literature. His works have become a part of libraries in the entire English-speaking world. For his books were his creations—authentic, yes, but not a mere relating of dates and places; he was writing literature, not merely recording happenings.

ALICE AS A TOWNSHIP

Alice, as a community with a post office, had been recognized as such by this name for more than a decade before deciding to incorporate into a township.

This matter of the incorporation of the town of Alice is included in the minutes of the Commissioners Court of Nueces County, signed by Judge W. B. Hopkins, filed, and recorded on June 17, 1904 at 5 o'clock in the afternoon. H. E. Luter was County Clerk.

The following paragraph is a summary of these minutes:

> An election to determine whether or not its citizens wanted to incorporate Alice into a township was held June 2, 1904. There were 41 votes in favor of incorporating and 13 against. These returns were received by Judge Hopkins June 16, 1904, and on that day, in the Nueces County Commissioners Court he did order, adjudge and decree that the area of Alice (with its boundaries described in detail) be and are hereby incorporate within the said boundaries under the name of the Town of Alice.

The cost of entry and record of this order, plus the certified copy to be filed, had to be paid by the town of Alice. F. B.

Nayer had, on April 3, 1903, for $1.00 and other considerations, given land for use as a Fraternal Cemetery. This cemetery became the official Alice cemetery and formed part of the boundary of the original township.

The record book, titled "The Minutes of the Town Council of Alice, Nueces County, Texas," has many blank pages. Writing begins on page 3, where it is recorded that on June 28, 1904, an election was held at which the following officers were declared by the County Judge to be elected: Mayor, P. A. Presnall; Aldermen, F. B. Nayer, S. B. Mosser, G. W. Newberry, L. G. Collins, and Phil Hobbs; and A. F. Clark, Marshal.

These elected officers met at the Nayer-Ellis Company building on July 11, 1904 and were sworn in. Frank W. Ellis served as clerk. He and Mayor Presnall signed these statements as an organizational meeting record—not as minutes. The record of the July 22 meeting, after F. W. Ellis had been appointed officially the Town Secretary at a salary of $5.00 a month, was designated as the first minutes. F. B. Nayer was appointed the Mayor Pro Tem because Presnall was out of town. The town marshal's salary was set at $25.00 a month, and the mayor and aldermen were paid $1.00 a year.

The next meeting was held July 25 for the purpose of accepting bids to print and publish the Town Ordinances. D. S. Boothe of *The Echo* bid $2.00 per page, but A. D. Smith of *The Sun* bid $1.50 per page and was awarded the contract. Both bids were to specifications.

Phil Hobbs was appointed Town Treasurer and bonded for $200.00 at the July 30 meeting. The Mayor made important committee appointments, and the Town Marshal was instructed to be provided with dog license tags.

On September 7, the Town Council adopted a resolution to collect occupational tax which was to be no less than that collected by the County. Alderman Newberry was fined $3.00 for being absent.

Then the Council started having hog trouble. They passed an ordinance which required residents to keep their hogs penned and only under specified conditions. The Town Marshal was directed "to inform F. G. Vela that the Council does not deem it advisable to change the ordinance in regard to hogs." On September 15, a petition signed by 136 persons in regard to the hog ordinance was read. The petition was filed.

At the January 12, 1905 meeting, a committee of three was

appointed to draft a new HOG ORDINANCE (sic). The following resolution was adopted at this meeting: "Resolved that the Alice, Wade City, and Corpus Christi Telephone Company be granted permission to erect telephone poles on the streets of Alice . . ."

Revenue in the guise of fines was increasing. On February 8, 1905, Ildefonso Lopez was fined $4.00, Teofila Barrera $5.00, and B. P. Gilman $5.00. No reasons were given for these fines.

Minutes of the next several meetings were short and routine or non-existent. On June 15, 1905, Trinidad Salazar's petition asking for a bridge over the arroyo to the north of his store on Reynolds Street was read. The request was referred to a committee to investigate and report the costs of such at the next meeting. Also at this meeting, L. G. Collins' resignation was accepted and G. R. Adams was appointed in his place. Twenty dollars was allowed the Street and Alley Committee to buy tools and pay the labor to cut down the weeds in the streets and alleys. Also passed was the motion "for the Sanitary Committee to prepare an ordinance relating to closets, and to report on same the next regular meeting."

The minutes of July 19th stated, "No report was made on the closet ordinance or the Salazar bridge." But decisions to close the Santa Gertrudis Public Road north of Sidbury Avenue, and to collect the ad valorem tax of ¼ of 1% for the year 1905 were made. A penalty of 10% was to be collected if the tax was not paid before October 1, 1905. Notice of these ordinances were to be printed in the *Alice Echo* and in *El Sol*, local newspapers . . . "Provided the town could get reasonable rates."

No more minutes are recorded until March 19, 1906. These contained almost no business of any kind and were the last minutes recorded in the first "Town Council of Alice, Nueces County, Texas" record book until February 23, 1910. The pages between numbers 47 and 101 were left blank. Recorded on page 101 were the facts that the City Council met and that Mayor F. B. Nayer and Commissioners G. R. Adams and A. F. Holmgreen were present. It is interesting that members of the Council, other than the Mayor, are now referred to as "Commissioners" rather than "aldermen."

Although not recorded here, an election must have been held, for it was noted that these men filed their oaths of office. At this time, also, P. S. Anderson was elected clerk with a salary of $40.00 per month, and that he was placed under bond for two thousand dollars. (The cost of government was rising rapidly.) The City rented the Kendall property, consisting of lots 11 and 12 in Block 12, for $4.00 a month. No reason was given for use of this property. The Council adjourned to meet again February 26th at 10 a.m. at the City Hall—but there is no record of their having done so.

At the next recorded meeting on March 4, 1910, Mayor Nayer gave a check for $536.61 to City Clerk Anderson. It was a refund by the County of Nueces for the account credit of the previous administration, and was to be placed in the General Fund. Five dollars was allowed for the purchase of Studer's *Texas Municipal Corporation Laws,* which the clerk was authorized to buy. These were the last recorded minutes of the Town Council. On March 23, 1910, the first minutes of the City of Alice begin, for the Township of Alice was now incorporated into a city.

MUSTANG PLAINS TOOK BACKWARD STEP WITH 19th CENTURY CHANGES

Political boundary lines in the Mustang Prairies took a step backward just before the Twentieth Century. On March 12, 1899, the Texas Legislature abolished Encinal County. Since February 1, 1856, Encinal County had vegetated. No one had bothered to organize the county, so after forty-three years it finally became apparent to the red-tape makers that local residents were not interested in organizing the area into a county, so its area was incorporated into Webb County.

No more new counties were created south of the Nueces until 1911, when Jim Wells, Brooks, and Willacy Counties were created in separate bills by the 32nd Legislature.

Jim Wells County was created from Nueces County on Groundhog Day. William Adams, W. T. Wright, W. W. West, Charles Premont, and James F. Scott were named Commissioners to organize the county. Sam Rayburn was Speaker of the House and A. B. Davidson was President of the Senate when House Bill 119 creating Jim Wells County was passed, as well as when the other two named counties were created. The Senate tacked some amendments onto the bill, and it passed with a vote of 25 yeas and one nay. It was finally approved and signed by Governor O. B. Colquitt, and received in the Department of State on March 11, 1911 at 10:10 a.m. The Commissioners were given ten days to organize themselves into a court and hold their first meeting.

The first recorded minutes of unorganized Jim Wells County are dated March 18, 1911. The first election to fill the county offices was held May 6, and canvassed May 8, 1911. The first minutes of organized Jim Wells County are dated May 15, 1911.

James B. Wells, Jr., for whom Jim Wells County is named, was born on St. Joseph's Island in 1850. His father participated in the Texas Revolution, and served in the Texas Navy, and became Sailing Master of the "Brutus." He resigned government service when the ship was destroyed by a storm at Galveston in 1837, and soon moved to St. Joseph's Island.

James B. Wells, Jr. received the LL.B. degree from the University of Virginia in 1875. After practicing law and dealing in land speculation, "Jim" accepted a partnership in law with Judge Stephen Powers of Brownsville. His first work was defending owners of original land titles in this area.

He was influential in the economic development of the Lower Rio Grande Valley. However, his greatest contribution was in fostering the improvement of relations between the original settlers and newer settlers who came into the region after the development of irrigation and railroads.

Both Brooks and Willacy Counties were created March 11, 1911. Falfurrias, which was started in 1883 and given the Spanish name for the beautiful "Heart's Delight" desert flowers that grow in the immediate vicinity, was designated county seat of Brooks County. Sarita was named county seat of Willacy County.

Brooks County was named for James Abijah Brooks, who came to Texas from Kentucky when about 2 years old. He first settled in Collin County where he farmed and ranched and drove cattle up trail. In 1880, he moved to San Antonio. He joined the Texas Rangers in 1882, and was commissioned Captain in 1889. He was stationed in Alice as Captain of Company A in 1902, and was active in stopping cattle rustling, especially from the King Ranch. In 1906, he resigned from the Rangers and settled in Falfurrias. James A. Brooks represented the 95th District in the House of Representatives until 1911, and served as Judge of Brooks County from 1911 until 1939.

Willacy County was created from Cameron and Hidalgo Counties. The area was occupied by Spanish colonizers during the 1780's, and a survey was made in the area by July, 1790. The San Juan Carricitos Grant was made, by order of the Spanish Government on October 28, 1793, to José N. Cavazos. Heirs still hold much of the grant. El Sal del Rey and La Sal Vieja supplied all South Texas and North Mexico with salt until after the Civil War.

General Philip H. Sheridan, on reaching the hot, shifting sands around the Baffin Bay vicinity, is reported to have exclaimed, "If I possessed both Texas and Hell, I'd rent out Texas and live in Hell!"

Raymondville was made the county seat of Willacy County when Kenedy County was created out of the northern portion of Willacy County, which included Sarita, and took Sarita for its own county seat.

Willacy County was named for John G. Willacy who came to Texas from Louisville, Kentucky, and settled near Corpus Christi. He served in the Texas Legislature from 1899 until 1914, serving two terms in the House and the rest in the Senate. During the early 1920's, he was State Tax Commissioner under Governor Pat M. Neff.

John G. Willacy died on September 19, 1943, at the age of 84.

GEORGE CLEGG, HORSEMAN

George Austin Clegg, a resident of Alice from 1904 until his death in 1959, was one of the nation's most successful raisers of fine Quarter Horses. "Old Sorrel," foundation stallion of the King Ranch herd, was from Clegg's stock.

Clegg, being a native South Texan from near Cuero, was naturally interested in horses—riding, racing, roping. When a young man, he considered himself an expert, until about 1895— to use Mr. Clegg's own words in an interview of several years ago, "Clay McGonigal came through our part of the country on a roping tour, and cleaned us all out. Right then and there I decided to get myself the fastest horse I could find."

On July 12, 1897, he married Letitia Nichols of Cuero. The couple moved to Alice in 1904. It was here in 1905 that he laid the foundation for his success as a Quarter Horse breeder. He purchased "Little Joe," when a yearling colt, from Dow Shely, who was co-owner of the famous "Traveler." His partner bought four mares in Del Rio.

157

In 1911, Clegg was racing some of their offspring, using a jockey named Pap Rebo. Rebo told Clegg of the death of Samuel Watkins, owner of the world's fastest Quarter Horses, and that Watkins' horses were going to be put up for sale. Clegg bought two of the mares, and a racer named "Hickory Bill." His really good Quarter Horses started with the breeding of the Little Joe and Hickory Bill mares.

Cesar Kleberg bought a suckling colt sired by Hickory Bill from Clegg in 1913. This colt became "Old Sorrell."

Mr. Clegg was an established Quarter Horse breeder by 1916. He was also a "big time" cattleman. During the early 1920's, he had about 300 brood mares, all of which carried the blood of outstanding horses in their pedigrees. But he gradually drifted into the quarter-mile racehorse game exclusively.

In 1921, the Cleggs were involved in an automobile accident and Mrs. Clegg was killed. Then the depression hit and Mr. Clegg lost his horses, his cattle, and his ranch properties— which had been extensive. In 1934 he entered the sheriff's race, but lost the election.

Clegg began working for the King Ranch and handled their race horses for many years, and became a judge at horse shows. Because of his great knowledge of horses and his integrity, he was much in demand and became nationally recognized.

In June of 1952, he took a boatload of cattle to Cuba for the King Ranch.

George Clegg died of cancer January 10, 1959, at the home of his daughter, Mrs. Christine Clegg Philips of Alice.

In appreciation for Clegg's many accomplishments in the Quarter Horse field, the King Ranch donated the George Clegg Memorial Trophy to the Jim Wells County Fair, which is held in Alice annually, in 1959. The trophy was to be presented to the grand champion of the Quarter Horse Show at the fair each year and to be received permanently by anyone whose animals had won the grand championship three times. It was won permanently in October of 1965 by L. M. Pearce, Jr., of Beeville.

1913 COUNTY CREATIONS—ONE A "GHOST"

Kleberg County was created February 27, 1913 and organized June 27, 1913. It was named for the first Robert Justus Kleberg, a German immigrant to Texas in 1834, who was a participant in the Battle of San Jacinto. He was a graduate of the University of Goettingen, Germany. Following his graduation, he married and moved to Texas.

His son, Robert J. Kleberg, II, was an attorney whose chief client was Richard King. Kleberg married Richard King's daughter, Alice, in 1886.

Kleberg County was formed from the south half of what remained of Nueces County after Jim Wells County had been created out of it in 1911. Baffin Bay and Los Olmos Creek form the south boundary of Kleberg County. During early Texas days, "Smugglers' Pass" followed this boundary line.

The King Ranch comprises most of Kleberg County. Richard King started his ranch in 1852, when he bought the Santa Gertrudis Spanish Land Grant from the heirs of brothers José Domingo, José Lorenzo, and José Julian de la Garza, who were the original grantees.

Kingsville, established in July, 1904, is the county seat. Rivera Beach, in the south part of the county on Baffin Bay, was quite a resort town from 1913 until destroyed by a hurricane in 1916.

Jim Hogg County, created on March 31, 1913 and organized soon afterward, was named for Texas' first native-born governor, James Steven Hogg. The county was created from a part of newly organized Brooks County, and a bit of Duval County. Its county seat, Hebbronville, was started in 1881 by W. R. Hebbron as a station stop on the Texas-Mexican Railway. Peña's Station, about one-half mile to the east of the railroad station, was a well-known freight station for ox-wagon freighters. An 1893 description of the road south of Peña's Station leading to Rio Grande City states that "mile after mile of nopal cactus is seen, some of it fifteen feet tall with leaves as large as a man's body."

James Steven Hogg was born in Cherokee County on March 24, 1851, and died in Houston on March 3, 1906. Modern Texas historians generally consider him one of Texas' best governors. He was orphaned when twelve years old, and soon took a job splitting wood to help pay for his school tuition. He got a job in a newspaper office as general flunky, and was soon setting type. He studied to perfect his spelling and to improve his vocabulary.

While helping the Quitman sheriff in his fight against lawlessness, Hogg was shot in the back from ambush. He soon recovered, and resumed his newspaper work. He ran two newspapers of his own, one in Longview and one in Quitman, with which he fought subsidies to railroads, corruption in the U. S. Grant administration, and local lawlessness. He had been studying law whenever possible, and passed the state bar examination in 1875.

After holding several lesser public offices, Jim Hogg ran for attorney general of Texas, and won the election. During his tenure, he forced "wildcat" insurance companies out of Texas, recovered one and one-half million acres of school lands fraudulently held by railroads, helped write the nation's second State Anti-Trust Law, and forced the rich railroad companies to respect and obey Texas laws. He was elected governor on the platform of advocating the establishment of the Texas Railroad Commission, to insure continued regulation of railroads.

A *School History of Texas* (prepared from *The General History* written by John Henry Brown), by Mrs. Mary M. Brown, published in 1894, states that, "The Legislature in 1891 passed two laws of great importance, upon which the public became divided. These new laws were, one creating a State Railroad Commission . . . The other law was in relation to foreigners or aliens holding land in Texas . . . Great changes have been made in the constitution and laws in the judicial department of the government, favorable to a more prompt and less expensive administration of justice."

Perhaps Texas is in dire need of another Jim Hogg, with like political views, as summed in his address made in honor of President Theodore Roosevelt at Dallas, April 5, 1905. This was his last important public address. He said, "I should like to see: Rotation in office permanently established; nepotism forbidden; equality of taxation a fact; organized lobbying at Austin suppressed; the free pass system honestly, effectively abolished; oil pipelines placed under the commission's control; insolvent corporations put out of business; all bonds and stocks of every class of transportation limited by law; corporate control of Texas made impossible; and public records disclose every official act and be open to all, to the end that everyone shall know that, in Texas, public office is the center of public conscience."

Dunn County was created August 21, 1913, from the lower half of Duval County. However, Dunn County was not organized within the allotted time, so its creation became null and void. Oil had been discovered on the Piedras Pintas Ranch in the western part of Duval County, southwest of San Diego.

Plans to develop these findings probably influenced the attempted division of the thinly populated county. Another attempt to divide the county of Duval was made in 1915. An act was introduced into the Legislature to divide the county along similar lines to those of Dunn County and to name the new county, "Lanham." However, this bill died in committee. Samuel William Tucker Lanham, for whom it was to have been named, was Texas' last governor who had been a Confederate soldier and the 22nd governor of Texas. Thus, nothing came of Lanham County—an analogy of the Confederacy.

JUDGE ROBERT "BOB" ROLAND MULLEN

In the spring of 1914, a tall, handsome, black-haired man, with his wife and three children, moved to Alice. He had been a railroad man for about fifteen years, and was now relocating because he wanted to practice law. For several months, he had been checking South Texas towns, and chose Alice because it seemed the most promising.

This man was Judge Robert Roland Mullen, a Canadian by birth, but an Alician Texan by choice. He had been born in Kingston, Ontario on December 4, 1876.

When Robert Roland was five years old, his parents moved southwestward to Oneil, Nebraska. In 1897, he graduated from Fremont Normal in Fremont, Nebraska.

Shortly after his graduation, Mullen married Ella Kindell and moved to Kansas City, Missouri. Early in 1901, he moved to Saginaw, Texas, where he was the agent for both the Santa Fe and the Fort Worth and Denver Railroads.

In 1911, Mullen moved to Cresson, Texas as agent for the Santa Fe Railroad. While living in Cresson, he began studying law at home. He passed the state bar examination and was admitted to the bar on July 1, 1913. A couple of months later, he moved with his family to Corpus Christi, and began looking for a place to locate permanently.

Although Mullen had just moved into Jim Wells County in the spring, he decided to enter the race for county attorney in the fall election. It was the county's second election, because Jim Wells County had just been organized in 1911. Mr. Mullen had impressed the people of the county to the extent that he won the election from the incumbent. He was reelected in 1916.

During Mullen's first term of office as county attorney, he

worked with Philip Pope Price, who was commissioner of Precinct 2. Later as judge, he, W. T. Wright, Sr., and Price served together for five consecutive terms while Mr. Price was county school superintendent, from January 1925 until January 1935.

In 1918, Mullen had won the election for county judge, and W. T. Wright, Sr., had won the election for commissioner of Precinct 2. These two men of high integrity and intelligence were fellow travelers and won the next twelve elections, also. Judge Mullen retired in 1945, but Wright continued in office one more term.

The first paved highways criss-crossing Jim Wells County, including Highway 281, were built while Judge Mullen was in office. Jim Wells County also developed one of the soundest financial structures in Texas during these years under Judge Mullen's leadership. When he retired, he left the county entirely free of debt.

Judge Mullen was also active and influential in business and civic affairs throughout the Mustang Plains.

Judge and Mrs. Mullen were the parents of three children: Robert Raymond, who lives in Alice and is president of the Alice Savings and Loan Association and also of the Sandia State Bank, which is the county's oldest bank; Marie (Mrs. Jim Young))of Houston; and F. M., also of Alice and a business man.

"Old Judge Bob Mullen," as he is fondly remembered by his many longtime friends and associates, loved the Mustang Plains. Until shortly before his death, he actively managed his Jersey farm near Alice.

Judge Robert Roland Mullen died at his home in Alice of a cerebral hemorrhage on January 26, 1947.

TEXAS' LAST COUNTY CHANGE IN THE MUSTANG PLAINS

The last county in Texas to be created and organized was Kenedy, deep in the Llanos Mesteñas region. It occupies the middle third of the coast between Corpus Christi and Brownsville. Much of it is the hot, shifting sands section known as "Wild Horse Desert" to early settlers. During summers, wagon trains and stage coaches came through these sands at night, because horses and mules could not stand the daytime heat.

Kenedy County was created by the Legislature in 1921 from the land that had been Willacy County since 1911, except for a narrow strip five to ten miles wide along its south boundary. This strip contains La Sal Vieja, a salt lake that had furnished salt for Spanish explorers and settlers as well as for countless generations of Indians before its discovery by the Europeans.

The east corner of Hidalgo County and an uneven section along Cameron County's north boundary line, consisting of about one-fourth of the area of Cameron County at this time, were joined with the remaining strip of Willacy County to form present Willacy County. Raymondville, sliced off of Cameron County, was named county seat of reapportioned Willacy County to replace Sarita that was made the county seat of Kenedy County.

Mifflin Kenedy, for whom the new county was named, was a native of Chester County, Pennsylvania. He became acquainted with Richard King during the 1840's, while both were working for riverboat companies. Both aided General Zachary Taylor in the transporting of men and supplies from New Orleans to Corpus Christi, and later to points along the Lower Rio Grande.

In 1850, Kenedy and King formed a partnership to operate riverboats on the Rio Grande from Brownsville to Rio Grande City. This enterprise proved to be very profitable. The two men dissolved their partnership in 1852, and King bought extensive ranch lands along Santa Gertrudis Creek and adjoining areas.

Mifflin Kenedy bought half interest in the huge ranching venture in 1860, but the partnership was dissolved in November of 1867. Kenedy took the southern land, called the Laureles Ranch, and began fencing it in 1868. He was the first rancher in the Mustang Plains to begin fencing ranch lands.

*   *   *

COUNTY SEAT SIDELIGHTS — The earliest settlements that exercised local government over sections of land in this area were founded during the mid-1700's and were called municipalities. Except for Laredo and Old Dolores (now a ghost town with rock ruins extant), these were located south of the Rio Grande. However, Dolores was destroyed by Indians about the turn of the 18th Century but rebuilt nearby, and Laredo was a part of Coahuila rather than Nuevo Santander.

Refugio became a municipality in 1825, and San Patricio

in 1834. When Texas became a Republic and named the Rio Grande as its south and west border, San Patricio was named the county seat of this vast area south of the Nueces. Other counties of the Mustang Plains were all carved out of these two original counties—San Patricio and Refugio, except for a little bit of the southwest portion of Bexar County. Some of these early counties still use their original county seats as such. Laredo began as a Spanish municipality, and San Patricio and Refugio as Mexican municipalities.

Those county seats whose names have remained the same, but whose sites have been changed are Beeville and Edinburg. Beeville was removed from its original site along Medio Creek to its present site in 1860; and Edinburg was removed from the Rio Grande, presently called Hidalgo, to its present site near the center of Hidalgo County in 1908.

The only one whose name, but not site, was changed is Zapata. It had been known since Spanish days as Carrizo, but its name was changed to Zapata about 1890.

La Salle, by old Fort Ewell on the Nueces in the south-central part of La Salle County, was county seat for only two years. Then Cotulla was named county seat in 1882.

In 1893, San Patricio, bypassed by the San Antonio and Aransas Pass Railroad in 1885, finally lost to Sinton as county seat.

In 1919, the county seat of Live Oak County was removed from Oakville to George West, soon after a fine new courthouse had been built.

Sarita is unique in that it retained its original site and name, but changed counties: from Willacy to Kenedy County, and kept its status as county seat.

LAGARTO COLLEGE

In the west, the wide orange sunset was blending into soft purples toward the north and the south, while in the east the perfectly round October moon was mirroring the sunset in a hazy nest of palest gold.

The two sisters in calico were so overcome by the absolute beauty of the South Texas autumnal spatial scene that their throats ached at the sheer wonder of it all. They stood back to back, trying to lose none of the glorious east-west scene.

Zadie and Kate Adams had arrived a day early at Lagarto

College, which was built on just about the highest flat-topped hill along the Lower Nueces River.

Tomorrow there would be several hundred more students here, and little time for musing. And a whole year would pass before another such October moon.

And on another Saturday in October 80 years later, Kate's and Zadie's daughters—along with about 200 other sons and daughters and other descendants of the former students of Old Lagarto College—would stand on the same hill now long bereft of college buildings and witness the unveiling ceremonies of a State marker commemorating the old college.

These ceremonies were held on October 7, 1967 on the actual site of the college grounds. The old fireplaces that were still standing a year ago are now gone. However, Hurricane Beulah was not the culprit that destroyed them. According to several of those attending the ceremony, a rock dealer drove in with his big truck during the summer, razed the chimneys, and hauled off the rocks.

Lagarto College was in operation from 1884 until 1895, with A. G. Heaney as president. Dr. Gordon Heaney of Corpus Christi is his grandson.

The first plot of ground for the college was given by John W. Raymond.

The grandfather of Mrs. Happy Sanguinet of Live Oak County was vice-president.

The main college building was a two-story building with a fireplace at each end. The first term opened with nine professors and about 250 students. Its peak enrollment was 800 students.

Such a school would now be called an academy, for all levels from upper elementary through junior college were taught.

Lagarto College boasted a professor from England and one from Washington, D. C., as well as several others from out of Texas. The college faculty and students were mighty proud of their music department, which had an orchestra that numbered as many as 26 members.

Members of several pioneer families in the present Jim Wells, Nueces and Kleberg County areas attended Lagarto College. Among these were the Adams, Bell, McNeill, Miller, Hinnant, Reynolds, Grover, Wright, Newberry, Cox, Gilpin, Dix, Wade, Goodwin, and Dobie families. There are probably many more such families in the area.

165

The dedication ceremonies of the Lagarto College marker consisted of the following program.

Master of Ceremonies ....S. T. Brown, Jr., Chairman
                                        of Live Oak County Histor-
                                        ical Survey Committee

Welcome ....Honorable Judge L. Hinton
                                        Live Oak County Judge

Invocation ....Dr. Gordon Heaney
                                        Corpus Christi, Texas

Introduction of Special Guests ......Mrs. Happy Sanguinet
                                        Member of Live Oak County
                                        Historical Survey Committee

Introduction of Speaker ....Mrs. Lela Beall Porter
                                        Argenta, Texas

Dedicatory Address ....Dudley R. Dobie, Jr.
                                        San Marcos, Texas

Unveiling of Historical Marker ....Descendants of First
                                        Families of Lagarto, Texas

Benediction ....Mrs. Willie Hinnant
                                        Member of Live Oak County
                                        Historical Survey Committee

BIBLIOGRAPHY
PRIMARY SOURCES

Manuscripts:

Broeter, Miss Tillie, "Beginning of Alice, Texas" (MS., privately held by Agnes G. Grimm, Alice, Texas).

Miss Broeter (deceased) was born in Old Collins, now a ghost town, grew up in the Mustang Plains and was a school teacher and administrator for many years. This manuscript is the speech she wrote for a program, probably for the Booklovers Club of Alice, commemorating Alice's fiftieth anniversary as an incorporated community. It was written in 1954. Alice was incorporated into a township in 1904. (This manuscript will be a part of the Jim Wells County archives when they are set up.)*

Mendiola, Enrique, "Ben Bolt—Palito Blanco" (MS., privately held by Agnes G. Grimm, Alice, Texas).

Mr. Mendiola was a member of the Jim Wells County Historical Survey Committee which turned in a report to the State Survey Committee in the Spring of 1963 about historical highlights of the county. This report was based on reports handed in by individual members. This manuscript is the report of this member, a teacher, who grew up in the Ben Bolt-Palito Blanco vicinity and who was doing graduate work at A & I University at that time.*

Price, Josephine, "History of Alice" (MS., privately held by A. G. Grimm, Alice, Texas).

Miss Price is a native of the Alice area and a descendant of an English immigrant settler who was among the first shipload of settlers from Europe to enter this area through the port of Corpus Christi rather than Indianola or Galveston. This was in 1852. She was also a member of the County Historical Survey Committee in 1963. This manuscript has been previously used by her for a club program. She still lives on a portion of the huge ranch her grandfather started, and her father improved.*

Reynolds, Seana McCoy, "History of Northeastern Jim Wells County" (MS., privately held by A. G. Grimm, Alice, Texas).

Miss Reynolds is a descendant of an English immigrant settler who was aboard the first ship bringing European settlers directly into the port of Corpus Christi in 1852. She has restored and is living in the ranch house that was built of hand-cut caliche blocks in 1867, on the Ventana Ranch west of Orange Grove. She wrote this manuscript for the County Historical Survey Committee in 1963 to be a part of the report to be sent to Austin.*

Schubert, Joseph A., "History of Alice Schools" (MS., in possession of author, Alice, Texas).

Dr. Schubert, a native of Alice, is now a local dentist. He wrote this paper when a senior in high school in 1952, for his English teacher. His father has been a local dentist for about twenty-five years. The paper is well authenticated.

Stubblefield, Park L., "Development of the Premont Area" (MS., in possession of A. G. Grimm, Alice, Texas).

Mr. Stubblefield, recently deceased, wrote this manuscript for the 1963 County Historical Survey Committee report. It is taken from his extensive notes about the Premont area, which he had planned to organize for publication at an early date.*

Government Documents and Records:

Abstract Number 1, Cameron County; "La Feria Grant to José María Balli from the King of Spain (Old Deed Book Number 1, property of M. Bryan Glasscock, La Feria, Texas).

This is a translation of the Spanish Deed Book Number 1, and consists entirely of this La Feria Grant, beginning with the King's grant and bringing the abstract to the 1920's.

Abstract Number 1393, District of San Patricio, Under the Confirmation Act of 1860, Austin (File No. 563, General Land Office); Filed in Zapata County, January 14, 1861.

Deed Record Books, Nueces County, A to Z, 1 to 6, County Courthouse, Corpus Christi, Texas.

These Deed Record Books include pertinent information from the State of Tamaulipas, Mexico and the Republic of Texas. Original Books A, B, C, D were in Spanish; parts of Republic of Texas and early State records were in both Spanish and English. Most of these have now been replaced with English translations.

Deed to Lots 5, 6, 7, 8 in Block 2, in the Town of Kleberg (in possession of Lucille Hobbs (Mrs. Goode S.) Wier).

These lots were sold by the San Antonio and Aransas Pass Town Site Company for $600.00 to George Hobbs. They are signed by Mifflin Kenedy, President, and dated August 30, 1888. This was the original name of Alice, but the Post Office Department refused to accept it because of duplication.

Deed to Survey Number 9 (in possession of owners, Mr. and Mrs. Roman Escobar, San Diego, Texas), in Duval County.

Mrs. Escobar is a daughter and granddaughter of former owners of La Mota Ranch; Mr. Escobar was a resident of La Mota when a child and attended La Mota School.

Field Notes from Survey made by Felix S. Blucher, District Surveyor of Nueces District, and recorded in Corpus Christi April 25, 1854, in Deed Records Book E, pages 42, 43, 44.

(The original is in the General Land Office in Austin, in a packet. When found, it was not recorded in a book; it was in a cubbyhole, and the clerk said she had not known it was there.)

Quit Claim Deed showing sale of Lichtenstein Hotel of Alice, Texas to Trinidad Salazar in 1896 (in possession of daughters Miss Guadalupe Salazar and Mrs. Beatrice Salazar Lopez).

Alice's first newspaper carried an advertisement in regard to this hotel and continued to carry it for three or four years.

Land of The La Donna Plat out of La Blanca Grant and Llano Grande Grant in Hidalgo County, Texas, Abstract of Title (in possession of and property of M. B. Glasscock of La Feria, Texas).

Minutes of Commissioners Court, Jim Wells County, Vol. 1 (County Courthouse, Alice, Texas).

This book contains both the minutes of Unorganized Jim Wells County and the first minutes of Organized Jim Wells County.

Minutes of Town Council of Alice, Book 1 (City Hall, Alice, Texas).

These minutes are of Alice as a township, and later of its organization into a city and selection as county seat.

Supplemental Records, Book X (Cameron County (property of M. B. Glasscock of La Feria).

Original record book covering various deeds.

Books and Pamphlets:

Boethel, Paul C., *The History of La Vaca County*, San Antonio (Naylor Publishing Company), 1936.
>   This book was of interest in its trade route connection with the Mustang Plains.

Bonnell, George W., *Topographical Description of Texas*. [Reprint with new material added, Waco (Texian Press), 1964], Austin (Clark, Wing, and Brown), 1836.
>   Contains excellent descriptions of this Llanos Mesteñas region as it existed in 1836.

Brown, John Henry, *Life of Henry Smith*, Dallas (A. D. Aldridge and Company, Stereotypers, Printers, and Binders), 1887.
>   Especially helpful in connection with description and location of ports and coastal settlements during the Mexican and Republic of Texas Eras. Also, some names are mentioned not found elsewhere.

Casteñeda, Carlos E., Ph.D., *Our Catholic Heritage in Texas*, Vol. II, III, IV, Austin (Von Boeckmann-Jones Company), 1939.
>   The Nuevo Santander Era, especially in Volume III, Chapter IV, is clearly explained and wonderfully readable. Other events having bearing on this Llanos Mesteñas region are mentioned, if not fully discussed, in other volumes and chapters.

Chatfield, Lt. W. H., *The Twin Cities of the Border*, New Orleans (E. P. Brando, Printer), 1893.
>   Lt. Chatfield was stationed in Brownsville for two and one-half years, and this large 48-page paperback booklet is a well organized compilation of his observations. A limited number were reprinted in 1959 by local historical organizations. It contains a map of Matamoros, Brownsville and Fort Brown and is well illustrated with "photo-engravings." It includes statistics through 1891.

Conner, John Edwin and Jack E. Conner and Robbie C. Harper, *Your Texas and Mine*, Oklahoma City (Harlow Publishing Corporation), 1960.
>   A state-adopted textbook for high schools. Dr. Conner is professor emeritus of the history department at the Texas Agricultural and Industrial University at Kingsville. He has been actively interested in Texas history for many years.

Cox, Mamie Wynne, *The Romantic Flags of Texas*, Dallas (Banks-Upshaw and Company, Publishers), 1936.
>   Miss Cox tells of some early settlers along the Nueces who also participated in the Texas Revolution. The husband of the designer of the first tricolor lone star flag of Texas settled near Mathis. His descendants grew up in this region, and he is buried near Alice.

Da Camara, Kathleen, *Laredo on the Rio Grande*, San Antonio (The Naylor Company), 1949.
>   Especially informative of Laredo vicinity through Republic of Texas Era.

Daniell, L. E., *Types of Successful Men of Texas*, Austin (Eugene Von Boeckmann, Printer and Bookbinder), 1910.
>   Biographies of men prominent in this region during the late 1800's. Printed by subscription, so not a very large number exists.

Davis, M. E. M., *The Story of Texas Under Six Flags*, Boston (Ginn and Company), 1897.
>   Descriptive and well written.

Dobie, J. Frank, *Coronado's Children*, New York (The Literary Guild of America), 1931.
>   Very descriptive of area.

Dodge, Colonel Richard Irving, *Hunting Grounds of the Great West*, London (Chatte and Windus), 1877.
> Colonel Dodge, when a very young man, had accompanied Zachary Taylor's army and had joined the march to the Rio Grande.

Dodson, Ruth, *Don Pedrito—"Curandero,"* San Antonio (Los Talleres de La Casa Editoria Lozano), 1934.

Dunn, William E., *Spanish and French Rivalry in the Gulf Region of the United States, 1678-1702*, Austin (University of Texas Bulletin), January 20, 1917.

Fields, F. T., and E. M. Schiwetz, *Texas Sketchbook*, Revised Edition, Houston (Humble Oil Company), 1955.
> Short histories and beautiful sketches of early settlements and interesting ruins along the lower Rio Grande.

Fisher, Orceneth, *Sketches of Texas in 1840* [Reprint with new material added, Waco (Texian Press), 1964], Springfield, Ill., (Walters & Weber, Printers), 1841.
> A vivid account of the geographical features of Texas in 1840, from the Rio Grande to the Sabine.

Ford, John Salmon, *Rip Ford's Texas*, Edited by Stephen Oates, Austin (University of Texas Press), 1963.
> Memoirs of J. S. Ford as a Texas Ranger from 1849, when he assumed command of the Texas Rangers in the Mustang Plains, until the end of his career. It also includes some experiences during the Mexican War. His vivid descriptions are invaluable.

Galvez, Bernardo de, *Instructions for Governing the Interior Provinces of New Spain* (Translated by D. E. Worcester), 1786.
> This book is in the Barker Library in Austin, at the University of Texas. It discusses the Spanish presidios of the later 18th Century and offers suggestions for meeting needs of the frontier. Galvez was Spain's last really strong military leader.

Garriga, Mariano S., D.D., Ll.D, *St. Joseph's Church, Alice, Texas* (with historical sketch by Hector S. Lopez of Alice, a souvenir booklet), October 18, 1953.
> The historical sketch begins with the ghost town of Collins, which was about two miles east of present Alice, and discusses local history largely pertaining to church growth and development (Catholic).

Haggard, J. Villasana, *Handbook for Translators of Spanish Historical Documents*, Oklahoma City (Photoprinted by Semco Color Press), 1941.
> Contains practical aids and suggestions for those attempting to read Spanish historical documents. Of especial help are the translations of many Spanish words and phrases, as well as the meanings of abbreviations, that are not found in modern dictionaries.

Hawkins, Wallace, *El Sal del Rey*, Austin (Texas State Historical Association), 1947.
> Discusses the Spanish salt mine in use by the Spanish during their entire occupation of the New World. Contains maps that are important in the Llanos Mesteñas region's history. Well documented.

Holley, Mary Austin, *Texas* [a facsimile reproduction of original, Austin (The Steck Company), 1935], Lexington, Kentucky (J. Clark and Company), 1836.
> Written and published by Mrs. Holley after a visit to Texas with her brother, Stephen F. Austin, in 1834. It is descriptive of the Texas area of that period, and is generally sympathetic toward Texas. It tells of the Copano Bay area, whose history was a part of the Llanos Mesteñas.

170

Holworthy, Sister Mary Xavier, *A Century of Sacrifice*, Corpus Christi (Private Printing), 1953.
> This book gives the early history of the Catholic Church in the Diocese of Corpus Christi. It is well documented and is interwoven as a basic part of the area's history. The first priests in this region, other than the very early Franciscan monks, were from France.

Holworthy, Sister Mary Xavier, *Father Jaillet, Saddlebag Priest of the Nueces*, Corpus Christi (private printing), 1948.
> Biography of first Pastor of the Parish and Missions of San Diego, and Pastor elsewhere in the Mustang Plains for more than 50 years altogether.

Horgan, Paul, *Great River, The Rio Grande In North American History*, Vol. II, New York (Rinehart and Company, Inc.), 1954.
> Especially good discussions of Mexican and Republic of Texas days in Copano and Rio Grande areas. Good descriptions of building of Fort Brown and Fort Polk.

Huson, Hobart, *Refugio*, Vol. I, Woodsboro, Texas (The Rooke Foundation, Inc.), 1953.
> Very carefully detailed and authentic work about area in vicinity of Refugio from earliest records.

Ikin, Arthur, *Texas: Its History, Topography, Agriculture, Commerce, and General Statistics*. [Reprint with new material added, Waco (Texian Press), 1964], London (Sherwood, Gilbert, and Piper), 1841.
> Excellent description of Republic of Texas days.

Linn, John J., *Reminiscences of Fifty Years in Texas*, New York (Sadlier Company), 1883.
> Anecdotes and descriptions of Texas before and after the Civil War. Seems somewhat exaggerated at times.

Lott, Virgil N. and Mercurio Martinez, *The Kingdom of Zapata*, San Antonio (The Naylor Company), 1953.
> Zapata County area history by native residents. Detailed.

McCampbell, Coleman, *Saga of a Frontier Seaport*, Dallas (Mathis Publishing Company), 1935.
> Story of early Corpus Christi.

Manry, Beatrice, *The History of Fort Brown*, Austin (University of Texas Bulletin), December 8, 1927.
> Informative and authentic.

Miller, Mrs. S. G., *Sixty Years In the Nueces Valley*, San Antonio (Naylor Printing Company), 1930.
> First-hand observations before and after the turn of the century. Quite a few names of early settlers and happenings.

Moore, Walter, and James M. Day, *The Texas Almanac, 1857-1873, A Compendium of Texas History*, Waco (Texian Press), 1967.
> Reprinting of **The Texas Almanac** as title indicates. Is especially sympathetic of President Mirabeau B. Lamar and critical of President 'Sam Houston.

Newell, Reverend C., *History of the Revolution In Texas*, New York (Wiley and Putnam), 1838.
> Author a Methodist minister who spent some time in Texas and was truthfully encouraging about Texas' future and present.

Oberste, William H., *Texas Irish Empresarios and Their Colonies,* Austin (Von Boeckmann-Jones Company), 1953.

Father Oberste of Refugio based his book largely on church records. It is very informative and more comprehensive of the Texas Irish and their area in Texas than his **History of Refugio Mission.**

O'Shay, Elena Zamora, *El Mesquite,* Dallas (Mathis Publishing Company), 1935.

El Mesquite Rancho is located in the Llanos Mesteñas southwest of present Concepción. It was an important stop on the Spanish travel and trade route between northern Mexico and La Bahía and the lower Texas coast.

Pierce, Frank Cushman, *Texas Last Frontier,* Menasha, Wis. (George Banta Publishing Company), 1917.

A brief history of the Lower Rio Grande Valley of Texas by a Brownsville resident of 1859 until after the publication of this book. It begins with the Spanish Era.

Rankin, Melinda, *Texas In 1850* [a reprint, Waco (Texian Press), 1966], Boston (Damrell and Moore), 1850.

Strongly biased religiously and preaches a lot, but has some good descriptions of conditions in Brownsville and other parts of Texas.

Reed, S. G., *A History of the Texas Railroads and of Transportation Conditions Under Spain and Mexico and the Republic of Texas and the State,* Houston (The St. Clair Publishing Company), 1941.

Early methods of transportation through this deep South Texas region as richly descriptive and informative as title.

Richardson, Dr. R. N., *The Comanche Barrier to the South Plains Settlement,* Glendale (Private Printing), 1933.

Tells of the enormity of the damage and killing by these Plains Indians in this area, which is generally ignored by United States historians and military reports. Well authenticated.

Rickard, J. A., and Maurine Bullock, *Your Texas History,* Austin W. S. Benson and Company, Publishers), 1962.

School textbook richer than usual in regard to the Mustang Plains region, because Dr. Rickard was a history professor at the Texas Agricultural and Industrial University at Kingsville until his death.

Rock, James L., and W. J. Smith, *Southern and Western Texas Guide For 1878,* St. Louis (A. H. Granger), 1878.

Good geographic descriptions, and early forts.

Root, Honorable Elishu, Ed., Sec'y of War, Brig. General Fred C. Ainsworth, and Joseph W. Kirkley, *War of the Rebellion, Official Records of the Union and Confederate Armies,* Series IV, Vol. 7, Washington, D. C. (Government Printing Office), 1900.

Rich in coastal warfare.

Ryan, William, *Shamrock and Cactus,* Houston (The Young Company), 1936.

About the Irish settlers in Texas; especially informative of Lipantitlan and 1835.

Scott, Florence J., *Old Rough and Ready On The Rio Grande,* San Antonio (The Naylor Company), 1935.

Consists of three stories: "The Mier Expedition," "Old Rough and Ready On the Rio Grande," and "The Last Battle of the Civil War." All three of these happenings took place in the Mustang Plains, climaxing along the Rio Grande. Well authenticated.

Sowell, A. J., *Early Settlers and Indian Fighters of Southwest Texas*, Austin (Ben C. Jones Company, Printers), 1900.
Incidental bits related to the Mustang Plains.

Sutherland, Mrs. Mary A., *The Story of Corpus Christi*, Corpus Christi (The Corpus Christi Daughters of the Confederacy, Publishers), 1916.
Detailed, and relates several incidents known to the author that are not found in other early histories of the city.

Stambaugh, J. Lee, and Lillian J. Stambaugh, *The Lower Rio Grande Valley of Texas*, San Antonio (The Naylor Company), 1954.
Ambitious undertaking; begins with Escandon Era and Indians of that time; sympathetic, but more from angle of observer or reader of chronicles than "lived in."

Steen, Ralph W., *Texas, A Story of Progress*, Austin (The Steck Company), 1942.
Textbook; one of the best of all times to date.

Steen, Ralph W., and Frances Donecker, *Texas: Our Heritage*, Austin (The Steck Company), 1962.
Meager; strictly Seventh Grade, but excellent pictures and bibliography.

Sterling, William Warren, *Trails and Trials of a Texas Ranger*, United States of America (Private Printing), 1959.
Largely written in Alice, Texas where Texas Rangers were stationed during the 1890's and early 1900's. Excellent descriptions of area during Captain Sterling's active participation; too subjective and loosely organized, but good source material.

The Grolier Society, *The Book of Knowledge, Vol. XXI, The Book of Texas*, Dallas (The Colonial Press), 1929.
Factual; good discussions about the Nueces River Valley participation in the Texas Revolution.

The Writers' Round Table, *Padre Island*, San Antonio (The Naylor Company), 1950.
Deeply researched by local historians.

Tiling, Moritz, *History of the German Element in Texas, 1820-1850*, Houston (Published by Author), 1913.
Well researched and a labor of love and pride; gives a good insight into plans and lives of early Germans.

Weaver, Sarah Sanborne, *The White Buck*, San Antonio (The Naylor Company), 1957.
Fictionized local intermingling of Texas and Mexican history, legends, and facts along the Rio Grande from Mier to Corpus Christi and Beeville; captures the local spirit of post Civil War times, but reader must be a native to understand and appreciate it.

Webb, Walter Prescott, and H. Bailey Carroll, and Others, *The Handbook of Texas, Vol. I, II*, Austin (The Texas State Historical Association), 1952.
Ambitious work, well organized; some mistakes due largely to local historians; needed by all Texans.

Wilbarger, J. W., *Indian Depredations In Texas*, Austin (The Steck Company), [Facsimile of Original], 1888.
First-hand information, but seems exaggerated in places; very interesting.

Wooten, Dudley G., Ed., *A Comprehensive History of Texas—1685 to 1897*, Vol. I, Dallas (William G. Scarff, Publisher), 1898.
    Especially informative about French activity in the Matagorda and Copano Bay areas, as well as in the Bay of St. Bernard; also tells of Spanish-French clashes in area.

Wurzbach, Emil Frederick, *Life and Memoirs*, Translated by Franz J. Dohmen, San Antonio (Yanaguana Society), 1937.
    Route of early roads detailed; discussion of forts along Rio Grande.

Yoakum, H., Esquire, *History of Texas—1685-1846* [facsimile (The Steck Company), Austin], Redfield, New York (Published by Author), 1855.
    Tells about forts or camps at Arkokisa and Matagordo vicinity; generally very well written and authoritative.

Periodicals:

Barrett, Arrie, "Western Frontier Forts of Texas, 1845-1861," *West Texas Historical Association Yearbook*, Vol. VII (1931), (West Texas Historical Association).

Crimmins, M. L., Ed., "Posts in Existence in Texas in 1856" (taken from J. K. F. Mansfield's Inspection Report of Texas), *The Southwestern Historical Quarterly*, Vol. XL, Austin (The Texas State Historical Association).

Crimmins, M. L., Ed., "W. G. Freeman's Report On the 8th Military Department," *The Southwestern Historical Quarterly*, Vol. LII, Austin (The Texas State Historical Association).

Fitzsimmons, Joseph, County Judge of Nueces County, and Others, "The Mexican and Indian Raid of '78" (Address of the Committee of People to Secretary of State of the United States), *Quarterly of the Texas State Historical Association*, Vol. V (1901-1902), Austin (The Texas State Historical Association).

Gardner, William H., "From Dragoons to Dudes," Austin, *Texas Parade*, May 2, 1948.

Graf, Leroy P., "Land Grants in Texas South of the Nueces," *Southwestern Historical Quarterly*, Vol. L, Austin (The Texas Historical Association).

King, Alma D., "The Political Career of William Simpson Oldham," *The Southwestern Historical Quarterly*, Vol. XXXIII, Austin (The Texas State Historical Association).

Taylor, Paul S., "Historical Notes on Dimmit County, Texas," *Southwestern Historical Quarterly*, Vol. XXXIV (October, 1930), Austin (The Texas State Historical Association).

The Dallas Morning News, The Texas Almanac, Dallas (A. H. Belo Corporation), 1934-1966.

Wilcox, Seb S., "Laredo and Fort McIntosh Furnish Much Colorful History," *Epic Century*, September, 1938.

............., "History of Fort Ringgold," *Texas Highway Bulletin* (Vol. 9, No. 4), April, 1927.

174

Newspapers:

El Latino Americano (Alice, Texas), January 21, 1921.
 Featured Catarino Garza: paper in possession of his granddaughter, Miss Amelia Perez of Alice.
The Brownsville Herald, May 10, 1936.
The Corpus Christi Caller-Times, Sunday, January 18, 1959.
 Corpus Christi history featured in this edition.
The Corpus Christi Gazette, January 8, 1846; March 8, 1946 (extra).
The Corpus Christi Star (Spanish and English), 1848-1849.
 (Available copies, University of Texas Archives).
The Eagle Pass Guide, August 20, 1931.
The Harlingen Star, August 19, 1931.
The New York Daily Tribune, June 10, 1846.
The Nueces Valley, October 10, 1857; December 5, 1857.
The San Antonio Express, December 13, 1931; September 22, 1935; July 23, 1939.
The Texas State Gazette (Austin), December 1, 1849.

Microfilms:

Mercer Log, Number 1 (April 21, 1866-August 27, 1866), (at Retama Library, Corpus Christi). Newspaper copies in possession of author.

Maps:

Austin, Stephen F., "Texas With Parts of the Adjoining States," Philadelphia (H. S. Tanner, Publisher), 1835 (from copy published by Ginn and Company, 1897).
 (Also from photostatic copy of Map in General Land Office, Austin).
Blucher, Felix von, "San Patricio District (A Compilation of Surveys, published in 1870). (General Land Office Archives, Austin).
 Mr. Blucher was the first District Surveyor; and also a private surveyor south of the Nueces, for more than 30 years.
Brue, A., "Corte du Texas—Extraite de la Grande Carte du Mexique, Paris (Geographe du Roi), 1840.
Bureau of Topographical Engineers, "Texas and Part of New Mexico, 1857," Austin (W. S. Benson and Company, Publishers), 1862. (State Archives.)
Burr, David H., "Texas," New York (J. H. Colton and Company), 1834. (State Archives.)
Chief Engineer's Office, M. D. of C., "Description of the Best Route from Fort Ewell to Ringgold Barracks" (Seal dated September, 1865). (State Archives.)
File Number M976.409, "Texas, 1881 (tentative date)," (University of Texas Archives).
Gartoryski, Stanislaw, Pvt., Camp F, First Louisiana Cavalry, "Best Route from the Nueces River to Laredo by Way of Fort Ewell" (Undated), (State Archives).

Homanno, Joh Baptista, "Regni Mexicani Sen Novae Hispaniae Ludoviciana, N. Angliae, Carolinae, Virginiae, et Pensylvaniae" (Noribergae), 1730 (University of Texas Archives).

Lara, Padre José Antonio Gutierres de (Cartographer unnamed), "Mapa de Mier y Su Jurisdiccion," 1831.
    Donated to the Texas Archives by Perry W. Steele, Jr. of Roma, Texas.

Mesur, E. S., Lith., "Map of the Southern Part of Texas," New York, Before 1834. (University of Texas Archives.)

Official Map, "San Diego, Duval County" (not dated).
    It shows city plat laid over old existing roads; supposed to be first city planning map of San Diego. In possession of Mrs. N. A. Hoffman, Sr. of San Diego in 1967.

Pressler, Charles W., and A. B. Langermann, "Pocket Map of the State of Texas," Austin, 1879. (University of Texas Archives).

Roessler, A. R., Assistant Engr., Division of the Gulf, "Best Route for the Movements of Troops from Laredo to Ringgold Barracks" (not dated). (State Archives.)

Zannoni, M. Rizzi (Cartographer unnamed), "Carte Geo-Hydragraphique—Du Golfe du Mexique e De Ses Isles," Paris, 1780. (University of Texas Archives.)

Official Texas Highway Maps, Road Maps, and County Maps, 1957-1967.

Signed Statements (To author): (Dated).

Appling, Mrs. R. L. (Ester), March 1, 1962. (In possession of author.) (Native of Orange Grove, Jim Wells County.)

Bell, Mr. Van, June 30, 1959; August, 1963. (In possession of author.)
    Resident of Carrizo Springs since 1894.

Bitterman, Mrs. Hester, September 9, 1965; April 3, 1966.
    Native of Lagarto and resident of Old Collins and Alice; attended school in all three places, also Nuecestown.

Black, Mrs. R. M., May, 1960; June 3, 1963.
    Early Collins and Alice Resident; daughter of circuit-riding Methodist minister.

Escobar, Hermelinda Bazan (Mrs. Roman), February, 1967, San Diego.
    Native of LaMota, Duval County, and descendant and part owner of LaMota Ranch.

Escobar, Mr. Roman, February, 1967, San Diego.
    Child resident of La Mota, where he attended school; present husband of Hermelinda Bazan, and part owner of ranch.

Frazier, Mrs. Michel Florence Malinda Dickens, Easter, 1958; June 30, 1959.
    Carrizo Springs resident since 1886. Lived in old Fort McLaughlin when first married.

Garcia, Mrs. Mary (Maria Rosales), February 10, 1962, Alice.
    Taught in Alice and San Diego areas 50 years plus.

Hinojosa, Mr. Clemente, October 25, 1966.
    Owner of Old Amargosa rock house and part of ranch since 1923; attended school here. 80+ years old.

Hoffman, Mrs. N. A., Sr., November 10, 1961; San Diego.
Early Alice resident; lived in vicinity all her life.

Hollan, Georgia Glover, August 10, 1965, Alice.
Grew up in Ramireña, near south bank on Nueces River; descendant of Irish Colonists along Nueces (McGloins).

Lopez, Mrs. Beatrice Salazar, December, 1965, Alice.
Daughter of Trinidad Salazar and native of Alice since 1890's.

Moos, Adolf, April 3, 1966, Alice.
In Alice since 1915; in Mustang Plains since 1890's.

Mullen, Robert Raymond, July 29, 1967, Alice.
Moved to Alice when a child; his father was Jim Wells County's second Judge and remained so for thirteen consecutive terms.

Palacious, Josefa Perez de, September 4, 1961. (Translated by Mrs. N. A. Hoffman, Sr.) San Diego and Amargosa.
Was Abraham Perez' only living granddaughter when interviewed; lived on Old Amargosa Ranch when a child.

Price, Miss Josephine, March 1, 1962, Alice.
Descendant of first English immigrants to Corpus Christi, on ship arriving in 1852; lives on and manages ranch established by grandfather (part).

Reynolds, Seana McCoy (Mrs. R. R.), May, 1964; December, 1965.
Descendant of early English immigrants to Corpus Christi; lives in and restored 1867 Ventana Ranchhouse, near Orange Grove.

Roddy, Mrs. Henry (Susie Dodson), December, 1965, Corpus Christi.
Descendant of Archelaus Bynum Dodson and Nueces Valley pioneers.

Salazar, Miss Guadalupe, December, 1965; March 12, 1963, Alice.
Daughter of Trinidad Salazar, pioneer store owner and prominent early resident of Alice.

White, Mr. Ive, August, 1963; June 30, 1959, Carrizo Springs.
Son of first Precinct No. 1 Commissioner of Dimmit County in 1888, who built first bridge to span the Nueces River, and also Commissioner of Precinct 1 for several years.

Wright, Halsey, June 10, 1966, Alice.
Son of Pioneer W. T. Wright and perennial Jim Wells County sheriff; born and reared in Alice vicinity.

Wright, W. T., Sr., July 11, 1961; October 22, 1962; June 29, 1963, Alice.
Parents on board first English immigrant ship to Corpus Christi in 1852; cowboy extraordinary, County Commissioner of Nueces County and later of Jim Wells County; appointed by Governor to assist with organization of Jim Wells County.

Published, Unbound Papers:

..............., "The Adams Brothers of Jim Wells County" (papers removed from a book, brochure, or small magazine with no date, author, or name of source. In possession of Mrs. Goode S. Wier of Alice and formerly owned by her parents. Published about 1920).

Scrapbooks:

Old one belonging to Mrs. W. T. (Bertha Halsey) Wright, Sr., with following inscription on inside front cover: "From Seana for My Birthday."
>Some dated clippings near 1900, but most have date and source cut off; several rare clippings, but most concern marriages of family and friends.

Personal Interviews: (Furnished pictures, source material, anecdotes and such but no signed statements).

Adams, N. O., Sr., of Alice, Texas.
Albert, Dr. Richard O., of Alice.
Beasley, Ricardo, Ben Bolt.
Cheshire, Mrs. Walter (Zainta Gibson) of Alice, whose father drove cattle uptrail to Kansas eight times.
Chote, Mrs. Dover Dell (Bertha Wright).
English, Mrs. ...., Santa Maria, restored and owns Rancho Blanco near present Santa Maria.
Guerro, Mrs. Reynaldo (Old Dot), Carrizo Springs.
Herrera, Mrs. Aurelino, San Ygnacio (lives in old fort).
Hinnant, Mrs. R. L., Seven Sisters (lives on ranch on which Picacho Hill is located).
Johnson, Mr. and Mrs. Bill, Carrizo Springs (recently acquired Old Lemon Ranch).
Maley, Mrs. Clyde (Louisa Broeter), Alice (parents moved to Alice from Old Collins).
Perez, Miss Amelia, Alice (granddaughter of Catarino Garza).
Shelby, Mrs. Harry (Barbara Wittman), Alice (lived in San Diego, Texas when a child).
Wade, Mrs. Wallis, Sandia (owns old Spanish fort ruins).
Walt, George, Alice native.
White, Mrs. Ive, Carrizo Springs.
Wier, Mrs. Goode (Lucille Hobbs), Alice (native of Alice).
Word, Mrs. McGehee, Sr. (Edith Garrett), Alice native.
Wright, Mrs. W. T., Sr., Alice (early teacher and resident).
And others.

SECONDARY SOURCES

Manuscripts and Typescripts:

Pollard, Neva Virginia, "Short History of Jim Wells County" (M.A. Thesis, Texas University of Arts and Industries, 1934), MS. (In Alice Library.)

Unsigned, "San Diego de Abajo and Arriba" (given to author by A. L. McIntosh for planned County Archives; MS given as introduction of Rafael Garcia, President, San Diego Lions Club, program), 1966.

Unsigned, "From a Clipping Out of Paper of January 10, 1896—
'Cornerstone Laid for the Church of the Advent at Alice,
Texas'," (given to author by Rector John Covey), 1963. Typs.

Unsigned, "In Regard to Pedro Saenz Bazan (supposed to have
been information furnished by uncle of Mrs. Roman Escobar,
but not known whether he wrote it or just told it). 1967. MS.

Unsigned, no title (MS of talk for Club Program for Texas Day,
in possession of Mrs. McGehee Word, Sr. of Alice).

Books and Pamphlets:

Lane, J. J., "Transportation Report" (United States Treasury Expert in Texas in 1888 to Secretary of Treasury of the United
States; Government Printing Office).

Picardo, Ed. Hackett, *Limits of Louisiana and Texas,* Vol. II, Austin (University of Texas Press), 1934.

South Texas Chamber of Commerce, *1959 South Texas Vacation
Land Guide,* San Antonio (301 Texas Centennial Building).

Periodicals:

Allen, Henry Easton, "The Parilla Expedition to the Red River in
1759" (from H. E. Bolton), *The Southwestern Historical
Quarterly,* Vol. XLIII, Austin (The Texas State Historical
Association).

Dobie, Dudley R., "A Son of the Texas Revolution," Vol. 9, No. 12
(September 1932), Bandera, Texas (J. Marvin Hunter)
(taken from an earlier article in *The San Antonio Express*).

Maps:

Hunt, Richard S., and Jesse E. Randal, "From a Map of Texas
compiled from surveys on record in the General Land Office
of the Republic of Texas to the Year 1839" (from *El Sal del
Rey,* page 16).

Index

182

183

Villarreal, Jose: 29
Vivian Ranch: 51, 132
Vivian, Uncle Charlie: 51

Waco: 149
Wade City: 154
Wadeville: 23
Wade, Wallis: 14, 15, 23
Walker, Lt.: 65
Wallace, Capt.: 117
Webb County: 25, 26, 55, 72, 73,
    80, 97, 122
Webb, James: 55
Welch: 69
Wells, James, Jr.: 156
Werbiski, Al: 7
West Texas State College: 107
West, W. W.: 155
White, Grey: 51
White, Ive: 51
Wier, Lucille Hobbs: 41, 83, 146
Wilcox, Gen. C. M.: 93
Wild Horse Desert: 162
Wilke, Georgia Adams: 41
Willacy County: 156, 164

Willacy, John G.: 157
Wilmot Proviso: 57
Woll, Adrian: 81
Wood, Gov. George T.: 46, 65
Woods, Mary: 91
Word, Edith Garrett: 41, 120
World War II: 66
Worth, Brig. Gen. W. J.: 53
Wright, Bertha Halsey: 116
Wright, Halsey: 83
Wright, John: 34
Wright, T. C.: 8, 115
Wright, W. T., Sr.: 105, 115, 130,
    155, 162

Yellow fever: 102, 103, 136
Yorktown: 112
Young, John: 80
Young, Marie Mullen: 162

Zapata: 95, 143, 164
Zapata, Col. Antonio: 95
Zapata County: 5, 13, 28, 49, 50,
    95, 122
Zúnega, Tomás: 130

189

Grimm, Agnes Glasscock.
   Llanos Mestenãs: Mustang Plains [by] Agnes
G. Grimm.   [Waco, Tex., Printed by Texian
Press, 1968]
   xii, 189p. illus., maps, ports. 24cm. index.

   Bibliography: p.167-179.

1.Texas-History. I.Title.